Close Relationships

THE STUDY OF LOVE AND FRIENDSHIP

DUNCAN CRAMER

Reader in Psychological Health,
Loughborough University

ARNOLD

A member of the Hodder Hea

LONDON • NEW YORK • SYDN

First published in Great Britain in 1998 by
Arnold, a member of the Hodder Headline Group
338 Euston Road, London NW1 3BH

http: // www.arnoldpublishers.com

Co-published in the United States of America by
Oxford University Press Inc.
198 Madison Avenue, New York, NY 10016

British Library Cataloguing in Publication Data
A catalogue entry for this book is available from the British Library

Library of Congress Cataloging-in-Publication Data
Cramer, Duncan, 1948–
    Close relationships: the study of love and friendship/Duncan
Cramer
    p. cm.
    Includes bibliographical references and indexes.
    ISBN 0–340–62533–3 (hardcover). — ISBN 0–340–62534–1 (pbk.)
    1. Love. 2. Friendship. 3. Interpersonal relations. 4. Man–woman
relationships. 5. Intimacy (Psychology) I. Title.
BF575.L8C7 1998
158.2—dc21   98–13915
                                                                     CIP
                    ISBN 0–340–62533–3 (hb)
                    ISBN 0–340–62534–1 (pb)

Production Editor: Wendy Rooke
Production Controller: Helen Whitehorn

Typeset by Phoenix Photosetting, Chatham, Kent
Printed and bound in Great Britain by MPG Books, Bodmin, Cornwall

Contents

Preface

This book aims to provide an outline of some of the major ideas and research on the factors that are thought to lead to satisfying and enduring close personal relationships. Because of the importance of empirically assessing and establishing the relevance and value of these factors, much of the substance of this book describes studies which have tried to do this. As most of the work has been on dating and marital heterosexual relationships, the content of this text largely reflects this concern. To give a chronological context for the topics covered, some of the earliest studies on a particular topic have been identified. Unlike many other books on close relationships, specific information has been provided when available on the sample, the measures and the size of appropriate findings of the research outlined. While presenting these details may make the text more difficult to read initially, they give the reader important information which should help them evaluate the significance of these studies without having to turn to alternative sources for this information. Furthermore, this information should assist the reader in deciding whether they need or wish to read the study in its original form.

Details on the sample include the number of females and males taking part, whether the sample was recruited from the community or from particular groups such as students, whether some form of probability sampling was used and the country where the sample was obtained. Information on the size of the sample is necessary for estimating the likelihood of the results being statistically significant and not due to chance. Big effects may not be statistically significant in very small samples while very small effects may be significant in very large samples. Other things being equal, studies with large samples have been selected wherever possible to exemplify a given line of research. The other information on the sample enables the reader to determine certain important aspects of the population on which the findings have been based and may be intuitively used to estimate the extent to which the findings may be generalizable to other populations of interest. Details on measures generally provide some indication of their content to illustrate what they may be assessing. While there was not enough space in a book of this kind to present fuller information, wherever available references have been cited where further details may be obtained. Finally, to give the reader some idea of the potential and relative importance of a finding, the size of the statistical association between two variables has been reported where this information was provided or where it could be calculated from the information provided. Many factors have been found to be associated with relationship compatibility; simply reporting this information gives no indication of the size of the association. While verbal descriptors such as 'weak', 'moderate' and 'strong' is more informative it is not as specific as giving the correlation coefficients.

In reading this book it should become clear that while we have gained much knowledge about the important factors that bring about satisfying and enduring close relationships, our understanding of this inherently interesting subject is limited, and that there are many more questions remaining to be answered. It is the author's hope that this book will help stimulate the search for these answers.

1

Unravelling Close Relationships

Close or personal relationships occupy a major part of the lives of most people. For example, many people have a close relationship with someone. In a representative sample of 1,416 British adults interviewed in 1986, 67 per cent said they were married and living with their spouse (Jowell *et al.* 1987, p. 238). Another 4 per cent reported they were not married but were cohabiting with their partner, while 6 per cent stated they were married or had a steady partner but did not live with them. Twenty per cent said they did not have a steady partner while the remaining 3 per cent presumably did not answer the question. Excluding partners and family, half the sample reported that they had four or more close friends and only 14 said they had none (Jowell *et al.* 1987, p. 239). About 54 per cent estimated they saw their closest friend at least once a week. In other words, many of us are in frequent contact with our partner and closest friends. Similar questions have been asked of nationally representative samples in the United States, Australia, West Germany, Austria, Hungary and Italy but the results do not seem to have been published (Jowell *et al.* 1989).

The central aim of this book is to discuss some of the principal factors thought to affect the development, maintenance and dissolution of these close relationships and to examine the way in which these factors have been studied scientifically, since our knowledge of them is based on the way in which they have been investigated, as should become apparent. An accurate understanding of these factors may, in turn, enable us to have more realistic expectations of our own relationships and to make our relationships more fulfilling as well as to help others do so.

THE NATURE OF SCIENCE

One of the main objectives of science is to establish laws or principles about a particular phenomenon such as close relationships. While the natural sciences appear to have been very successful in developing a wealth of such laws or principles, it is debatable whether it is possible to derive principles to describe and explain human behaviour. Many people certainly sometimes talk about certain aspects of human behaviour as if they were lawful. Two frequently quoted examples from the field of human relationships are the sayings 'Birds of a feather flock together' and 'Opposites attract'. The first proverb implies that individuals who are similar in certain respects are drawn together, while the second suggests that people who have opposite characteristics are attracted to one another. While these two rather general maxims appear to be contradictory, they are not necessarily so if they are seen to apply to different personal characteristics. The first adage has been called the principle of *homogamy* and the second that of *heterogamy*. As mentioned in Chapter 5, some of the earliest studies on close relationships looked at homogamy in mate selection (Anonymous 1903). Many social scientists see it as their task to develop and to test principles that explain various features of human behaviour. This book describes and evaluates principles put forward to explain the nature and development of close relationships as well as empirical studies that have endeavoured to test these principles.

It is important to make three related points about the nature of these scientific principles at this stage. The first point is that the exact conditions under which they apply may not be known at this time. Initially it may be assumed that they operate in the conditions in which they were first observed. So, for example, we may begin by assuming that the principle that similarity leads to attraction applies to many, if not most, physical, psychological and social characteristics. The second point is that the principle most probably does not apply in all conditions at all times to all people. So, this particular principle may not always apply, or may not apply at all, to your behaviour although it may generally apply to the behaviour of other people. The third point is that no indication is often given of how much of the behaviour in question is explained by a particular principle. Thus, for instance, similarity may not be the most important factor in accounting for attraction between people in the sense of being the factor that explains the greatest part of interpersonal attraction.

Although the research on the role of similarity in close relationships is described in Chapter 5, the way in which social scientists generally go about testing scientific principles can be more specifically illustrated by some of the ways in which they have studied similarity in attitudes between people. In many ways the easiest approach is to give to pairs of individuals who are close, such as married couples, a questionnaire which measures attitudes and to work out how similar the couples are in their attitudes. This kind of study is often referred to as a *cross-sectional survey* since it collects information across one section of time. A statistical test which is often used to assess how similar pairs of individuals are is Pearson's product moment correlation coefficient, often simply called a *correlation* for short and symbolized as r (Cramer 1998). This measure varies from -1 through 0 to 1. A correlation of 1 indicates that there is a perfect positive (linear) relationship between two sets of values such as the attitude scores of wives and husbands. In other words, the wife with the most positive attitude is married to the husband with the most positive attitude, the wife with the next most positive attitude is married to the husband with the next most positive attitude, and so on. A correlation of –1, on the other hand, shows that there is a perfect negative or inverse (linear) association between two sets of values. That is to say, the wife with the most positive attitude is married to the husband with the most negative attitude, the wife with the next most positive attitude is married to the husband with the next most negative attitude, and so forth. A correlation of 0 or close to 0 suggests that there is no (linear) relationship between the attitudes of wives and husbands. In most social science research we do not find perfect correlations of ±1. Usually they are in the region of ±0.2 or 0.3. A positive correlation indicates that wives and husbands are similar in attitude, a negative correlation shows that they are dissimilar, while a correlation close to 0 demonstrates that there is no linear relationship between them. It is useful to know the exact value of the correlation as it gives us an idea of how similar their attitude scores are for the sample as a whole, and it enables us to compare this correlation with correlations obtained in other studies as well as correlations for different characteristics such as physical attractiveness and intelligence. Because of their informativeness, correlations will often be reported in this book where they are available in the original study or where they can be calculated from the information given.

An example of a cross-sectional study which investigated attitude similarity in 566 married British couples was reported by Hans Eysenck and James Wakefield (1981). Attitudes were measured with an 88-item questionnaire (Eysenck 1976) which assessed two broad groups of attitudes called *conservatism* and *tough-mindedness*. These two groups of attitudes represent two unrelated dimensions which can be thought of as two axes lying at right angles to one another, as shown in Figure 1.1.

In other words, a person's score on conservatism is unrelated to their score on tough-mindedness. The conservatism dimension ranges from extreme left-wing (radical) views at one end to extreme right-wing (conservative) views at the other end. The tough-mindedness dimension varies from extreme tough-minded attitudes at one pole to extreme tender-minded attitudes at the other pole. Two examples of items measuring conservatism are 'Sex crimes, such as rape and attacks on children, deserve more than mere imprisonment; such criminals ought to be flogged or worse' and 'In taking part in any form of world organisation, this country should make certain that none of its independence and power is lost'. Those agreeing with these two statements tend to be conservative or right-wing and those disagreeing with them radical or left-wing. Two items assessing tough-mindedness are 'The idea of God is an invention of the human mind' and 'Sex relations except in marriage are always wrong'. Tough-minded people tend to endorse the first item and reject the second while tender-minded people do the opposite. Wives and husbands held similar attitudes on both conservatism (the correlation being 0.51) and tough-mindedness ($r = 0.56$).

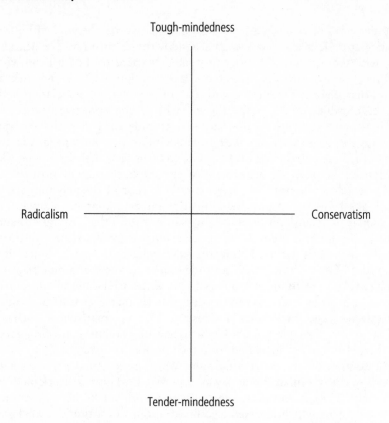

Figure 1.1 Two unrelated attitude dimensions of conservatism and tough-mindedness

Finding that wives and husbands have similar attitudes at one point in time does not, of course, tell us whether there is a causal connection between being married and having similar attitudes and, if so, what the direction of the causal relationship is. Are we, for example, more attracted to people with similar attitudes and so more likely to marry someone with similar attitudes? In other words, does attitude similarity lead to liking? Or, on the other hand, do we tend to make our attitudes more similar to those we like, so that liking someone causes us to have similar attitudes? These two explanations need not, of course, be mutually exclusive. We may both like people with similar attitudes and make our attitudes more similar to those of people we like. Finally, it is possible that there is no causal connection between being married to someone and having similar attitudes to them, but there appears to be a connection because both the person we are married to and the attitudes we hold are related to one or more other factors such as age or socio-economic background. For example, older people may hold more conservative attitudes than younger ones. If our sample contains individuals differing widely in age and if the age of wives and husbands are similar, then the finding that a person is married to someone with similar attitudes may be due to the fact that older people are more likely to be married to one another and to have more conservative attitudes. Although Eysenck and Wakefield found that their married couples were similar in age ($r = 0.77$), older people were not more conservative than younger ones, so this particular explanation does not apply to their finding. However, it is possible that some other factor, such as socio-economic status or educational level, which they did not look at, may have been responsible for this finding.

Statements about causality, then, cannot be made from a cross-sectional survey in which information on various characteristics has been gathered at one point in time. A design which yields more information about causality than a cross-sectional study has been called a *longitudinal, panel* or *follow-up* survey and is one in which individuals are tested on two or more occasions. If, for example, people with similar attitudes are more likely to remain married later on, then clearly the later marital state could not have been responsible for the earlier attitude similarity. However, the relationship between prior attitude similarity and subsequent marital state may be mediated by other factors, such as prior socio-economic status or educational level. In other words, people with similar socio-economic backgrounds may be both more likely to have similar attitudes and to marry. It may be the similarity in socio-economic background and not the similarity in attitude which makes them more likely to marry. Consequently, in analysing such data it is preferable that potentially confounding characteristics such as these are controlled, which is usually done statistically.

Despite their value, there are relatively few longitudinal studies because they are more costly to carry out and require a commitment which it may not be possible to give. An example of a longitudinal study investigating attitude similarity in married couples was reported by Peter Bentler and Michael Newcomb (1978). This study, however, did not control for factors such as socio-economic status and educational level. Bentler and Newcomb had 162 newly married American couples complete the Bentler Psychological Inventory which measures 28 personality characteristics with 680 pairs of statements. Respondents have to select which of each pair of statements more closely describes them. One of these characteristics or variables was called *liberalism*, which may be measuring attitudes similar to Eysenck's dimension of conservatism. Four years later, they managed to contact 77 of the original couples of whom 53 were still married and 24 were separated or divorced. When they looked to see how similar these couples originally were in terms of their liberalism scores, they found no difference between those who were still married ($r = 0 .44$) and those who were separated or divorced ($r = 0.40$). In other words, similarity in these attitudes did not predict who was likely to remain married four years later. However, as they did not also measure attitude similarity four years later, we do not know whether the separated and divorced couples held less similar attitudes at this stage than the still married couples. If they did, then it might imply that attitude dissimilarity leads to marital break-up. Consequently, it is preferable in such longitudinal studies to assess the same characteristics of interest at each point in time.

One study which did this was reported by Timothy Curry and David Kenny (1974). They selected six groups of eight students living in the same hall and who initially did not know each other. Each group lived together in a residential unit consisting of four two-person bed/study rooms, a living room and a bathroom. Each person in the group had to complete the same measures after one, two, four, six and eight weeks of living together. Included among these measures was the Spranger Value test which requires participants to rank-order, in terms of their importance to them, the following six areas of interest: political, theoretical, economics, aesthetic, social and religion. To this list was added a seventh area of physical-athletic. Participants also had to rate each member of their group on a 100-point scale ranging from feeling least to most favourable towards them. This was a measure of how much they liked each member of their group. The degree of similarity in the ranking of the interests between any two people in a group was correlated with the level of attraction a member of each pair felt for the other. Since each person in a group evaluated the other seven group members and since there were eight people in a group, there were 56 ratings of attraction for each group and 336 for the six groups.

To keep matters more simple, the relationship between similarity of interests and attraction will only be described for judgements made after being together for the shortest period of one week and the longest period of eight weeks. The correlation between similarity of interests and attraction for these two time-points are displayed in Figure 1.2. As might be expected, after living with someone for only one week there is no relationship between similarity of interests and attraction ($r = -0.04$). People do not appear to be more attracted to others with similar interests, possibly because they have not yet had sufficient time to find out about their common interests. After eight weeks of being together there appears to be a relationship between similarity of interests and attraction ($r = 0.17$). Members tended to like those with similar interests. However, this relationship is weak or small.

To find out what percentage of the variation in liking another group member can be accounted for by having similar interests, we square the correlation and convert this proportion to a percentage by multiplying it by 100 which gives a value of about 3 per cent. In other words, about 3 per cent of the variation in liking another group member is explainable in terms of holding similar interests. There may be various reasons why the relationship between liking someone and having similar interests is not stronger. First, the measure of interests is fairly crude, having only seven points or rank positions. Second, there may have been little variation among group members in terms of how they ranked these seven interests so that attraction was based on other characteristics. In addition, psychological measures, like most measures, are unreliable to some extent. That is, if you ask someone the same question twice over a short period of time or if you ask that person what seem to be similar questions you will find that the answers are not always the same. If the reliability of

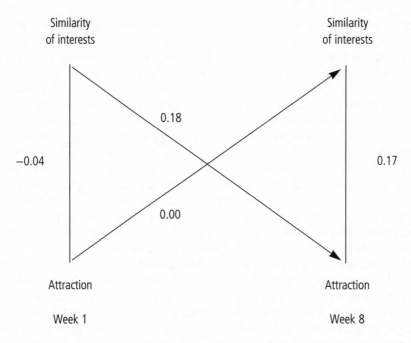

Similarity
of interests

Similarity
of interests

0.18

−0.04

0.17

0.00

Attraction

Attraction

Week 1

Week 8

Figure 1.2 Correlations between similarity of interests and attraction at one and eight weeks of living together

the measures is known, the correlation between the two measures can be statistically adjusted for this unreliability, which will increase the correlation (Cramer 1998). Since the reliability of the two measures at the two points in time is not given for this study, correcting the correlations between attitude similarity and liking for unreliability of the measures is not possible.

Turning to the correlations between the two different variables over the eight-week period, there is no relationship between how much one likes a group member after one week of knowing someone and how similar one's interests are to theirs after eight weeks ($r = 0.00$). This suggests that liking someone does not lead us to make our interests more similar to theirs. On the other hand, there is a positive relationship between how similar one's interests are after one week of living with someone and how much one likes them after eight weeks ($r = 0.18$). In other words, it appears that we grow to like those who have similar interests to ourselves. This kind of analysis is known as *cross-lagged panel correlation* (Campbell 1963) and seems to be useful in exploring the temporal direction of statistical relationships between two variables. However, its application depends on certain conditions being met (Kenny 1975) which are described in Chapter 3. A critical paper by Rogosa (1980) may have, in at least my own and Tom Cook's judgement (Campbell and Reichardt 1991, p. 204), inappropriately discouraged its use.

The most suitable method for determining whether one variable has an effect on another is a *true experimental* design as opposed to a *non-experimental* design (Campbell and Stanley 1966). A true experimental design has two essential features. First, only the variable thought to be the cause of an effect should be varied or manipulated. For example, if attitude similarity is expected to affect liking then the degree of attitude similarity should be varied so there may be two or more levels of attitude similarity, such as very similar, moderately similar and very dissimilar. Although more than one variable can be systematically varied in a single study, everything else should be kept as similar and as constant as possible. For instance, the kind of attitudes being varied should be the same, as should the way in which this similarity is conveyed.

Second, participants should be assigned *at random* to the different levels of the variable being varied (or to the order in which these levels are presented if participants experience more than one level). When there is a reasonable number of people taking part in a study (say, 10 or more to each condition), random assignment makes it more likely that the individuals in each condition will be similar. For example, people agreeing to participate in a study are likely to differ in terms of the extent to which they generally like others. Assigning participants at random to, say, two conditions in which they expect to judge a stranger with either similar or dissimilar attitudes increases the probability that the participants in those two conditions will generally be similar in terms of how much they would have liked the stranger if they had no information about their attitudes. This is important because if, for the sake of argument, participants expecting to judge a stranger with similar attitudes generally disliked others, then they may like the stranger with similar attitudes less than those participants expecting to judge a stranger with dissimilar attitudes. If this happened it would appear that people liked others with dissimilar rather than similar attitudes.

If random assignment has been successful, so that participants in the two conditions are similar, and if the only difference between the two conditions is that participants in one condition anticipate judging a stranger with similar attitudes while participants in the second condition expect to judge a stranger with dissimilar attitudes, then the two essential features of a true experiment have been met. If, under these conditions, participants expecting to judge the stranger with similar attitudes like this person more than the participants expecting to judge the stranger with dissimilar attitudes, then the most likely cause of this effect is the difference in attitude similarity.

A study like this was reported by Donn Byrne (1961, 1971). In this study 34 introductory psychology students at the University of Texas initially indicated on a seven-point scale their beliefs on 26 issues ranging from important ones (such as their attitudes towards racial integration, God and premarital sex) to less important ones (such as their views on cowboy films and TV programmes, classical music and politics). Two weeks later they were told that students in another class had also completed this attitude questionnaire. What they now had to do, on the basis of seeing one of these students' opinions, was to try and guess this person's intelligence, knowledge of current events, morality and adjustment. They also had to say how much they thought they would like this person if they met them and how much they thought they would like to work with this person in an experiment. The answers to these last two questions were used as an indication of how much participants thought they would like the other person. The person they had to form an impression of was described as being of the same sex.

In effect, participants in this study had been deceived since students in another class had not been given the attitude questionnaire. What Byrne did was to create two experimental conditions by randomly assigning participants to one of these two conditions. One group of participants received attitude questionnaires which had been completed exactly as they had done while the second group were given questionnaires which expressed exactly the opposite views of the participants. Participants who were provided with questionnaires endorsing the same views as themselves both liked more and were keener to work with the stranger than participants who were handed questionnaires voicing opinions opposite to their own. Although Byrne did not do this, it would be useful to express the difference in liking between the two conditions as a correlation so that we can compare the results of this study with those of others (to find out how to carry out this simple calculation, see Cramer 1998, p. 153). For liking the stranger, the correlation with attitude similarity is 0.97 while for wanting to work with them the correlation is 0.81. In other words, there is a very strong relationship between attitude similarity and liking. Perhaps this is not surprising as the participants had no information about this person other than their attitudes.

Steve Duck (e.g. 1995), who has written at length on relationships, has criticized these kinds of experimental studies of initial attraction to strangers based on limited and atypical information as being not very informative about human relationships. This view seems to misunderstand the purpose of these studies, which is to try to determine the causal direction of a relationship that has been observed between two variables such as attitude similarity and liking. This is often difficult to achieve without resorting to what may appear to be a very artificial situation. Prior to the study by Byrne, a number of non-experimental studies had found that similar attitudes were held by friends (e.g. Winslow 1937) and by wives and husbands (e.g. Schiller 1932). For example, in one of the earliest studies on self-reported psychological similarity between wives and husbands, Belle Schiller (1932) reported a tetrachoric correlation of 0.65 on opinions on current topics for a relatively similar group of 46 married couples in New York. (Note that the tetrachoric correlation differs from Pearson's correlation and so cannot be compared with it.) In view of this research, determining the causal direction of this association provides a valuable contribution to our understanding of this finding. It is not immediately obvious in what other way Byrne could have tackled this important question. Although the experimental design may appear artificial, it should be said that it is not too far removed from the real-life situation in which we have to select candidates for interview, and hence the findings may be directly relevant to this context.

Of course, showing as Byrne did that attitude similarity leads to attraction does not exclude the possibility that attraction may also bring about similar attitudes. This idea does not seem to have been investigated. It would be relatively easy to do so using a similar design to Byrne's, in which participants had to make judgements about someone they had not met. As before, we initially measure the attitudes of the group of participants. Since we want to measure the extent to which our participants change their attitudes, we have to present them with a person who has dissimilar attitudes to them. We also have to manipulate the variable whose effect we want to study, which is the extent to which our participants feel positive towards this person. One way of doing this may be to vary the attractiveness of the other person with the expectation that participants will like an attractive person more than an unattractive one. We cannot do this by manipulating their attitude dissimilarity since we want to measure how much participants change their attitudes and it is possible that the extent of any change might be affected by the degree of dissimilarity. Consequently, we have to do it in some other way such as describing them more positively.

So, in this study we would have at least two conditions to which participants are randomly allocated. In one condition participants are presented with an attractive person and in the other condition with a less attractive person. After this we ask them to report their attitudes again to see if participants presented with the attractive person have made their attitudes more similar to those of this person than the participants in the other condition. It is also important to check that our manipulation of initial attraction has worked and that participants presented with the attractive person like that person more than participants presented with the less attractive person.

Although the true experimental design enables us to determine if one variable affects another, we need to be careful in making sure that we have manipulated only the variable that we wanted to vary and that we have not inadvertently manipulated another variable at the same time which may, in fact, have caused the effect we measured. For example, in the above study we tried to manipulate how much participants might like another person by varying the attractiveness of that person. There are several ways in which we could do this. The easiest way would be to vary the other information that we provided on this person. For example, we could describe the person who was supposed to be more attractive as being more honest. But if we did this and if we found that participants changed their attitudes more to a person described as honest than as dishonest, then we could not be sure whether this change was due to the fact that the person was described as honest or that they liked honest people. We would have more confidence that it was due to liking this person if we found a similar effect when we manipulated liking in other ways.

Regardless as to whether the design of a study is a non- or a true-experimental one, we should be more confident about a finding if it has been replicated in different settings and in different ways because we can then be more certain that the finding is not dependent on a particular set of circumstances. In other words, the finding would appear to be generally true. In some cases, a finding may be based on only one published study in which case we do not know how reliable that finding is. In other cases, conflicting results may have been obtained from different studies and may be due to differences in the way the studies have been carried out. In a book of this nature, it is not possible to list all the studies that have reported a particular result. Consequently, I have carefully selected the studies that are described in this book according to various considerations. In general, however, I will choose the best-designed studies of their type I know of and to point out what I see as their limitations if any. Two other kinds of studies will also be briefly mentioned. To give a little 'historical' or chronological perspective to the work on a particular issue, studies which were among the first to examine that topic will be included. Although most of the research cited in this book has been carried out in the English-speaking industrialized countries of the world, studies investigating the same topic in other cultures will be outlined where relevant and available.

SUMMARY

The scientific study of close relationships attempts to generate propositions which explain the development, maintenance and dissolution of such relationships and to empirically test the validity of these propositions. A better understanding of close relationships should enable us to have more realistic expectations of our own relationships and to make our relationships more fulfilling as well as to help others do so. In its simplest form a causal proposition states that one variable affects another, such as the causal proposition that similarity leads to attraction. The strength of a linear relationship between two variables can usually be described in terms of a correlation or a squared correlation. The ideal way of testing a causal proposition is by carrying out a true experiment in which the causal variable is manipulated and all other variables are held constant. Under these circumstances the effect that occurs is likely to be due to the manipulated variable. To achieve such control true experiments may appear contrived and somewhat removed from everyday life. Non-experiments, on the other hand, often entail simply measuring variables either at one point in time or, less commonly, across time. Correlations between variables in a non-experiment indicate that variables may be related but do not allow us to determine the causal nature of the relationship between the variables. The conclusions that we can draw from the scientific study of close relationships depend on how those studies have been conducted and written up. Consequently, it is necessary to be familiar with the strengths and weaknesses of the studies on which conclusions are based.

2

Classifying Close Relationships

There are various ways of trying to classify close relationships, none of which are entirely satisfactory on their own or are mutually exclusive. One way is in terms of kinship (such as wife and husband) and friendship (such as close or best friend). There are several problems with this simple distinction. It excludes people who are not married but who may have a strong or developing emotional commitment to one another, such as couples in love. For some relationships these two broad categories are not mutually exclusive in that a family member or relative may also be seen as a friend: for example, someone may say that 'My mother is my best friend'. While it is clear how to describe relationships between family members (such as wife–husband, mother–daughter and so on), a similar system cannot be applied to friendships. A second way of classifying relationships is in terms of romantic relationships and friendships. Once again these two categories are not necessarily mutually exclusive as your lover could also be your closest friend. Furthermore, if the term 'romantic' is not seen as applying to loveless marital relationships, then there is no category for describing these relationships.

A third and more recent way of categorizing close relationships is in terms of same- and cross-sex relationships. While most romantic relationships are cross-sex ones, most close friendships are same-sex ones. None the less, there are substantial numbers of same-sex romantic relationships and cross-sex close friendships. In terms of determining the percentage of cross-sex close friendships, a question asking whether their closest or best friend (excluding partners or family) was a man or a woman was included in nationally representative surveys carried out in the United Kingdom, the United States, Australia, West Germany, Austria, Hungary and Italy (Finch 1989, p. 94). The number of men whose best friend was a woman varied from zero in Hungary to 21 per cent in Austria. The number of women whose best friend was a man ranged from 7 per cent in the United Kingdom to 23 per cent in Austria, Hungary and Italy. Some idea of the number of same-sex romantic relationships may be obtained from the number of people who say that they have had sexual experience mostly or only with people of the same sex or who see themselves as being homosexual. Two recent surveys of nationally representative samples in Britain and the United States provide some evidence on this point. In the British survey 1 per cent of 8,384 men said that they had some sexual experience only or more often with males compared to 0.3 per cent of 10,492 women who had some sexual experience only or more often with females (Johnson *et al.* 1994, p. 187). In the United States' survey 2 per cent of 1,401 men and 0.9 per cent of 1,732 women reported that they think of themselves as homosexual (Laumann *et al.* 1994, p. 311). It is important to determine if and how the nature of same-sex romantic relationships differs from that of cross-sex ones, and if and how the nature of opposite-sex close friendships differs from same-sex ones. Most research, however, has been carried out on married couples, cross-sex romantic relationships and same-sex friendships, making it difficult to draw adequate comparisons.

RELATIONSHIP SATISFACTION

An alternative way of classifying relationships is in terms of their quality. However, most of the tests are concerned with romantic relationships and so cannot be applied unaltered to friendships. The early tests were developed to assess the quality of marital relationships (Hamilton 1929) while more recent tests have been reworded to measure the quality of romantic relationships (S. Hendrick 1988). The quality of these romantic relationships has been variously called success, adjustment, happiness, satisfaction or some such synonym (Spanier 1976). The most widely used test of marital adjustment has been the Marital Adjustment Test which was developed by Harvey Locke and Karl Wallace (1959) in Los Angeles. It consists of 15 items. The first item asks respondents to rate the happiness of their marriage on a 35-point scale varying from 'very unhappy' to 'perfectly happy'. The next eight items require respondents to rate on a six-point scale the extent of their agreement on matters such as money, sex and display of affection. The remaining six items tap various other aspects of their relationship such as whether they had ever wished that they had not married and if they had to relive their life whether they would marry the same person again. They gave this test to a middle-class sample of 118 wives and 118 husbands who were not married to one another. Forty-eight of them were thought to have problems in their relationship in that they were either receiving marital counselling, were separated or were recently divorced. These individuals were compared with 48 others who were matched for age and gender and who were judged to be happily married by friends who knew them well. The overall score on the 15 items added together for the unhappily married group was considerably lower than that for the happily married group suggesting that this test can be used to distinguish the two groups.

More recently, Graham Spanier (1976) has developed the Dyadic

Adjustment Scale which measures relationship adjustment in married and cohabiting couples and which consists of 32 items, 12 of which are the same as or similar to those in the Marital Adjustment Test. The Dyadic Adjustment Scale was completed by 94 recently divorced individuals, who were asked to answer it in terms of the last month they spent with their spouse, and by 218 married people, all living in Pennsylvania. A statistical technique generally called factor analysis (Bryman and Cramer 1997) was used to find out whether the items were grouped into smaller and related factors. Four related factors were found which were called dyadic consensus, dyadic satisfaction, dyadic cohesion and affectional expression. The meaning of a factor is usually determined by the content of the items which correlate most highly with that factor. To indicate the meaning of these four factors the three items which correlated most strongly with each factor are shown in Table 2.1.

Dyadic consensus

8 Indicate the approximate extent of agreement or disagreement between you and your partner on philosophy of life.

2 Indicate the approximate extent of agreement or disagreement between you and your partner on matters of recreation.

5 Indicate the approximate extent of agreement or disagreement between you and your partner on friends.

Dyadic satisfaction

20 Do you ever regret that you married? (or lived together)

16 How often do you discuss or have you considered divorce, separation, or terminating your relationship?

18 In general, how often do you think that things between you and your partner are going well?

Dyadic cohesion

25 How often do you have a stimulating exchange of ideas with your mate?

27 How often do you calmly discuss something with your mate?

26 How often do you laugh together?

Affectional expression

4 Indicate the approximate extent of agreement or disagreement between you and your partner on demonstrations of affection.

6 Indicate the approximate extent of agreement or disagreement between you and your partner on sex relations.

30 Has not showing love caused differences of opinion or problems in your relationship during the past few weeks?

Table 2.1 The three items correlating most highly with each of the four factors of the Dyadic Adjustment Scale

The divorced individuals scored significantly lower than the married people on all four sub-scales, showing that they differed on all four of them. The overall score on this test had a very high correlation of 0.93 with the Marital Adjustment Test, demonstrating that these two tests seem to be measuring the same construct. Mark Eddy and his colleagues (1991) provided additional support for the four factors with a confirmatory factor analysis carried out separately for 1,515 women and 1,307 men from Oregon in the United States.

One problem with these two tests of relationship adjustment is that the different aspects of a relationship being measured are all assumed to reflect relationship adjustment. For example, including items on the extent of agreement between couples implies that agreement between couples contributes towards relationship adjustment. This is an assumption that needs to be tested. As Spanier only presented the average intercorrelations between the scores on the four sub-scales (which was 0.68), it is not possible to tell which of the factors were most closely related.

Many individuals in Western societies have romantic relationships with and marry people they love. For example, Ernest Burgess and Paul Wallin (1953) asked 998 engaged couples living in Chicago in the late 1930s whether a person should ever marry someone they did not love. About 80 per cent of the women and 82 per cent of the men said 'No' (p. 394). Further asked whether married people should continue to live together when they were no longer in love, about 84 per cent of 911 of the women and about 81 per cent of 913 of the men answered 'No' (p.395). In the 1986 British Social Attitudes Survey mentioned at the beginning of this chapter, 75 per cent of the sample said that ceasing to love one another was a sufficient reason for divorce (Ashford 1987, p. 126). Younger people were more likely to endorse this view than older ones: 82 per cent of people aged 18–34 agreed with this view compared with 66 per cent of people aged above 54. Consequently, it is surprising that neither of these two tests include such a measure.

Asking people questions such as whether they and their partner agree on how to show affection does not, of course, assess how affectionate they are. We can agree with our partner not to be very physically affectionate in our relationship but that does not mean that we do not feel great affection for each other. A study by Joan Broderick and Daniel O'Leary (1986) looked at the relationship between the Locke–Wallace Marital Adjustment Test and a measure of love in 55 couples living in the state of New York and found that this measure correlated very strongly with marital satisfaction in both women ($r = 0.87$) and men ($r = 0.89$). In an earlier study Ernest Burgess and Paul Wallin (1953) found that love was strongly positively correlated with both marital happiness ($r = 0.65$) and marital satisfaction ($r = 0.64$) in the 666 couples they followed up three to five years after they had married (p. 504).

Shorter scales have been developed and used to measure relationship satisfaction. For example, Susan Hendrick (1988) devised a seven-item scale which included a question on how much one loved one's partner. This scale was strongly positively correlated with the Dyadic Adjustment Scale ($r = 0.80$) in a sample of 114 psychology undergraduates. In terms of the Dyadic Adjustment sub-scales, it was most strongly related to the satisfaction sub-scale ($r = 0.83$), followed by the consensus ($r = 0.62$), cohesion ($r = 0.57$) and affectional expression ($r = 0.51$) sub-scales. Walter Schumm and his colleagues (1986) produced the three-item Kansas Marital Satisfaction Scale which was found to be highly related to the Dyadic Adjustment Scale ($r = 0.83$) in a small sample of 61 wives living in Kansas. This scale was most strongly related to the satisfaction sub-scale ($r = 0.77$) of the Dyadic Adjustment Scale, followed by the cohesion ($r = 0.72$), consensus ($r = 0.63$) and affectional expression ($r = 0.58$) sub-scales. A single item has been used to assess marital happiness in the General Social Survey carried out in the United States (Glenn and Weaver 1978). A major problem with a single-item scale is that the reliability of a person's view on the issue at that time cannot be estimated. When asked how happy their marriage is, most people say that their marriage is very happy. For example, in a nationally representative survey in the United States in 1976, of the 1,167 who had been only married once 53 per cent said their marriage was very happy, 28 per cent reported it was above average, 17 per cent replied it was average and only 2 per cent said it was not too happy (Veroff *et al.* 1981, p. 163). Similar results were found in another survey where 4 per cent of the women and 2 per cent of the men said that their marriage was not too happy or not at all happy (Gove *et al.* 1983).

ROMANTIC LOVE AND LIKING

The most widely used measure of the romantic love felt towards one's partner is Zick Rubin's (1970) Love Scale. In order to determine whether his Love Scale could distinguish between liking and loving someone, he also developed a Liking Scale. Both scales consist of 13 items. Examples of three items from each of the two scales is presented in Table 2.2.

Rubin asked 158 dating couples at the University of Michigan to complete

---

Love

9 I would forgive _____ for practically anything.

6 If I could never be with _____, I would feel miserable.

4 I would do almost anything for _____.

Liking

9 I think that _____ is one of those people who quickly wins respect.

3 I would highly recommend _____ for a responsible job.

2 I think that _____ is unusually well-adjusted.

Table 2.2 Examples of three items from Rubin's (1970) Love and Liking Scales

the items in terms of their partner and a close, same-sex friend. He found that his couples loved their partner more than their close friend, suggesting that his Love Scale can distinguish these two close relationships. Couples also liked their partner more than their close friend, although this difference was smaller than that for love.

If we look at the items that make up the Liking Scale, they seem to convey feelings of respect and admiration more than those of liking. To determine the extent to which the items on these two scales corresponded to simple statements of attraction such as 'I really love you', 'I really like you' and 'I respect you as a person', I gave these scales (together with another 74 items on affection) to 225 16- to 17-year-old British adolescent females and factor-analysed the results (Cramer 1992b). Seven of the Love Scale items correlated quite strongly with one factor and six of the Liking Scale items correlated quite highly with a second factor, suggesting that items on the two scales can be distinguished in this way. The items shown in Table 2.2 are the three Love Scale items which correlated most highly with the first factor and the three Liking Scale items which correlated most strongly with the second factor. I called the first factor Love and the second one Respect. Although these next findings were not published, the item 'I really love you' correlated most strongly with the Love factor confirming this was the meaning of this factor. The item 'I really respect you as a person' was more strongly related to the Respect than to the Love factor while the item 'I really like you' was more highly correlated with the Love than the Respect factor, implying that the majority of items on Rubin's Liking Scale may be assessing respect rather than liking as such. It is possible that loving is simply a stronger form of liking and that apart from a difference in strength, the two concepts cannot be distinguished. In other words, it may be more appropriate to view liking and loving as lying on the same dimension with disliking and hating at the other end and indifference in-between (Swensen 1972) (see Figure 2.1).

Other concepts and measures of romantic love are discussed in Chapter 10.

RELATIONSHIP CLOSENESS OR INTERDEPENDENCE

An important dimension of close relationships, which has received insufficient attention, is the extent to which the members within a close relationship voluntarily engage in behaviour together or spend time together. To some extent this aspect of the relationship is indirectly measured by the dyadic cohesion

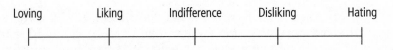

Figure 2.1 Single bipolar dimension of attraction

component of the Dyadic Adjustment Scale (Spanier 1976). Answering 'more often than once a day' to the kind of dyadic cohesion items shown in Table 2.1 (such as 'How often do you have a stimulating exchange of ideas with your mate?') implies that these activities occur frequently in the relationship. However, the score on the five items that go to make up this scale is restricted to the activities mentioned, which is a very limited selection of the full range of activities that people might engage in, such as watching television or travelling. Furthermore, the items give no indication of the time that people might voluntarily spend together.

There appear to have been relatively few attempts to assess this aspect of close relationships. In developing his model of friendship, Paul Wright (1969) at the University of North Dakota defined friendship in terms of 'the extent to which the plans, activities, and decisions of one of the acquaintances are contingent upon those of the other when both members of the pair are free to exercise a certain amount of choice' (p. 297). He measured this criterion of voluntary interdependence with 10 items such as 'When I plan for leisure time activities, I make it a point to get in touch with ____ to see if we can arrange to do things together' (p. 301). People seen as better friends obtained higher scores on this scale than those rated as less good friends.

One of the three dimensions used by Mary Anne Fitzpatrick (1988) to create her typology of marital relationships (the Relational Dimensions Inventory) was interdependence/autonomy. This dimension consisted of the four sub-factors of sharing, autonomy, undifferentiated space and temporal regularity. Examples of items from these four sub-scales are shown in Table 2.3. Items are answered on a seven-point scale ranging from 'Always' to 'Never'. The scales were based on a factor analysis of responses from 1,448 married American individuals (Fitzpatrick and Indvik 1982).

The two other dimensions Fitzpatrick used to classify couples were ideology and conflict. Ideology consisted of the two sub-factors of traditionalism (e.g. the woman should take the husband's last name) and uncertainty (e.g. there should be no constraints on individual freedom within the marriage), while conflict constituted the two sub-factors of conflict avoidance (e.g. avoiding conflict and arguments) and assertiveness (e.g. being persuaded or forced by your partner to do things you don't want to do). Using a statistical technique called cluster analysis (which groups together individuals who share characteristics), Fitzpatrick found that individuals and their marriages could be categorized into one of three types called traditional, independent and separate. The characteristics of the individuals falling into each of these three categories are presented in Table 2.4. For example, both the traditionals and the separates have more conventional views about marriage and have more fixed times for doing things together than the independents.

In one study Mary Anne Fitzpatrick and Patricia Best (1979) investigated the marital adjustment, using the Dyadic Adjustment Scale, of 60 married American couples according to their marital type. Traditionals tended to be more satisfied with their marriages than the separates and independents.

Sharing (23 items)

2 We talk about the future of our relationship.

3 We share responsibility for deciding when, for how long, and at what speed chores around the house should be completed.

4 We go out together to public places in the community such as zoos, sporting events, public parks, amusement parks, museums, libraries and so on.

Autonomy (6 items)

6 My spouse/mate has taken vacations without me (even if only for a day or two).

27 I have my own private workspace (study, workshop, utility room, etc.).

30 I have taken separate vacations from my spouse/mate even if only for a day or two.

Undifferentiated space (8 items)

1 We try to make our guests feel free to enter any room of our house.

17 I open my spouse's/mate's personal mail without asking permission.

18 I feel free to interrupt my spouse/mate when he/she is concentrating on something if he/she is in my presence.

Temporal regularity (4 items)

24 We eat our meals (i.e. the ones at home) at the same time every day.

33 In our house, we keep a fairly regular daily time schedule.

39 We serve the main meal at the same time every day.

Table 2.3 Examples of three items from each of the four sub-factors of the autonomy/ interdependence dimension of the Relational Dimensions Inventory

However, since the classification of independents is based on the sub-scales of the two other dimensions as well as the interdependence sub-scale, it is not known to what extent the lower marital satisfaction of the independents is due to their scores on these other sub-scales. To determine this it would have been preferable if marital satisfaction had simply been correlated with the sub-scales.

Ellen Berscheid and her colleagues (1989) developed a test of interdependence called the Relationship Closeness Inventory. This test measured the following three aspects of interdependence: (1) the amount of time during the day that the two people spent alone together; (2) the number of 38 different activities (such as watch TV or go on a trip) that the two people did alone together; and (3) the extent to which the one person influenced the other in terms of 34 different issues (such as how they spend their money or free time). These three aspects were positively intercorrelated (average $r = 0.35$) in a sample of 241 introductory psychology students at the University of Minnesota who were asked to complete the questionnaire in terms of the person with whom they currently have 'the closest, deepest, most involved, and most intimate relation-

Scales	Traditional	Independent	Separate
Ideology			
Traditionalism	High	Low	High
Uncertainty	Low	High	High
Interdependence			
Sharing	High	Moderate	Low
Autonomy	Low	High	High
Undifferentiated space	High	High	Low
Temporal regularity	High	Low	High
Conflict			
Conflict avoidance	Low	Low	High
Assertiveness	Low	High	High

Table 2.4 Fitzpatrick's three types of marital relationships

ship'. A second sample of 75 students completed the questionnaire for a 'not close' as well as their closest relationship. The total score on the questionnaire and the scores on the three sub-scales were significantly higher for the closest than for the not-close relationship, showing that the questionnaire could discriminate between the two types of relationship. For the closest relationships these scores were not correlated with Rubin's (1970) Loving and Liking scales. In the initial sample, however, the answers to the two simple questions of 'How much do you love _____' and 'How much do you like _____', when combined, did correlate to some extent with the overall closeness score ($r = 0.20$). These results imply that interdependence is weakly related to feelings of affection. There was also no relationship between the overall closeness score and a measure of the experience of positive as opposed to negative feelings in the relationship.

RELATIONSHIP DURATION OR STABILITY

For marital relationships at least, many people expect them to last 'till death us do part' (Book of Common Prayer). For example, every year since 1976 a nationally representative survey of high school seniors has been carried out in the United States called 'Monitoring the Future' (Thornton 1989). One of the questions asked in this survey is how likely the respondent thinks it is that they will stay married to the same person for life if they marry or are married. For the years 1985–86, about 88 per cent of the women and 81 per cent of the men thought it very or fairly likely that they would remain married to the same person for life (p. 880). However, it has long been recognized that remaining married until one of the partners dies is unrealistic for some relationships and that in many societies ending the marriage is legally permitted (Goode 1993). Information on this is available from a representative survey carried out on values in 1981 in 10 Western European countries: Belgium, Denmark, Eire, France, Great Britain, Holland, Italy, Northern Ireland, Spain and West Germany. Only 8 per cent of the total sample believed that there were no circumstances which justified divorce, although this figure reached 32 per cent in the Irish Republic (Harding *et al.* 1986, p. 117). Respondents were asked which of the 10 reasons shown in Table 2.5 were sufficient for divorcing one's spouse. The percentages giving these reasons as sufficient for divorce are presented in this table for women and men separately for the European sample and together for a British sample questioned again in 1986 (Ashford 1987, p. 126). Violence and consistent unfaithfulness were seen as being the strongest reasons for seeking a divorce.

Because many government agencies keep national statistics on marriages, divorces and deaths, considerable information exists on the duration of marriages and their chances of breaking up. There are various ways of estimating the chances of a marriage ending in divorce (England and Kunz 1975), the main ones of which are outlined below.

Crude Divorce Rate

The crude divorce rate is the number of divorces per 1,000 of the population for a particular year. This figure can be misleading because it depends on the number of people in the population who are married and who therefore may

| Reasons | Western Europe | | Britain |
	Women (5,951)	Men (6,512)	(1,552)
Violence	79	75	92
Consistently unfaithful	73	71	94
Cessation of love	58	58	75
Consistent over-drinking	57	50	59
Incompatible personalities	44	47	42
Unsatisfactory sex	21	26	28
Can't have children	7	7	7
Financially broke	4	4	4
Problems with in-laws	3	3	4
Long illness	3	3	3

Table 2.5 Percentages agreeing with reasons as sufficient for divorce in two surveys

be susceptible to divorce. If a large proportion of the population is unmarried (perhaps because they are too young to be married), the crude divorce rate will be low. The crude divorce rate for the United Kingdom in 1991 was about 3 (United Nations 1995, p. 559). In other words, in 1991 there were about 3 divorces per 1,000 people.

Refined Divorce Rate

A better measure is the refined divorce rate which is the number of divorces per 1,000 married women (or couples) for a particular year since this takes account of the number of people in the population who are eligible to divorce. The refined divorce rate, for instance, for England and Wales in 1991 was about 14 (Office of Population Censuses and Surveys 1995, p. 1). That is, in 1991 about 14 out of 1,000 marriages (i.e. 1.4 per cent) were dissolved. A major problem with this measure is that it is not sensitive to the age composition of the married population. It has been found that younger married couples are more likely to divorce than older ones. For example, John Haskey (1982) has calculated the refined divorce rate for divorces in England and Wales in 1979 for women marrying at different ages. He noted that for marriages which had lasted for at least three years, the refined divorce rate for women who married aged under 20 was about twice as high as for those who married between 20 and 24 and almost three times as high as for those who married between 25 and 29.

Ratio of Divorce to Marriage Rates

A widely used measure of divorce is the number of divorces per 1,000 marriages which, in other words, is the ratio of the divorce rate to the marriage rate for a particular year. In the United Kingdom in 1991 the number of marriages was 350,000 and the number of divorces was 171,144, so the divorce–marriage ratio was 0.49. The disadvantage of this index is that very few of the people who have divorced in that year were also married in it. In other words, in all but a few cases, the two populations are not the same. For example, with other things being equal, a population which has a large number of unmarried people is likely to have a lower divorce–marriage ratio than a population which has a large number of married couples, because more people are likely to become married in any one year in the first than in the second case.

Age-specific Divorce Rates

To take account of populations with different age distributions, the age-specific divorce rate is used which is the number of divorces per 1,000 married women or couples for a particular age.

Standardized Divorce Rates

A disadvantage of the age-specific divorce rate is that it does not give a single statistic or index which summarizes the rate for a population. This is provided by the standardized divorce rate. This measure assumes a fixed age distribution for married women which is used to estimate the expected number of divorces in each age group. These numbers are added for all age groups, divided by the standard population size and multiplied by 1,000.

Marital Life Status

The most appropriate way of calculating the divorce rate is to calculate the percentage of marriages which end in divorce rather than in the death of the partner. These data are based on following from birth to death a group or cohort of people born in a particular year or range of years. Where the group of people is too young to get married, get divorced or die, the chances of these events happening are estimated. The analysis is obviously complicated and details can be found elsewhere (Preston and McDonald 1979; Schoen 1975; Schoen and Nelson 1974).

Using this technique, Robert Schoen and John Baj (1984) worked out that for England and Wales in 1975 the percentage of marriages that were likely to end in divorce was about 22 per cent for women and 28 per cent for men. The average duration of marriage was estimated to be about 30 years for both women and men. Robert Schoen and his colleagues (1985) also calculated the percentage of marriages that were likely to end in divorce for Americans in 1975. This was about 42 per cent for women and 44 per cent for men. The average duration of marriage was about 24 years for both women and men. Using more recent figures, Robert Schoen and Robin Weinick (1993) estimated that for American women and men in 1988 the percentage of marriages ending in divorce was about 43 per cent and that the marriages would last for 25 years on average. For those marrying in England and Wales in 1987, John Haskey (1989) has calculated that the percentage of marriages likely to end in divorce was about 37 per cent. About 50 per cent of the couples would be married for 26 years.

For those marriages ending in divorce, the probability of divorce is greatest in the early years of the marriage. Table 2.6 shows the number of complete years married for those marriages in England and Wales which ended in divorce in 1993 (Office of Population Censuses and Surveys 1995, pp. 60–1). The percentage of divorces increases up to 7.15 per cent at four years of marriage and then decreases to 2.45 per cent at 16 years of marriage. About a fifth of all divorces in 1993 occurred after four years of marriage, half of them after nine years of marriage and about three-quarters after 16 years of marriage. The median duration of marriages ending in divorce in the United States has for many years been about seven years, leading to the expression of 'the seven-year itch' (U.S. Bureau of the Census 1995, p. 103).

Duration of marriage (years)	Percentage of divorces	Cumulative percentage
0	0.05	0.05
1	2.85	2.90
2	5.64	8.54
3	6.88	15.42
4	7.15	22.57
5	6.75	29.32
6	6.27	35.59
7	5.47	41.06
8	5.14	46.20
9	4.57	50.77
12	3.64	62.39
16	2.45	74.30

Table 2.6 Duration of marriage for divorces in England and Wales in 1993

Most people who divorce, however, do not remain divorced but remarry. Robert Schoen and Robin Weinick (1993) estimated that for American women in 1988 the percentage of divorcees remarrying was about 72 per cent and that the average duration of a divorce was about 13 years. For American men in 1988 the percentage of divorcees remarrying was about 78 per cent and the average duration of a divorce was about eight years. For England and Wales in 1975 Robert Schoen and John Baj (1984) worked out that the percentage of divorcees remarrying was about 80 per cent for women and 89 per cent for men. The average duration of divorce was about nine years for women and five years for men.

Another indication, therefore, of the nature of a relationship is how long it has lasted. But because some people are reluctant to break up an unsatisfactory relationship, a long relationship is not necessarily a happy, loving or close one. Tim Heaton and Stan Albrecht (1991) reported that 7 per cent of a nationally representative sample of Americans taking part in the 1987/8 National Survey of Families and Households were involved in an unhappy but stable marriage in the sense that they did not say that they were very or moderately happily married and they rated the likelihood of separation or divorce as being low or very low.

CHANGES IN MARITAL STATUS DURING THE TWENTIETH CENTURY

Changes in the estimated likelihood of marriage, divorce, remarriage and the average duration of marriage during the course of the twentieth century may need to be taken into account when interpreting studies which have used marital status or duration as the sole indication of the state of the relationship. The peaks and troughs of some of the changes documented by Robert Schoen and his colleagues (Schoen *et al.* 1985; Schoen and Weinick 1993) are presented in Table 2.7.

	Year of birth						Annual statistics	
	1888–1892	1923–1927	1928–1932	1933–1937	1938–1942	1943–1947	1975	1988
Women								
Percentage ever marrying of those surviving to age 15	91.9			97.3	97.3			87.9
Age at first marriage	23.0			21.0				25.1
Percentage of marriages ending in divorce	16.7							43.2
Duration of marriage (years)	28.6		31.1				23.9	24.8
Number of marriages	1.25						1.63	1.51
Percentage of life spent married	47.1		53.0					41.2
Men								
Percentage ever marrying	88.8				96.2			83.5
Age at first marriage	26.5			23.3	23.3	23.3		27.5
Percentage of marriages ending in divorce	17.5							42.7
Duration of marriage (years)	28.0	29.9					23.6	24.5
Number of marriages	1.34						1.74	1.58
Percentage of life spent married	50.9			58.4				44.8

Table 2.7 Peaks and troughs of aspects of the twentieth-century American marriage

The percentage of Americans who survived to the age of 15 and who married was relatively low at the beginning of the century, peaked in the late 1930s and has since steadily decreased to its lowest point. For women, the percentage ever marrying was 91.9 for those born in 1888–92, 97.3 for those born in 1933–42 and 87.9 in the 1988 statistics. For men, the percentage ever marrying was 88.8 for those born in 1888–92, 96.2 for those born in 1938–42 and 83.5 in the 1988 statistics.

The average age of Americans marrying for the first time has shown a similar pattern, generally decreasing at first and then increasing. For women, the average age was 23 for those born in 1888–92, 21 for those born in 1933–37 and 25 in the 1988 statistics. For men, the average age was 26.5 for those born in 1888–92, 23.3 for those born in 1933–47 and 27.5 in the 1988 statistics.

The percentage of American marriages ending in divorce has generally steadily increased with some fluctuations for those born after 1952. For women, it was 16.7 for those born in 1888–92 and 43.2 in the 1988 statistics, while for men it was 17.5 for those born in 1888–92 and 42.7 in the 1988 statistics. The average duration of marriage first increased and then decreased with some fluctuations after 1975. For women, it was 28.6 years for those born in 1888–92, 31.1 for those born in 1928–32, 23.9 years in the 1975 statistics and 24.8 in the 1988 statistics. For men it was 28 years for those born in 1888–92, 29.9 for those born in 1923–27, 23.6 in the 1975 statistics and 24.5 in the 1988 statistics.

Finally, the number of times an American has married and the percentage of their life spent in the married state has at first increased and then generally decreased. For women, the number of times they married was 1.25 for those born in 1888–92, 1.63 in the 1975 statistics and 1.51 in the 1988 statistics. The percentage of their life women spent married was 47.1 for those born in 1888–92, 53.0 for those born in 1928–32 and 41.2 in the 1988 statistics. For men, the number of times they married was 1.34 for those born in 1888–92, 1.74 in the 1975 statistics and 1.58 in the 1988 statistics. The percentage of their life men spent married was 50.9 for those born in 1888–92, 58.4 for those born in 1933–37 and 44.8 in the 1988 statistics.

What these figures do not take account of is the increased tendency of people to cohabit prior to becoming married and after becoming divorced. Based on a large national survey carried out in the United States in 1987/8, Larry Bumpass and James Sweet (1989) calculated that the percentage of people who cohabited before their first marriage quadrupled from 11 per cent for marriages that occurred in 1965–74 to 44 per cent for those in 1980–84. For second marriages they almost doubled from 34 per cent for marriages in 1965–74 to 60 per cent for those in 1980–84. Within a few years, most cohabiting couples have either married or stopped living together. The median duration of cohabitation was 1.3 years. Sixty per cent of those who first cohabit with someone marry that person and 50 per cent of those who do so marry within three years. In a second paper Larry Bumpass and his colleagues (1991) found that the decline in the marriage rate was largely offset by the increase in cohabitation. For those aged 20–24, 24 per cent fewer people married in 1985 than in 1970 while the percentage of people who either lived together or married decreased by only 6 per cent during that period. In other words, about 75 per cent of the decrease in marriages between 1970 and 1985 was due to people cohabiting. Sixteen per cent fewer of those who separated between 1977 and 1981 remarried within five years of separating compared with those who separated between 1963 and 1967 while the percentage of people who either lived together or remarried increased by 7 per cent between those two periods. In other words, the decrease in remarriage was fully compensated for by the increase in cohabitation.

In some countries cohabitation is and has been more common than in the United States. For example, in Sweden in 1965 some 59 per cent of women cohabited before marrying compared with some 96 per cent of women in 1977 (Hoem and Hoem 1988). About half of those women cohabiting in 1965 married within a year compared with less than 5 per cent of those cohabiting in 1977.

LENGTH OF PRE-MARRIAGE RELATIONSHIP AND MARITAL DURATION

Couples who cohabit before marrying are more likely to separate after they marry, although this may only be true for those who cohabited when this was less common. In the United States, for example, Larry Bumpass and James Sweet (1989) found that couples who cohabited before their first marriage were more likely to break up after marriage than couples who did not cohabit. Ten years after marrying, 57 per cent of the couples who cohabited split up compared with 30 per cent of the couples who did not cohabit. However, Robert Schoen (1992), analysing the same data, found that while the probability of a marriage breaking up was greater for those born between 1943 and 1947 and who cohabited before marrying, there was no difference between those who cohabited prior to marriage and those who did not for those born since then. For example, for those born between 1953 and 1957 the probability of a marriage breaking up in the first four years was 0.17 for those who cohabited before marriage and 0.19 for those who did not. The length of time the couple know each other before marriage may be related to whether they remain married. In a recent five-year longitudinal study of 286 newly-wed couples living in Ohio, Lawrence Kurdek (1993) found that the number of months the couple had known each other was lower for the 64 couples who split up (28.74) than the 222 couples who stayed together (44.06 months).

RELATIONSHIP QUALITY AND RELATIONSHIP DURATION

To what extent are the three relationship qualities of satisfaction, love and closeness positively related to the duration of a relationship? We may expect that in relationships where there are fewer external pressures to maintain the relationship (such as friendships) there will be a weaker association between the length of the relationship and any of these three measures since we may be more likely to discontinue relationships which we feel are unsatisfactory. On the other hand, in relationships where there are greater external pressures to maintain the relationship (such as marriages) we may expect to find a stronger tendency for there to be less positive feelings about the relationship the longer it has lasted. We can investigate this question in at least two ways. First, we can correlate the three measures with the length of the relationship. A major disadvantage of this method where the age of the individuals within the sample differs widely is that age differences are confounded with cohort differences. In other words, older people will have obviously been born in an earlier year and as a result may have had different experiences from those born at a later date.

The second and more time-consuming way of collecting information on the association between these three measures of the state of the relationship and its duration is to follow up a group of individuals over time and to examine whether more positive relationships have a greater chance of being maintained and whether the feelings about those relationships have changed. An advantage of the second approach is that it enables us to determine whether we can predict which relationships are likely to endure. To make full use of this advantage it is preferable to know whether individuals whose relationship broke up also *wanted* that relationship to break up, since it is possible that they were satisfied with the relationship but their partner was not. Where the concern is to reduce the likelihood of a relationship such as a marriage breaking up, it would be useful if we could predict the probability of the marriage dissolving prior to the couple becoming married. However, even after the couple have married this information could be used to determine which couples may need help.

MARITAL SATISFACTION AND LENGTH OF MARRIAGE

Studies investigating marital satisfaction over the course of a marriage have produced conflicting results. Some have suggested there is a general decline in marital satisfaction over the years. For instance, Peter Pineo (1961) reported that the marital adjustment of 400 of the 666 married couples who had taken part in the study of Ernest Burgess and Paul Wallin (1953) was lower after they had been married up to 20 years (the middle years) than after they had been married up to six years (the early years). Robert Blood and Donald Wolfe (1960), in their study of 909 wives living in Detroit or the nearby countryside, noted that marital satisfaction declined the longer the wives had been married (p. 264). This decline was also found when the data were analysed in terms of the family life-cycle which was divided into the six following stages based largely on the age of the eldest child: (1) honeymoon (childless and married for less than four years);

(2) preschool (oldest child under 6); (3) preadolescent (oldest child 6–12); (4) adolescent (oldest child 13–18); (5) postparental (oldest child older than 18); and (6) retired (unemployed husbands over 59). Marital satisfaction was measured with five items on satisfaction with standard of living, understanding of problems and feelings, love and affection, companionship and number of children, weighted according to their importance (p. 102).

Other studies have suggested a curvilinear relationship between marital satisfaction and marital duration with an initial decline in satisfaction followed later by an upturn. In one of the first studies looking at this issue, Jessie Bernard (1934) reported that, although marital happiness was negatively correlated with length of marriage for both wives ($r = -0.27$) and husbands ($r = -0.34$), when happiness was plotted against the duration of marriage there appeared to be a curvilinear trend. However, as the number of people in some of her sub-groups was as small as four, the reliability of this observation must be questioned.

A later study by Boyd Rollins and Kenneth Cannon (1974) assessed marital satisfaction with three measures: the Blood–Wolfe index, a single item and the Locke–Wallace Marital Adjustment Test. They gave these three tests to 489 married Mormons selected according to gender and the following eight family life-cycle stages: (1) newly married; (2) infant; (3) preschool; (4) school-age; (5) teenage; (6) launching (children leaving home); (7) launched (all children left home); and (8) retired. The results for women and men were similar and so are not presented separately. In terms of the Blood–Wolfe index there seemed to be a decline followed by a levelling off, while for the other two measures a curvilinear trend was more apparent with an initial decline followed by a later upturn. However, when corrections were made for the way in which the Blood–Wolfe index was composed a curvilinear trend was observed for the items dealing with love, understanding and companionship.

Using three different samples, Graham Spanier and his colleagues (1975) found a curvilinear relationship in one sample (an Ohio sample of 196 couples), a negative relationship in another (a Georgia sample of 326 couples) and no relationship in the third (an Iowa sample of 265 couples). In a 40-year longitudinal study of 169 Harvard University graduates, Caroline and George Vaillant (1993) also reported there was no evidence of a curvilinear or a negative trend when length of marriage was divided into three 15-year periods.

In a later study Graham Spanier and his colleagues (1979) compared grouping individuals according to age, to length of marriage and to the stage of the family life-cycle, and found little difference between the three methods on 14 different measures such as age of youngest child and number of children. These results suggest that using the more complex index of the family life-cycle may not further enhance our understanding of the processes represented by age or length of marriage. However, Stephen Anderson and his colleagues (1983) found a significant curvilinear relationship between marital satisfaction and five stages in the family life-cycle, but no significant relationship between marital satisfaction and length of marriage in a relatively small sample of 196 wives living in an American midwestern city.

A few studies have found satisfaction with the premarital relationship to be related to marital satisfaction a few years later. Ernest Burgess and Paul Wallin (1953, p. 548) found that engagement success was positively correlated with marriage success three to five years after marriage for the 666 women ($r = 0.36$) and men ($r = 0.39$). Engagement success was measured with 24 items (pp. 305–9) such as the extent to which couples agreed on 11 issues, while marital success appeared to be assessed with eight components such as consensus (pp. 483–504). A more recent study by David Smith and his colleagues (1990) of some 80 white couples living in New York State and married for the first time found that relationship satisfaction as measured with the Marital Adjustment Test six weeks prior to marriage was positively correlated to it six months ($r = 0.58$), 18 months ($r = 0.38$) and 30 months ($r = 0.26$) after marriage. The correlation between marital satisfaction six weeks before and six months after marriage ($r = 0.58$) was lower than that between marital satisfaction 18 and 30 months after marriage ($r = 0.82$) despite being measured over a shorter time period (i.e. 7.5 vs 12 months), implying that relationship satisfaction may become more stable later on in marriage. In a more complete sample consisting of 264 couples Steven Beach and Daniel O'Leary (1993) found that relationship satisfaction at six weeks prior to marriage was positively related to it six months after marriage for both wives ($r = 0.63$) and husbands ($r = 0.53$).

Other studies have also found marital satisfaction to be stable to some extent within marriage. David Johnson and his colleagues (1992) found marital satisfaction to be moderately strongly correlated ($r = 0.52$) over eight years in an American national sample of 1,043 married individuals. John Gottman and Robert Levenson (1992) noted that marital satisfaction after about five years of marriage was positively correlated ($r = 0.63$) to marital satisfaction four years later in some 70 couples living in Bloomington, Indiana. Ted Huston and Anita Vangelisti (1991) reported that marital satisfaction measured two months after marriage was correlated to marital satisfaction two years later for both wives ($r = 0.51$) and husbands ($r = 0.34$) in 106 Pennsylvanian couples married for the first time. Steven Beach and Daniel O'Leary (1993) noted that marital satisfaction six months after marriage was moderately correlated to it 12 months later for both wives ($r = 0.68$) and husbands ($r = 0.69$) in their 264 couples. Frank Fincham and Thomas Bradbury (1993) found marital satisfaction to be highly stable over a year in 106 wives ($r = 0.70$) and their husbands ($r = 0.72$) who had been married for about nine years.

Several studies have shown relationship satisfaction to be related to subsequent stability. In the study by John Gottman and Robert Levenson (1992), 18 of the 70 couples separated and nine divorced during the four-year follow-up period. Earlier marital satisfaction was inversely related to both separation ($r = -0.24$) and divorce ($r = -0.22$). Lawrence Kurdek (1993) followed up 286 newly married couples in Dayton, Ohio over five years during which 64 of the marriages were dissolved. The correlation between marital satisfaction during the first year and subsequent marriage dissolution can be worked out from the F ratios presented (Cramer 1998), which was 0.20 for wives and 0.23 for husbands. In an earlier study Lawrence Kurdek (1992) followed up 71 gay and 43 lesbian couples over four years. The couples had been recruited from across North America. When first tested, the gay couples had lived together for about seven years and the lesbian couples for about five years. Over the four years, 10 gay and 12 lesbian couples separated. Once again using the F ratios, the correlation between relationship satisfaction during the first year and subsequent separation was calculated to be 0.30 for one partner and 0.39 for the other partner. Robert Sears (1977) reported the results of a follow-up study of 486 men who had initially been selected by Lewis Terman as children with IQs of 135 or over in 1921–23 when they were about 11 years old. In 1940 when they were about 30 years old, these men and their wives were asked to complete the Terman Marital Happiness Test when most of them had been married for a short time. In 1972 when they were about 62, they were asked about their marital status. About 71 per cent of them had unbroken marriages while about 21 per cent had a history of divorce or separation. Marital status in 1972 was correlated with both the wife's ($r = 0.28$) and the husband's ($r = 0.22$) marital satisfaction measured 32 years earlier.

MARITAL SATISFACTION AND THE NATURE OF THE PRE-MARITAL RELATIONSHIP

Studies which look at the relationship between marital satisfaction and length of marital relationship may need to take account of the duration and nature of the pre-marital relationship. Findings on whether people who have known each other for longer prior to marrying are more happily married are contradictory. Hans Eysenck and James Wakefield (1981) found that there was no relationship in their 566 married British couples between marital satisfaction and the length of time a partner was known prior to becoming engaged or the length of time between the engagement and the wedding. However, Kelly Grover and her colleagues (1985) reported a moderately strong correlation ($r = 0.39$) between length of dating and the Kansas Marital Satisfaction Scale in a small sample of 51 wives living in Kansas, indicating that those who had dated for longer were more happily married. A number of studies have found that there is no relationship between marital happiness and whether couples cohabited before marrying or the length of cohabitation (Booth and Johnson 1988; Thomson and Colella 1992). For instance, in a random-digit dialling telephone survey of 2,033 married people Alan Booth and David Johnson (1988) found no association between their 11-item measure of marital happiness and whether couples had cohabited.

ROMANTIC LOVE AND RELATIONSHIP DURATION

The strength of love and liking do not appear to be consistently related to the length of the dating relationship. Zick Rubin (1970) found that his Love and Liking scales were generally unrelated to the length of time the person had been dating their partner, apart from women showing greater love the longer they had been dating.

There is some evidence, however, that love decreases over time in the marital relationship. Peter Pineo (1961) reported that the love scores of 400 of the 666 married couples who had taken part in the study of Ernest Burgess and Paul Wallin (1953) were lower after they had been married up to 20 years (the middle years) than after they had been married up to six years (the early years). In 32 couples living in New York State and varying from just married to having been married for 17 years, Richard Cimbalo and his colleagues (1976) also found that the longer-married couples loved their partners less.

The strength of love has been found to predict the stability of dating relationships. Relationships characterized by greater love are more likely to endure. Charles Hill and his colleagues (1976) gave the Love and Liking Scales to 231 dating students in the Boston area. After two years 103 couples had broken up. They found that the Love Scale scores at the start of the study were significantly lower for both the women and the men who broke up later. For women the Liking Scale score was also significantly lower for those whose relationships ended. Women's love for their partner was a stronger predictor ($r = 0.32$) of the state of the relationship two years later than men's love for their partner ($r = 0.18$). Mary Lund (1985) gave nine of the 13 items of the Love Scale to 129 dating students in Los Angeles and asked them about their relationship four months later, by which time 29 of the relationships had ended. Students whose relationships ended had lower Love Scale scores at the start of the study than those whose relationships were still ongoing ($r = 0.46$). Similar results were obtained by John Berg and Ronald McQuinn (1986) in 38 American dating couples followed up over four months using a 10-item scale developed by Braiker and Kelley (1979).

CLOSENESS AND RELATIONSHIP DURATION

Ellen Berscheid and her colleagues (1989), in their development of the Relationship Closeness Inventory, found that overall closeness tended to decline the longer close friendships had lasted ($r = -0.33$) but that there was no relationship between closeness and the length of the close romantic relationships. They followed up at both three and nine months 74 of the 105 students who had described a romantic relationship as their closest and found that 25 of these relationships had ended by three months and a further 11 by nine months. The relationships of individuals with higher overall closeness scores were less likely to have ended nine months later.

RELATIONSHIP DURATION IN FIRST AND LATER MARRIAGES

The evidence on whether later marriages are more likely to break up than first marriages appears mixed. Teresa Martin and Larry Bumpass (1989), for example, found that for those marrying between 1980 and 1985 in the United States there was a greater probability for second marriages ($p = 0.27$) to break up in the first five years than first marriages ($p = 0.23$). The difference in this probability was smaller for those marrying in 1975 to 1979 (0.24 vs 0.22) and non-existent for those marrying in 1970 to 1974 (0.18 vs 0.18). For white women marrying in 1980 to 1985 there was no difference in the probability of first and second marriages breaking up when both the age at first marriage and level of education were taken into account. In other words, second marriages were more likely to break up when the wife had less education and had first married as a teenager. Alan Booth and John Edwards (1992) noted in their United States national longitudinal sample of 2,033 married persons who were first interviewed in 1980 that marriages where both partners had been divorced were more likely to end in divorce than marriages where one of the partners had been divorced, which in turn were more likely to end in divorce than marriages where neither partner had been married before. In this study the number of years couples had been married was controlled as marital dissatisfaction and divorce was found to increase during the course of marriage.

MARITAL HAPPINESS IN FIRST AND LATER MARRIAGES

Several recent studies have found no differences in marital satisfaction between that in first and that in later marriages. Alfred DeMaris (1984), in a sample of 295 wives and 277 husbands married in Gainsville, Florida in 1978/9, found that marital satisfaction (as measured by the Dyadic Adjustment Scale) did not differ significantly between first-married and remarried wives or husbands. Similarly, Alan Booth and John Edwards (1992), in their longitudinal study, found that there was no difference in marital happiness, interaction or disagreement between first-married and remarried individuals in 1980 controlling for years of being married. However, marital happiness and interaction declined more over the eight years in the remarried than in the first-married.

SUMMARY

Overall the state of a close relationship can be described in terms of the following four general characteristics: (1) satisfaction or happiness with the relationship; (2) attraction or strength of feeling towards the person in the relationship; (3) the closeness or voluntary interdependence of the behaviour of individuals in the relationship; and (4) duration or stability of the relationship. Research has been primarily concerned with explaining relationship satisfaction, attraction and duration, most of which has been carried out on dating and married couples. Relationship satisfaction has been found to be strongly related to attraction and both of these have been shown to be related to the likelihood of the relationship breaking up.

3

Well-being and Close Relationships

It has been known for over a century that being married is associated with living longer. Based on the 1851 mortality rates for single, married and widowed women and men in France, William Farr, the Superintendent of the Statistical Department of the Registrar's General Office for England, wrote in 1858 that 'Marriage is a healthy state. The single individual is more likely to be wrecked on his voyage than the lives joined together in matrimony.' (1885/1975, p. 440). In 1859 the French demographer, Adolphe Bertillon, using statistics on mortality, suicides and madness for France, argued that marriage resulted in better health. His son, Jacques Bertillon (1879, pp. 782–3), also thought that the association between marital status and health was due more to family life leading to better health than to healthier people marrying. The idea that marriage may have beneficial health effects is generally known as the protection hypothesis, while the notion that people who marry differ from those who do not in some way that enhances their health is often referred to as the selection hypothesis. Overall, Jacques Bertillon favoured the protection hypothesis since this also explained the higher mortality of the widowed and the divorced. Charles Letourneau (1891), on the other hand, supported the selection hypothesis in that he believed that physical ill health was partly responsible for celibacy and so presumably greater mortality (p. 350).

DURKHEIM'S ARGUMENT FOR SOCIAL PROTECTION

It was Emile Durkheim (1897/1952) who argued most persuasively for the protection hypothesis with respect to suicides. While acknowledging that some of the lower suicide rate of married people may be due to their greater 'health, fortune and morality' (p. 180), he believed that the greater part of it was due to the influence of the family. Largely based on the figures in Table 3.1, Durkheim presented the following two main facts to support his argument.

Age	Men			Women		
	Unmarried	**Married**	**Widowed**	**Unmarried**	**Married**	**Widowed**
Grand-duchy of Oldenburg						
0–20	7	769	—	4	95	—
20–30	71	49	286	39	17	—
30–40	130	74	77	32	17	30
40–50	189	95	286	53	19	68
50–60	264	138	271	67	31	50
60–70	243	148	305	63	37	56
70+	267	114	259	—	120	91
France						
15–20	113	500	—	79	33	333
20–25	237	97	142	106	53	66
25–30	394	122	412	151	68	178
30–40	627	226	560	126	82	205
40–50	975	340	721	171	106	168
50–60	1,434	520	979	204	151	199
60–70	1,768	635	1,166	189	158	257
70–80	1,983	704	1,288	206	209	248
80+	1,571	770	1,154	176	110	240

(Adapted from Durkheim 1952, pp. 177–8)

Table 3.1 Number of suicides per 10,000 for age of unmarried, married and widowed men and women in the Grand-duchy of Oldenburg (1871–1985) and France (1889–1891)

First, if suicide depends on the lower resilience of the unmarried, then the suicide rate of the unmarried compared with that of the married should increase with age up until about 40, by which age most of the eligible people have married and the proportion of weaker individuals in the remaining population of unmarried people should be greatest. However, this was not the case. The suicide rate of the unmarried compared with that of the married did not increase with age. For example, for French women aged 20–30 the suicide ratio of the unmarried to the married was about 2.1 (257/121) while for those aged 30–40 it was about 1.5 (126/82). For French men aged 20–30 the so-called coefficient of preservation was 2.9 (631/219) while for those aged 30–40 it was about 2.8 (627/226).

Second, if selection was responsible for the increased suicide rate of the unmarried, the suicide ratio of the unmarried to the married should be the same for both women and men as the weaker of both sexes will be less likely to marry. However, this ratio varied for the sexes from society to society implying that it was due to variations in the nature of the marital relationship. In France the suicide risk for married women was greater than that for married men while in the Grand-duchy of Oldenburg (in present-day northern Germany) it was greater for married men than for married women. For example, for those aged 20–30 the suicide ratio of the unmarried to the married in France was 2.1 (257/121) for women and 2.9 (631/219) for men, while in Oldenburg it was 2.3 (39/17) for women and 1.4 (71/49) for men. A lower ratio indicates a greater risk of suicide for the married. Furthermore, for French women the suicide ratio of the unmarried to the married decreased with age and so presumably with length of marriage.

Durkheim went on to argue that the lower suicide rate of the married in France was due primarily to having children rather than to being married. For men the suicide risk of husbands without children was greater than that of husbands with children and of widowers with children. Furthermore, the suicide risk of widowers without children differed little from that of husbands without children. The fact that the suicide rate of widowers with children was greater than that of husbands with children he thought was due to the widowed father having to 'shoulder a double burden and perform functions for which he is unprepared' (p. 188). For women the risk of suicide was lower for women with children than for unmarried women and for unmarried women than for childless wives.

Durkheim also drew attention to the adverse effects of widowhood which led to an increased risk of suicide for both women and men. For example, for French 60- to 70-year-olds the suicide ratio of the widowed to the married was 1.6 (257/158) for women and 1.8 (1,166/635) for men. He went on to suggest that the sex which was better protected by marriage would also be less affected by widowhood. In France the more protected sex was men while in Oldenburg it was women. For example, for French 60- to 70-year-olds the suicide ratio of the unmarried to the widowed was 0.7 (189/257) for women and 1.5 (1,768/1,166) for men. For 60- to 70-year-olds in Oldenburg, on the other hand, the suicide ratio of the unmarried to the widowed was 1.1 (63/56) for women and 0.8 (243/305) for men.

There are two problems with relying on the kind of data used by Durkheim in making inferences about the relationship between marital status and well-being. First there is concern about the accuracy of official statistics. With respect to suicide, Gregory Zilboorg (1936) suggested that many suicides are not reported as such. For example, many suicides are concealed by their families. If this is the case, then the suicide rate among the married is likely to appear lower than among the unmarried. There also appear to be errors in the accurate recording of marital status. Mindel Sheps (1961), for instance, found that the U.S. Census data stated that for 14-year-old boys, there were 1,670 widowers, 1,320 divorcés and 6,660 husbands. The marriage statistics from 24 states, on the other hand, reported that there were 45 marriages where the groom was under 15. It is not known how findings from official statistics are affected by these kinds of errors. Second, Durkheim's argument that the selection hypothesis implies an increase of the suicide rate for the unmarried as against that of the married until age 40 only holds if the mortality rate of the unmarried is similar to that of the married. If the mortality rate of the unmarried in relation to that of the married decreases with age as noted by Julia Zalokar (1960), and if the mortality rate reflects fitness to marry, then the selection hypothesis does not imply an increase in the suicide rate of the unmarried.

To determine the relationship between marital status and, say, mortality as an index of well-being, it is preferable to follow up a group of individuals over the same length of time and see whether more of the married survive than the non-married. However, even if more of the married do survive, this difference is not necessarily due to the protective effects of marriage but may be due to other factors which differentiate the married from the non-married, such as differences in income. Moreover, unless we determine at random who marries and who remains single, we will not be able to find out whether the life of people who would otherwise be single is, in fact, shortened by the experience of marriage and whether the life of people who would otherwise be married is lengthened by the experience of not marrying. Since it is unethical to decide at random who is to marry and who is to remain single, we have to try and rule out the influence of other factors which differentiate the married from the non-married by measuring them and showing that they do not account for the difference in mortality between these two groups.

A number of longitudinal studies have been carried out which have looked at the effect of marital status and other measures of social relationships on various indices of well-being including mortality and mental health. One of the advantages of mortality as an index of well-being is that it is generally obvious whether someone is dead or alive, although advances in medical technology mean that people can be kept alive even though they are capable of little else. Measures of mental health are more problematical in that they are usually based on what the individual says about their own behaviour, making it difficult to compare one person's experience with another's. However, there is evidence that psychological distress may be related to increased mortality from factors other than suicide.

RELATIONSHIP BETWEEN MORTALITY AND MENTAL HEALTH

Several recent studies have shown that depression and/or hopelessness is related to an increased risk of mortality. For instance, John Barefoot and Marianne Schroll (1996) found that mortality from heart disease or from all causes was higher in women and men who were depressed 17 or 27 years earlier, even when other risk factors were controlled and when items referring to somatic symptoms of depression were excluded. Relative risk of mortality from all causes varied from 1.35 to 1.65 depending on which factors were controlled. The sample consisted of 409 men and 321 women who were born in Denmark in 1914 and who were followed up until 1991. In 1964 and 1974 they were given various physical and psychological tests. Depression was measured with the 40-item obvious depression scale of the Minnesota Multiphasic Personality Inventory (MMPI) (Wiener 1948). Risk factors included age, sex, systolic blood pressure, level of blood triglycerides, smoking, forced expiratory volume of the lungs and signs of heart disease.

In Finland Susan Everson and her colleagues (1996) found that middle-aged men categorized as not having hope were more likely to die from various causes over a six-year follow-up even when risk factors were controlled. Men were classified into one of three levels of hopelessness based on only two items ('I feel that it is impossible to reach the goals I would like to strive for' and 'The future seems to me to be hopeless, and I can't believe that things are changing for the better'). Causes of mortality were defined as all causes, cardiovascular versus noncardiovascular causes, internal (e.g. disease or illness) versus external (e.g. violence, injury or accident) causes and cancer. The relative risk of men categorized as having high versus low hopelessness varied from 1.42 (for cancer) to 3.90 (for heart disease). Risk factors included age, systolic blood pressure, high and low density lipoprotein cholesterol, body mass index, physical activity, smoking, frequency of drunkenness, income, years of education, perceived health status, previous disease history, MMPI Depression Scale and quality and availability of social support and organizational participation.

In the United States Robert Anda and his colleagues (1993) found that middle-aged and elderly people who were depressed or who had no hope were more likely to die from heart disease over a 12-year period, controlling for various risk factors. The sample consisted of 2,832 people taken from the National Health Examination Follow-Up Study (Cornoni-Huntley et al. 1984) who were between 45 and 77 years old and who said that they had not been diagnosed as having a serious chronic illness such as heart disease or bronchitis. Depression was measured with four items which included one item on hopelessness ('During the past month have you felt so sad, discouraged, hopeless or had so many problems that you wondered if anything was worthwhile?'). Hopelessness was classified into three categories on the basis of a six-point rating scale, and depression was dichotomized as absent or present in terms of the cut-off point for defining clinical depression. The relative mortality risk was 2.2 for low to severe hopelessness and was 1.5 for depression when adjusted for age, sex, race, years of education, marital status, smoking, total cholesterol, systolic blood pressure, body mass index, alcohol use and physical activity.

PROSPECTIVE STUDIES ON MORTALITY AND CLOSE RELATIONSHIPS

The first longitudinal study examining the relationship between social relationships and mortality was reported by Lisa Berkman and Leonard Syme (1979). In 1965 a representative sample of 6,928 adults in Alameda County near San Francisco were surveyed, and the number of people in the sample who died in the subsequent nine years was noted. Mortality was related to each of the five following measures of social relationships: (1) whether they were married; (2) how many close friends and relatives they had and how often they saw them; (3) whether they belonged to a church; (4) whether they belonged to any formal or informal groups; and (5) a global social network index based on the first four measures in which the first two variables were weighted more heavily than the last two.

Table 3.2 presents the percentage of married and non-married women and men who died in three consecutive age groups as well as the relative risk of the non-married dying. As expected, more people die in the older age groups. People who were married lived longer than those who were not married, but this difference was only statistically significant for men. In other words, being married was more important for the longevity of men than of women. In the 30–49 age range, non-married men were almost three times as likely to die as married men, whereas there was little difference between married and non-married women in the same age group. The relative risk of dying for non-married men decreased with age from 2.9 to 1.3.

Table 3.3 shows the percentage of deaths and the relative risk of death for women and men with the highest and lowest social contact. People who had more frequent contact with close friends and relatives lived longer than those with fewer contacts. Although this difference was statistically significant for both women and men, it was greater for women. For example, in the 30–49 age group, women with the lowest contact were almost three times as likely to die as those with the highest, whereas men with the lowest were only almost twice as likely to die as those with the highest.

Church and group membership were also related to mortality but the differences were generally less marked than those for marital status and social contact. These four measures of social relationships predicted mortality independently of one another. So, for example, marital status was still related to mortality when the influence of the other three measures was controlled. The effect of not being married could be compensated for by having more contact with close friends and relatives. People who were not married but who had much contact with friends and relatives had mortality rates which were equal

Age	Women			Men		
group	Married	Non-married	Risk	Married	Non-married	Risk
30–49	3.0	3.8	1.3	3.0	8.6	2.9
50–59	7.1	9.6	1.4	12.1	25.5	2.1
60–69	14.4	20.7	1.4	26.9	33.7	1.3

(Adapted from Berkman and Syme 1979, p. 189)

Table 3.2 Percentage of deaths and relative risk of death in married and non-married women and men in three age groups

Age	Women			Men		
group	High	Low	Risk	High	Low	Risk
30–49	1.9	5.4	2.8	2.9	5.1	1.8
50–59	6.6	12.3	1.9	11.0	14.5	1.3
60–69	11.4	31.0	2.7	22.2	40.7	1.8

(Adapted from Berkman and Syme 1979, p. 189)

Table 3.3 Percentage of deaths and relative risk of death in three age groups of women and men with high or low close contacts

to those who were married but who had little contact with friends and relatives. When the four measures were combined into a single overall index, similar results were found. People with the lowest score on this index were more than twice as likely to die as those with the highest score.

Because this study is a non-experimental design, the association between these measures of social relationships and mortality could be due to one or more uncontrolled factors such as physical health. People who are physically unwell may have fewer social relationships and may also die sooner than those who are well. In other words, their physical health may determine both their social relationships and their longevity. The influence of a number of such factors on the relationship between the social network index and mortality were investigated. These factors were: (1) level of general physical health; (2) socio-economic status based on income and educational level; (3) smoking (current, past or never); (4) obesity; (5) alcohol consumption; (6) frequency of physical activity; (7) an index of seven health practices (such as sleeping seven or eight hours per night); and (8) use of health services. Mortality was still associated with the social network index when each of these factors was controlled. This finding suggests that none of these factors was responsible for the association between mortality and social involvement.

In most of the longitudinal studies on marital status and mortality, the married have been compared with the non-married as a whole and not with the different categories of the non-married, presumably because the numbers in these groups would have been too small for this purpose. For example, in the Berkman and Syme study 632 of the 2,496 women were in the non-married category. It is of interest to know whether the risk of mortality is higher in all the categories of the non-married group. Yoav Ben-Shlomo and his colleagues (1993) reported on such differences for 18,403 male Whitehall civil servants in London who were followed up for 18 years and who were aged 40–64 when they were initially tested between 1967 and 1969. Marital status was categorized as married, single, widowed or other, with the other category assumed to represent the separated and divorced men. The mortality rate per 1,000 person years adjusted for age was highest for the divorced/separated (21.0), followed by the widowed men (20.6), the single (16.9) and the married (13.9). In other words, the relative mortality risk or ratio of the non-married to the married was 1.51 for the divorced/separated, 1.48 for the widowed and 1.2 for the single.

When 12 factors which might influence the risk of death were controlled, the mortality ratio was reduced to 1.24 for the divorced/separated and the widowed and 1.05 for the single. In other words, there was little difference in the mortality risk for married and single men when these risk factors were controlled. The 12 risk factors were: (1) age; (2) employment grade; (3) height; (4) body mass; (5) smoking (current, past and never); (6) systolic blood pressure; (7) cholesterol level; (8) impaired glucose tolerance; (9) diabetes; (10) forced expiratory volume of the lungs; (11) forced vital capacity of the lungs; and (12) disease. With respect to the reported cause of death, widowed men were more likely to die of coronary heart disease and divorced/separated men of cancer.

Caution should always be exercised when generalizing from studies since they may give inconsistent results. For example, Shah Ebrahim and his colleagues (1995) followed up over 11 years 7,735 40- to 59-year-old men selected at random from one general medical practice in each of 24 British towns. When adjusted for 12 other factors, the relative risk of mortality was greatest for the single men (1.5), followed by the divorced/separated (1.2) and the widowed (1.1). The 12 factors that were controlled were: (1) age; (2) social class; (3) cigarette smoking; (4) body mass; (5) physical activity; (6) alcohol consumption; (7) systolic blood pressure; (8) blood cholesterol level; (9) forced expiratory volume of the lungs; (10) recall of doctor's diagnosis of heart disease or diabetes mellitus; (11) antihypertensive medication; and (12) employment status five years later.

The last two studies were restricted to men. Because of the longstanding interest in the effect of widowhood on health, there have been several longitudinal studies which have compared mortality in the married and the widowed in both women and men. In one of these studies, Knud Helsing and Moyses Szklo (1981) identified 4,032 white people living in Washington County in the American state of Maryland who were 18 years or older in 1963 and who became widowed in the subsequent 11 years. This group was compared with an equal number of married people who were matched for race, sex, age and geographic category of residence (urban, suburban or rural and small town). The crude or unadjusted mortality rate per 1,000 person years was significantly higher in the widowed than in the married sample for both women and men. The crude mortality ratio was 1.18 for women and 1.33 for men. When the mortality rate was adjusted for six other factors mortality was only significantly higher in the widowers. The adjusted mortality ratio was 1.04 for women and 1.26 for men. The six factors which were controlled were: (1) age; (2) years of education; (3) cigarette smoker currently; (4) age at first marriage; (5) frequency of church attendance; and (6) the number of bathrooms for their exclusive use. The relative risk of death was greater for men under 75. In addition, there was no tendency for widowers to die in the first 12 months following bereavement than in the subsequent years.

Ideally, of course, if one were examining the effect of marital status on mortality it is important to have information on the marital status of people in the study over time. So, for example, some of the married people may have become divorced and some of the divorced people may have remarried. In addition, it would be valuable to have data on how long people had been married. Lee Lillard and Linda Waite (1995) reported such a study. They analysed data from 1968 to 1988 from the Panel Study of Income Dynamics which is based on a representative sample of 5,500 American households. They noted that for men those who were widowed, divorced, separated or never married had approximately equal risks of dying and that these risks were significantly higher than for the currently married. For women those who were currently married were less likely to die than those who were not married. Compared with the never married, separated women were more likely to die while the widowed were less likely to do so. Women and men whose current marriage was longer were less likely to die and this relationship was stronger for women than for men. Note, however, that this study did not examine the relationship between mortality and the total length of time the person had been married.

Most longitudinal studies on social relationships and mortality have looked at the effect of marital status and the amount of social contact rather than the quality of those relationships. One exception is a study by Dan Blazer (1982) who in 1972 followed up over 30 months 331 people who were aged over 64 and who lived in Durham County in the American state of North Carolina. There were three measures of social involvement: (1) available roles and attachments based on marital status and the number of living siblings and children; (2) frequency of social interaction in terms of number of telephone calls and visits with friends or relatives; and (3) perceived social support measured with six items such as 'Enough contact with a confidant' and 'Someone would help if ill or disabled'. Mortality was compared in people scoring in about the lowest 10 per cent of these measures with those scoring above, and was greater in those with less social involvement both when unadjusted and when adjusted for the following 10 factors: (1) age; (2) sex; (3) race; (4) adequacy of income; (5) physical health; (6) self-care; (7) stressful life events; (8) symptoms of major depression; (9) cognitive dysfunction; and (10) current cigarette smoking. Relative risk of mortality was greatest for perceived social support (3.40), followed by available roles and attachments (2.04) and frequency of social interaction (1.88). This study suggests that quality of social participation is more strongly related to mortality than quantity.

A later study was reported by Bertil Hanson and his colleagues (1989) who in 1982–83 followed up over five years 500 men who were born in 1914 in Malmo, Sweden and who lived there. The men, therefore, were all about 68 years old at the time they were tested. Eight aspects of social participation were assessed. Each measure was dichotomized with most people categorized as having high social involvement. Of the eight measures, only availability of emotional support and adequacy of social participation were significantly related to mortality when adjusted or unadjusted for 12 other factors. The 12 factors were: (1) marital status (living alone/cohabiting); (2) social class; (3) hypertension; (4) physical activity; (5) alcohol consumption; (6) smoking (since 1969); (7) plasma cholesterol; (8) body mass index; (9) arteriosclerotic leg disease; (10) myocardial infarction (heart disease); (11) diabetes mellitus; and (12) cancer. When adjusted for all these factors together with the remaining social involvement measures, those with the fewest people to turn to for emotional support were 2.5 times more likely to die than those with more people to turn to, while those who were less satisfied with their participation in social events were 2.2 times more likely to die than those who were more satisfied. Those living alone were twice as likely to die during this period than those who were married or cohabiting. Adequacy of emotional support, on the other hand, was not related to mortality although it was not measured with similar items to those used to assess availability of emotional support. For example, one of the four items for measuring availability of emotional support was 'Do you have any friends or relatives whom you like very much and who like you very much?'. Adequacy of emotional support was not assessed in terms of how satisfied they were with these relationships but with a question such as 'Do you have enough good friends to be with?'. It may have been preferable to have measured adequacy of emotional support with a follow-up to the first question such as 'How satisfied are you with such relationships?' as done by Scott Henderson and his colleagues (1981) in their Interview Schedule for Social Interaction, rather than ask what may appear to be a question about the number of good friends.

LONGITUDINAL STUDIES ON MENTAL HEALTH AND CLOSE RELATIONSHIPS

There are a relatively large number of longitudinal studies which have investigated the relationship between mental health and various indices of social involvement. Many of them, which followed up people over a period of about a year, have shown an association between these two variables. Very few of these studies, however, have reported on the relationship between marital status and subsequent mental health. The results of some of these studies have been inconsistent. Peggy Thoits (1987) looked at the relationship between the separate categories of marital status in women and men and the two mental health measures of anxiety and depression in a representative sample of 1,106 adults living in Chicago who were first interviewed in 1972/3 and then re-interviewed four years later. Anxiety and depression were respectively measured by 12 and 11 items (Derogatis *et al.* 1971) taken from what is now known as the Symptom Checklist (Derogatis 1983). For women and men those married at time 1 had significantly lower anxiety and depression at time 2 than those unmarried for all categories of marital status, apart from widowed men where there was no difference. Although the results are not reported, these differences remained significant when the following variables were controlled: (1) age; (2) race; (3) education; (4) family income; (5) employment; (6) parental status; (7) presence of children under 6; (8) type of negative life event (controllable;

uncontrollable personal; uncontrollable network; deaths; and health-related); (9) sense of mastery; (10) time 1 anxiety; and (11) time 1 depression.

Other longitudinal studies have generally failed to find marital differences in mental health. George Kaplan and his colleagues (1987), in their nine-year follow-up of 6,928 adults in Alameda County, California, reported that marital status was not related to depression nine years later when controlling for the following factors: (1) initial depression; (2) age; (3) sex; (4) education; (5) income; (6) ethnicity; (7) physical health; (8) perceived health; (9) personal uncertainty; (10) anomie; (11) five acute events; (12) social isolation and (13) health practices. Marital status was analysed by comparing the married with either the never married or the previously married.

Thomas Oxman and his colleagues (1992), in their three-year follow-up of 1,962 65-year-olds or over living in New Haven in the American state of Connecticut, found that only people who were widowed prior to the follow-up were more depressed than the married when the factors of sex, housing, education, initial depression and initial functional disability were controlled. In other words, the never married or separated/divorced were no more depressed than the married. Depression was measured with the 20-item Center for Epidemiologic Studies (CES) Depression Scale (Radloff 1977). Using the same scale, Robert McCrae and Paul Costa (1988) compared depression in three groups of individuals who were followed up over about 10 years and who were initially aged between 65 and 74. The three groups were those who were (1) married at both times, (2) widowed during this period and (3) widowed at both times. The data came from the National Health and Nutrition Examination Survey I Epidemiologic Follow-up Study (Cornoni-Huntley *et al.* 1984) which was based on a national sample in the United States who were initially interviewed in 1971–75. There were no differences in depression between the three groups for both women and men when age and years of education were controlled. The failure to find a difference between the married and the widowed was not due to a greater tendency of the depressed to die during this 10-year follow-up period, because they also found no differences in mortality across the three groups.

Most of the longitudinal studies on the relationship between mental health and social involvement have looked at indices of social participation other than that of marital status. Only a few of these will be described to give an indication of their nature and findings. The first such study was reported by Marjorie Lowenthal and Clayton Haven (1968). In a sample of 280 people aged 60 or older and living in San Francisco, they found that people who were depressed were more likely to have lost a confidant in the previous year. While of interest, this study was relatively unsophisticated in that the presence of a confidant was measured with the single question of 'Is there anyone in particular you confide in or talk to about yourself or your problems?' and the data were simply reported as percentages. Depression was measured with eight items referring to satisfaction with life, happiness, usefulness, mood and planning.

A later and more sophisticated study was carried out by Scott Henderson and his colleagues (1981), who examined the relationship between psychological distress and four main measures of social involvement in a cross-sectional representative sample of 756 adults in Canberra, Australia, 231 of whom were followed up over three consecutive four-monthly intervals. The main index of psychological distress was the 30-item version of the General Health Questionnaire (Goldberg 1972), which is a widely used self-report measure of recent non-psychotic psychiatric disorder in community surveys. Two examples of questions from this test are 'Have you recently found everything getting on top of you?' and 'Have you recently been feeling unhappy and distressed?'. Three of the items, however, refer to social involvement which means that there is some overlap in content between this questionnaire and measures of social involvement. The three items are: 'Have you recently been able to feel warmth and affection for those near to you?'; 'Have you recently been finding it easy to get on with other people?'; and 'Have you recently spent much time chatting with other people?' The higher a person's score on this questionnaire the more likely they are to be diagnosed as having a non-psychotic psychiatric disorder, with people being defined as a psychiatric case with a score of 5 or more. Social involvement was measured with the Interview Schedule for Social Interaction mainly in terms of the availability and adequacy of close and less close relationships, which were respectively called attachment and social integration.

Availability of a particular social resource was generally assessed first, followed by a question on its adequacy. For example, availability of attachment was assessed with a question such as 'Is there any particular person you feel you can lean on?' which was then followed with the question 'Would you like to be able to lean more or less on this person?' to determine the adequacy of this attachment. Respondents who answered 'About right' to the second question were scored as being satisfied with this source, while those who replied 'Less', 'Depends on the situation' or 'More' were classified as being dissatisfied. Similarly, availability of social integration was assessed with a question such as 'These days, how many people with similar interests to you do you have contact with?' which was then followed with the question 'Would you like more or less of this or is it about right?' to establish the adequacy of this contact. Because not everyone had all eight of the forms of attachment they were asked about, adequacy of attachment was expressed in terms of the percentage of the attachments with which they were satisfied. The eight forms of attachment were with: (1) someone you intend to go on sharing your life with; (2) someone who knows you very well as a person and who lives in Canberra or nearby; (3) someone you can lean on; (4) someone who feels very close to you; (5) someone who will share your happy feelings and will feel happy because you are; (6) someone you can share your most private feelings with; (7) someone who has comforted you by holding you in their arms; and (8) people at home who really appreciate what you do for them. In addition, there were two other indices of social involvement. One was the degree to which a person accepted not having the eight forms of attachment. The other was whether the person had any unpleasantness or rows with one, two or three people who were close to them.

The validity of these measures was assessed in several ways. In the cross-sectional sample, the presumed relationship between these measures and marital status and length of stay in Canberra was examined. As expected, availability of attachment was highest in the married and lowest in the divorced and separated. Adequacy of attachment (expressed as a percentage) was highest in the widowed and married and lowest in the separated and divorced. The acceptance of not having attachments was highest in the widowed and least in the married and the divorced. Availability of social integration was similar in all groups except the widowed, who had the lowest level whereas the adequacy of social integration was similar in all groups. The relatively few people who had lived in Canberra for less than six months had less adequate social integration than the majority who had lived there longer. In the follow-up sample, extroversion was found to be positively related to the availability of social integration but not to that of attachment. Finally, people who knew one of 114 participants well were asked to answer the questions the way they thought the participant would have done. The correlation between the answers of these two people was highest for availability of social integration (0.59) and attachment (0.42) and lowest for adequacy of social integration (0.29) and attachment (0.39). Although these correlations are not as high as is desirable, they compare favourably with similar assessments in other studies.

The correlations between the six measures of social involvement assessed at the first interview and the General Health Questionnaire of psychological distress assessed at all four interviews are presented in Table 3.4 for the 177 participants who were not considered distressed at the first interview, as measured by the slightly more stringent criterion of six or less on the General Health Questionnaire. Adequacy of both social integration and attachment but not their availability was significantly associated with less psychological distress four and twelve months later. The correlations for the adequacy of social integration are slightly higher than those for the adequacy of attachment, although it is not reported whether this difference is statistically significant. The fact that the two correlations of −0.12 and 0.15 are not always given as being significant is presumably due to their being rounded up.

In another study Johanna Lackner and her colleagues (1993) reported on the relationship between five measures of social involvement and, six months later, two indices of psychological distress, in three consecutive six-month periods for 520 gay men who were at risk for AIDS and who were living in Chicago. The five measures of social involvement were: (1) perceived availability of emotional and material support (e.g. has someone to talk to when upset); (2) subjective integration (e.g. feels loved); (3) objective integration (e.g. number of group memberships); (4) validation (people in your personal life who approve of the way you do things); and (5) social conflict (e.g. feels misunderstood). The two measures of psychological distress were a modified

Social involvement	Time 1	Time 2	Time 3	Time 4
Availability of attachment	−0.09	0.01	−0.10	0.06
Adequacy of attachment (%)	−0.23**	−0.22**	−0.12	−0.15*
Acceptance of non-attachment	−0.02	0.04	0.10	−0.09
Availability of social integration	0.00	−0.10	−0.09	−0.09
Adequacy of social integration	−0.12*	−0.31***	−0.06	−0.21**
Rows with close others	0.15*	0.15	0.06	0.02

* p<0.05; ** p<0.01; *** p<0.001

(Adapted from Henderson *et al.* 1981, p. 147)

Table 3.4 Correlations between initial social involvement and initial and later psychological distress in people not distressed initially (n = 177)

version of the 58-item Symptom Checklist and its 11-item Depression subscale. Five of the 58 items refer to problems with others: (1) feeling critical of others; (2) feeling others do not understand you or are unsympathetic; (3) feeling inferior to others; (4) feeling people are unfriendly or dislike you; and (5) feeling lonely. At least one of these was included in the Depression subscale. Consequently, there was some overlap in content between the distress and social involvement measures. The most consistent relationship was between subjective integration and subsequent depression when five variables were controlled and when all the five indices of social involvement were examined together. The five variables which were controlled were age, race, income, HIV-serostatus and earlier psychological distress.

TEMPORAL RELATIONSHIP BETWEEN MENTAL HEALTH AND CLOSE RELATIONSHIPS

Most longitudinal studies which have looked at the relationship between social involvement and mental health have reported on the relationship between earlier social involvement and later mental health, controlling for earlier mental health. Generally, however, they have not also examined the relationship between earlier mental health and later social involvement. This is unfortunate because if the relationship between earlier mental health and later social involvement is significantly stronger than that between earlier social involvement and later mental health, then this finding implies that mental health may have a stronger effect on social involvement than social involvement has on mental health. Whatever the results, it is not possible to say that these relationships express a causal effect because they may be due to other factors which have not been controlled. However, they do provide some evidence of the nature of the relationship between these variables over time where it is difficult or not possible to carry out a true experiment in which people are randomly assigned to receiving different treatments, such as levels of social involvement.

Two ways of comparing the relative size of the temporal or cross-lagged relationships between two variables are cross-lagged panel correlation analysis and structural equation modelling. Few papers report using the first technique, presumably because of the critical review of it by Rogosa (1980). I used it in a study which investigated the relationship between self-esteem and having a close relationship seen as unconditionally accepting, understanding and genuine (Cramer 1988). Sixty-six undergraduates in their first year at Loughborough University in England completed the 10-item Rosenberg (1965) Self-Esteem Scale and the 64-item revised Barrett-Lennard (1964) Relationship Inventory on two occasions separated by 15 weeks. The results suggested that the quality of a close relationship has a stronger influence on self-esteem than self-esteem has on the quality of a close relationship, since the cross-lagged correlation between relationship quality at time 1 and self-esteem at time 2 ($r = 0.26$) was significantly more positive than that between self-esteem at time 1 and relationship quality at time 2 ($r = 0.03$).

This finding was unlikely to be due to the influence of other uncontrolled factors because the following four conditions proposed by David Kenny (1975) were met. First, relationship quality and self-esteem were measured at the same two points in time and referred to the same period of time which, in this case, was how they felt at the time of completing the questionnaires. If the measures reflected different lengths of time, they would not be comparable in this respect. Second, the correlation between relationship quality and self-esteem at the first point in time ($r = 0.14$) was similar to that at the second point in time ($r = 0.22$). Differing correlations would imply that the influence of other factors on the two variables was not the same. In other words, the two points in time would not be comparable. Third, the test-retest correlations were similar for relationship quality ($r = 0.72$) and self-esteem ($r = 0.82$). Differing test–retest correlations would suggest that the factors affecting relationship quality and self-esteem varied over time. And fourth, the internal reliabilities of the four measures were similar and high. Differing internal reliabilities would indicate that the variables were not being measured with the same reliability, which should bias the relationships between them.

It is likely that these conditions will not often be met, thereby restricting the use of cross-lagged panel correlation analysis. Certainly, they were generally not fulfilled when I re-analysed the data on adequacy of social support and mental health from the study of Scott Henderson and his colleagues. As a consequence, the results of this analysis were not reported (Cramer *et al.* 1996, 1997). A second disadvantage of this method is that it does not provide an index of the strength of the cross-lagged relationship which takes account of their other associations. These two drawbacks are not shared by the second method of structural equation modelling. A limitation of this second approach, however, is that it does not rule out the possibility that the stronger cross-lagged relationship may be due to other confounding variables which have not been controlled.

One way of using structural equation modelling to explore the temporal relationship between two variables is to compare the extent to which different temporal models provide the best fit to the data. In terms of our two variables of relationship quality and self-esteem, there are basically four such models, as shown in Figure 3.1. All four models assume that the variable at time 2 is affected by the same variable at time 1, so that self-esteem at time 1 influences self-esteem at time 2 and relationship quality at time 1 affects relationship quality at time 2. The first model assumes that relationship quality at time 1 affects self-esteem at time 2 and self-esteem at time 1 influences relationship quality at time 2. In other words, there is a reciprocal relationship between the two variables where each affects the other. The second and third models postulate a one-way relationship between the two variables. In the second model relationship quality at time 1 influences self-esteem at time 2 whereas in the third model self-esteem at time 1 influences relationship quality at time 2. The fourth model presumes no temporal relationship between the two variables. Using structural equation modelling, I found that the second model provided the best fit to the data, suggesting that relationship quality influenced self-esteem (Cramer 1990).

Looking at just the reciprocal model, Neal Krause and his colleagues (1989) also found evidence for a one-way effect in which satisfaction with social support was related to less depression 19 months later in a representative sample of 252 people aged 65 or older living in Galveston, Texas. Satisfaction with support was measured with a modified version of the Inventory of Socially Supportive Behaviors (Barrera *et al.* 1981; Krause 1986) in terms of informational, tangible and emotional support received from significant others, while depression was assessed with the Center for Epidemiologic Studies Depression Scale (Radloff 1977) but excluding items dealing with interpersonal difficulties. Dani Ulrich-Jakubowski and her colleagues (1988), however, found support for a one-way effect in which depression was related to less marital adjustment 15 months later in 78 men whose average age was 61. Depression was assessed with the 13-item scale of the Symptom Checklist (Derogatis 1983) while marital adjustment was measured with the Dyadic Adjustment Scale (Spanier 1976).

When I used structural equation modelling to re-analyse the data of Scott Henderson and his colleagues on mental health and adequacy of social support, I found that the best-fitting model was one of no temporal relationship for adequacy of attachment and mental health, and a one-way relationship for adequacy of social integration and mental health in which mental health influenced adequacy of social integration (Cramer *et al.* 1996, 1997). The reason

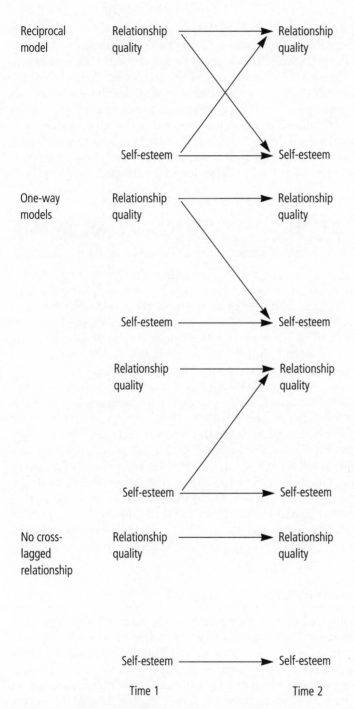

Figure 3.1 Four models representing reciprocal, one-way and no cross-lagged relationships between relationship quality and self-esteem

for these discrepant results is not clear. The three earlier studies defined support in terms of close relationships and so it is more appropriate to compare their findings with the measure of adequacy of attachment. One explanation may be that the close relationship measure does not assess whether there is a change in closeness in the relationship and who is primarily responsible for that change. For example, describing a relationship as less close may be the result of either withdrawing or being rejected from that relationship. Experiencing psychological distress may be more likely to lead to withdrawal, and being rejected to psychological distress. Samples which vary in terms of which of these two processes predominates may give differing results.

CONTROLLED INTERVENTIONS FOR TREATING PSYCHOLOGICAL DISTRESS

Longitudinal studies, of course, cannot determine whether the presence of a close relationship or an improvement in its quality enhances mental health. The only way to determine this is to carry out a controlled intervention in which people are randomly assigned to variations in the supportiveness of close relationships and to see if an improvement in mental health results for the more supportive relationships. This is obviously difficult to arrange. However, there are at least three situations in which this kind of opportunity has arisen. One concerns the evaluation of providing support to people, such as the bereaved, who are particularly vulnerable to suffering psychological distress. Another involves evaluating the effectiveness of psychological treatments in which there is an attempt to control for the effects of simply having a supportive relationship. In both these cases people are provided with a supportive relationship which may develop into a closer and more confiding relationship. The third situation is the most appropriate in that it endeavours to improve the close relationship itself. These three kinds of study do not, of course, tell us whether mental health affects social relationships. This question is addressed in research which includes measuring improvement in such relationships as part of the evaluation of the effectiveness of treatments for psychological distress.

Bereavement Interventions

One study which showed that providing the recently bereaved with supportive relationships enhances their mental health was reported by Mary Vachon and her colleagues (1980). They randomly assigned 162 recently bereaved widows in Toronto either to a control group which did not receive the intervention, or to the intervention which involved contact when needed with a trained widow on a one-to-one basis. The women were followed up six, 12 and 24 months after bereavement and the main measure of mental health was the 30-item General Health Questionnaire. Seventy per cent of the widows had a score of

5 or higher on this questionnaire, which is commonly used as the cut-off point for defining a psychiatric case (Vachon *et al.* 1982). The biggest difference between the two groups was at 24 months, when 58 per cent of the intervention group showed improvement compared with 34 per cent of the control group. The intervention appeared to be most effective with the widows who were initially the most distressed.

Several studies, however, have failed to find that support interventions enhance psychological well-being. Michael Caserta and Dale Lund (1993) found no differences in depression and grief for 286 recently bereaved women and men, aged 50 or over and living in Utah, who were randomly assigned to either eight weekly self-help group meetings, an additional ten monthly meetings or a control group without any meetings. Depression was measured with the 30-item Geriatric Depression Scale (Yesavage *et al.* 1983) and grief with the 13-item Texas Revised Inventory of Grief (Faschingbauer 1981). Participants were tested at the following four points after bereavement: 2–3 months; 4–5 months; 14–15 months; and 24 months. Thirteen of the 26 groups were led by people who had been widowed for four to five years and who had successfully coped with their own bereavement, while the remaining 13 groups were run by practitioners or doctoral students in counselling programs. The leaders did not act as counsellors or therapists but were there to facilitate the group process of coming to terms with their loss. About 43 per cent of the participants had a depression score indicating clinical depression. The failure to obtain an intervention effect may have been due to a 'floor effect' in that not enough participants were sufficiently depressed for a significant decrease in depression to occur.

Fred Tudiver and his colleagues (1992) also found no differences in mental health, social adjustment or social support for 113 recently bereaved widowers in Canada who were randomly assigned to either nine weekly mutual help groups or a waiting-list control condition which involved waiting eight months before being able to join such groups. Mental health was assessed with the 28-item General Health Questionnaire, the 13-item Beck Depression Inventory (Beck and Beck 1972) and the 20-item State Anxiety Scale (Spielberger 1983), social adjustment with the 42-item Social Adjustment Scale (Weissman and Bothwell 1976) and social support with the 27-item Social Support Questionnaire (Sarason *et al.* 1983). Participants were tested eight months after the orientation session at the beginning of the study. The groups were run by two of ten trained facilitators, most of whom were themselves widowed. The absence of differences between the two groups may have been due to the relatively short follow-up period of eight months and/or the possibility that the participants may not have been sufficiently severely distressed.

Placebo Control Interventions in Psychotherapy

Studies which evaluate the effectiveness of treatments should ideally have a control condition which is in all other respects similar to the treatment except that it does not contain the component or components that are thought to make the treatment effective. In the evaluation of drug treatments this control is known as a placebo control. The placebo takes the same form as the drug (i.e. a solution or pill) but does not contain the drug. In addition, it is preferable that the person administering the treatments does not know which one is the placebo. As some patients improve when receiving the placebo, it is important to have this control to find out whether the drug is more effective than the placebo. Unfortunately, we do not know what accounts for the effectiveness of the placebo. A similar kind of control is necessary in the evaluation of psychological treatments. However, unless we use an inert solution or pill, it is not possible to ensure that the person giving the placebo treatment is unaware of its nature.

One placebo control treatment that has been used in psychotherapy research is to allow patients to discuss their problems but without offering a therapeutic intervention. This kind of discussion may be similar to that offered by one's friends although they may be more inclined to give advice. If this control condition is more effective than no treatment or is as effective as a psychological intervention thought to be effective, then it is possible that social support may act in a similar way. One such study by Brian Shaw (1977) in Canada found that on the 21-item Beck Depression Inventory (Beck *et al.* 1961) depressed students attending a discussion group showed more improvement than those receiving no treatment, as much improvement as those receiving behaviour therapy but less improvement than those receiving cognitive therapy. In other words, the results of this study suggested that talking to others about your problem may reduce depression.

A few other studies have compared the effectiveness of professional psychotherapists and non-professional helpers and found little difference in effectiveness between them. Hans Strupp and Suzanne Hadley (1979) assigned 45 depressed and withdrawn male university students at Vanderbilt University in Nashville, Tennessee to either professional therapists or university teachers with a reputation for being warm and interested in students. Students who were unable to be treated at that time were asked to wait three months or to attend the university counselling centre for treatment. All of them opted to wait for treatment and formed the waiting-list control group. Treatment consisted of about 18 twice-weekly individual sessions. The five professional therapists had an average of 23 years of experience. Three of them were psychoanalytically oriented psychiatrists and the other two were experientially oriented psychologists. Therapeutic improvement was assessed in various ways immediately after treatment and about nine months later. In general, students receiving help showed more improvement than those on the waiting list but there was little difference in improvement between students being seen by either the professional or the non-professional helpers.

Charles Marmar and his colleagues (1988) in San Francisco found that 61 widows with unresolved grief who were randomly assigned to either 12 weekly individual sessions of brief psychodynamic therapy or 12 weekly meetings of mutual self-help groups generally showed equal improvement on various measures including social adjustment immediately after treatment, four months later and one year later. Each mutual self-help group was run by a trained widow who appeared to have successfully resolved her own loss.

Relationship Enhancement

The most pertinent kind of study for determining whether improved close relationships leads to increased mental health is one in which the effect on mental health of improving just the close relationship is compared with the effect on that relationship of improving only mental health. If improving the relationship is more beneficial to mental health than improving mental health is to the relationship, this finding implies that close relationships can enhance mental health. Three such studies have been published where mental health was defined in terms of depression. All three studies essentially showed that while marital therapy is as effective as non-marital therapy in reducing depression, marital therapy is more effective than non-marital therapy in enhancing the marital or marital-like relationship. In other words, while improving marital satisfaction decreases depression, reducing depression does not heighten marital satisfaction. Daniel O'Leary and Steven Beach (1990) in New York State compared the effectiveness of individual cognitive therapy and conjoint behavioural marital therapy against a waiting-list control in the treatment of depression in 36 wives with marital problems. Therapy consisted of 15–16 weekly sessions which were provided by the same three therapists. Depression was assessed with the Beck Depression Inventory and marital satisfaction with the Dyadic Adjustment Scale immediately before and after treatment and eight months later. Immediately after treatment and eight months later depression was lower in the two treatment groups than in the waiting-list control, but there was no difference between the two treatment groups. Marital satisfaction was greater in the marital therapy group than in the cognitive therapy group immediately after therapy and at follow-up, while there was no difference between the cognitive therapy and the waiting-list group.

Neil Jacobson and his colleagues (1991) in North America compared the effect of 20 sessions of conjoint behavioural marital therapy, individual cognitive-behavioural therapy and a combined treatment on depression in wives from 23 distressed and 37 non-distressed marital relationships. There were five therapists, all of whom treated at least two women in each of the three conditions. Among the measures used to assess depression and marital distress were the Beck Depression Inventory and the Dyadic Adjustment Scale which were administered immediately before and after treatment. Women selected for treatment had a higher score on the Beck Depression Inventory than those in the previous study but the cut-off point for classifying distressed and non-distressed marriages was similar. For the maritally distressed wives all three treatments resulted in a similar and statistically significant reduction in depression, while only behavioural marital therapy also produced a significant decrease in marital distress.

Lineke Emanuels-Zuurveen and Paul Emmelkamp (1996) in the Netherlands compared the effects of 16 weekly one-hour sessions of individual behavioural-cognitive therapy and conjoint behavioural marital therapy on depression in 27 maritally distressed wives and husbands. Depression was measured with the Beck Depression Inventory and marital distress with the Maudsley Marital Questionnaire (Crowe 1978) immediately before and after treatment. The therapists were advanced clinical psychology students, and as therapists did not seem to administer both treatments the results may have been due to the effects of therapists rather than the type of therapy given. However, the results were essentially similar to those of the previous two studies in that both treatments showed a significant decrease in depression while conjoint behavioural marital therapy resulted in significantly more improvement in the relationship than individual cognitive-behavioural therapy. Unfortunately, the last two studies did not include follow-up assessments so we do not know to what extent the improvement persisted.

No attempt was made in any of these three studies to ascertain whether the improvement in depression preceded or followed the increase in relationship satisfaction. Consequently, these studies did not directly address the issue of the causal relationship between depression and relationship satisfaction. One way of doing this may be to look at the immediate effects of trying to manipulate these two variables.

EFFECT OF PSYCHOTHERAPY ON SOCIAL ADJUSTMENT

A number of studies have evaluated the effectiveness of treatments for psychological distress in terms of social adjustment measured in various ways. The results of these studies have generally shown no improvement in social adjustment despite improvements in the main problem being treated. For example, Michael Gelder and Isaac Marks (1966) in London found little improvement in five-point clinician ratings of either family or other relationships in 20 agoraphobic patients randomly assigned to either behaviour therapy or psychotherapy for interpersonal problems, although agoraphobia had decreased. Patients were seen three times weekly for an average of 19 weeks for psychotherapy and 23 weeks for behaviour therapy and were followed up for a year after treatment. Similarly, Isaac Marks and his colleagues (1968) noted no improvement in clinician ratings of either family or other relationships in 28 phobic patients randomly assigned to three months of either systematic desensitization or hypnosis despite the phobias having improved. Michael Gelder and his colleagues (1973) also found no improvement in clinician ratings of either family or other relationships in 36 phobic patients randomly assigned to 15 weekly individual sessions of either flooding (asking patients to imagine being in the most frightening situations involving their phobia), systematic desensitization or a non-specific control treatment.

Bruce Sloane and his colleagues (1975) in the United States observed no improvement in clinician ratings of social isolation from start to end of treatment in 94 outpatients randomly assigned to either behaviour therapy, psychoanalytic psychotherapy or a waiting-list control condition, despite patients in the two therapy groups showing greater improvement than those on the waiting-list in their three main presenting symptoms. Treatment consisted of about 14 weekly individual sessions by experienced therapists. In the study previously described, Hans Strupp and Suzanne Hadley (1979) also found no differences between the three groups in the change in the clinician rating of the patients' interpersonal relationships or family adjustment from the start to the end of treatment, although the students in the two treatment groups improved in other ways. The lack of improvement in social adjustment in these studies may have been due to the relatively high level of social adjustment shown by the patients. On the other hand, Myrna Weissman and her colleagues (1974) in the United States found that of 150 moderately depressed women, those who were randomly assigned to eight months of weekly individual psychotherapy showed less social friction and better communication than those who were randomly allocated to monthly assessment and prescription interviews with a psychiatrist for the antidepressant drug, amitryptyline hydrochloride. Although the drug reduced depression it did not affect social adjustment. However, six and twelve months after treatment there were no differences in social adjustment between the two groups (Weissman *et al.* 1976).

MARITAL STATUS OR COHABITATION

There appear to be few relatively well-developed explanations of the ways in which marriage might enhance well-being. Emile Durkheim (1897/1952, p. 189) suggested that it was primarily due to the presence of children rather than marriage *per se*, particularly for women, and that the effect would be stronger the more children there were since this increased the cohesion of the family through the interchange and intensity of commonly shared views (pp. 201–2). On this basis, Frances Kobrin and Gerry Hendershot (1977) proposed that people living in families, who were not married, would have lower mortality than those living alone. They found that for both unmarried women and men mortality was lowest for people who headed a family and it was highest for unmarried women living as dependants in a family and for unmarried men living alone. Their data was an American national sample of about 20,000. More recently, I suggested that the poorer health of the non-married may be partly due to the fact that they were more likely to be living on their own (Cramer 1993a). If so, the well-being of those living alone should be worse than that of those cohabiting. Analysing a nationally representative sample of 6,572 British adults surveyed in 1984/85, however, I found no differences in physical or psychological health between those cohabiting and those living alone, controlling for age, education and income. Inez Joung and her colleagues (1994), on the other hand, noted that those living alone generally had poorer physical health than those cohabiting when age, sex, education, urbanization, religion and country of birth were controlled. Their data came from a representative survey of 18,973 people living in and around Eindhoven in south Holland, carried out in 1991.

Since none of these studies compared the well-being of the married with that of those cohabiting, it is not possible to determine whether those who are married have better health than those who cohabit. This comparison was made by Lawrence Kurdek (1991a) for depression using a nationally representative sample of 6,573 American adults surveyed in 1987/88. He found that married people were less depressed than those who were cohabiting who, in turn, were less depressed than those living without another adult, before and after controlling for age, income, race, education and presence of children. This finding suggests that any beneficial effects of marriage with respect to depression do not wholly depend on living together. However, the relationship between depression and whether one was married, cohabited or lived alone was small, accounting for only about one per cent of the total variance in depression.

SUMMARY

There is growing evidence from longitudinal studies that the presence or supportiveness of a close relationship is related to living longer and being less psychologically distressed. The causal direction of this association, however, is less easy to establish. One direction, sometimes known as the selection explanation, is that those who are physically and psychologically healthier are better able to form a close relationship. The opposite direction, sometimes called the protection explanation, is that having a close relationship leads to better physical and psychological health. A third possibility is that both causal pathways are operating to some degree. The few longitudinal studies which have compared the temporal association between close relationships and mental health have found either no temporal relationship between the two variables or one consistent with the protection explanation. Controlled clinical trials of the effectiveness of treatments for psychological distress have also generally lent support for the protection hypothesis, in that treating psychological distress has usually not enhanced social relationships. However, these studies may not be directly relevant to this issue as the measures of social adjustment were not specifically concerned with changes in close relationships and the patients may not have had unsatisfactory close relationships. Controlled clinical trials comparing treatments for improving marital relationships with those for reducing depression have supported the protection hypothesis in that while depression was reduced by both treatments, marital relationships were improved only by the relationship treatments.

4

Relationship Compatibility and its Prediction

Potentially there are a very large number of factors that might lead to the development or breakdown of satisfying close relationships. For example, having similar interests may cause people to spend time together engaging in activities which bring pleasure and enjoyment to the relationship. On the other hand, the loss of an interest once shared between two friends may result in their spending less time together, thereby diminishing their mutual enjoyment. It is possible that people know what the qualities are that generally make for good close relationships and that there is considerable agreement on what the most important characteristics are. Consequently, I will begin by looking at what people say are the major factors that are responsible for a successful relationship and for the break-up of such a relationship.

DESIRABLE AND UNDESIRABLE QUALITIES IN CLOSE RELATIONSHIPS

Ideally one would first of all ask people what they thought made for a good relationship or what qualities they looked for in a partner or friend, without the research worker asking about any particular qualities since doing this may bias what people say. A few studies have asked such open-ended questions. Geoffrey Gorer (1971) included three such questions in his survey on sex and marriage which was carried out in 1969 on an English random sample of 1,037 women and 949 men under 45. The sample also included 156 16- to 21-year-old children of some of the parents interviewed. The first question was what women thought were the three most important qualities a husband should have and what men thought were the three most important qualities a wife should have. The second question was what factors wreck a marriage, while the third question was what factors make for a happy marriage. Answers to these questions were grouped together into a smaller number of factors although Gorer does not report how reliable or how much agreement there was in doing this. The percentage of women and men whose answers to these three questions fell into these groups are respectively shown in Tables 4.1, 4.2 and 4.3.

The three most important qualities women thought a husband should have were consideration, affection and generosity while men reported that the three most important qualities a wife should have was being a good housekeeper and mother, and having various personal qualities such as being attractive and a good conversationalist (Gorer 1971, pp. 72–3). Lack of communication, inconsiderateness and infidelity were the three factors most commonly mentioned by both women and men as wrecking marriages (Gorer 1971,

Factors	Women/ husbands	Men/ wives
Understanding, consideration	52	24
Love, affection, kindness	44	22
Generosity	19	2
Sense of humour	18	11
Patience, level-headed	16	13
Love of home, co-operation	14	6
Faithfulness	12	12
Equanimity, good temper	13	10
Good father, love children	12	3
Tolerance	11	8
Thoughtfulness	10	1
Shares responsibility and interests	8	8
Fairness, justice	8	3
Good worker, ambitious	8	2
Moral qualities	7	12
Economical	5	2
Personal qualities	4	28
Treat wife as a person	4	2
Intelligence	2	6
Virility, strength	2	1
Good housekeeper	1	37
Good mother, love children	1	34
Good cook	0	14

Table 4.1 Percentage of English women and men citing the three most important qualities a spouse should have (Gorer 1971, pp. 72–3)

Factors	Women	Men
Neglect, bad communication	33	26
Selfishness, intolerance	25	25
Infidelity, jealousy	22	29
Poverty, money disagreements	19	15
Conflicting personalities, no common interests	12	13
Quarrelling	9	11
Sexual incompatibility, fertility	9	11
Lack of affection	8	7
Drunkenness, gambling	7	7
Lack of trust, untruthfulness	7	6
No house of one's own, in-laws	4	5
Don't know	1	2
Total	156	157

Table 4.2 Percentage of English women and men reporting factors that wreck a marriage (Gorer 1971, pp. 84–5)

Factors	Women	Men
Give-and-take, consideration	31	24
Comradeship, doing things together	30	27
Discussing things, understanding	30	26
Mutual trust and help	19	21
Love, affection	18	20
Shared interests	14	13
Children	11	17
Financial security	4	7
Equanimity, good temper	4	3
Sexual compatibility	3	7
Happy home life	3	7
Own home	0	1
Total	168	174

Table 4.3 Percentage of English women and men reporting factors making for a happy marriage (Gorer 1971, p. 64)

pp. 8 4–5). The three factors most frequently cited by women and men for making a happy marriage were consideration, understanding and doing things together (Gorer 1971, p. 64). With the exception of qualities that a wife should have, there appears to be general agreement that spouses should be affectionate, considerate and understanding.

In a smaller study in the United States Lawrence Weiss and Marjorie

Lowenthal (1975) asked 216 women and men, who were representative of an American city and of four stages in life, what their ideal close friend would be like. Their answers were reliably categorized into 19 groups. The percentage of answers falling into the 10 largest groups are displayed in Table 4.4. The three most common characteristics were being understanding, supportive and likeable. These qualities are generally similar to those found by Gorer as bringing about a good marital relationship.

A disadvantage of using open-ended questions is that the answers that people give are those which are immediately accessible and, unless we ask, we do not know their opinion on issues that they have not raised. Consequently, it is useful to know how everyone in a sample rates the importance of a particular factor. Several studies have done this. As described in Chapter 2, when various representative groups of Europeans were asked which of 10 reasons were sufficient for divorce, the five most common reasons were violence, consistent unfaithfulness, lack of love, consistent over-drinking and incompatible personalities (Harding *et al.* 1986, p. 118). The percentages of people endorsing the 10 reasons presented to them are given in Table 2.5. These characteristics can be seen as undesirable qualities in marital relationships. Respondents were also asked to rate which of 13 factors were very, rather or not very important to a successful marriage in the European survey while in a later British survey a fourth category of not at all important was added. The percentages saying these factors were very important are presented in Table 4.5 for the European sample as a whole (Harding *et al.* 1986, p. 120) and for British women and men separately when a different sample was questioned again five years later in 1986 (Ashford 1987, p. 144). Most people reported that faithfulness, mutual respect and appreciation, and understanding and tolerance were the most important factors and the fewest people chose agreement on politics, shared religious belief and same social background as the most important. There seems to be generally little difference in the popularity of these factors across

Understanding, accepting	16
Supportive, dependable	15
Likeable	14
Confidable	9
Easy to talk to	8
Similar interests	8
Similar personalities	6
Share activities	5
Trustworthy	5
Specific personality characteristics	4

Table 4.4 Percentages of qualities used to describe an ideal close friend in an American sample (Weiss and Lowenthal 1975)

Factors	Western Europe (*n* =12,463)	Britain	
		Women (*n* = 816)	Men (*n* = 736)
Mutual respect and appreciation	83	78	75
Faithfulness	81	87	85
Understanding and tolerance	78	72	65
Happy sexual relationship	65	51	50
Having children	55	33	29
Living apart from in-laws	50	57	53
Tastes and interests in common	46	21	20
Adequate income	39	35	33
Good housing	37	35	31
Sharing household chores	30	25	26
Shared religious beliefs	23	10	8
Same social background	22	13	10
Agreement on politics	10	3	2

Table 4.5 Percentages of people stating factors as being very important for a successful marriage in two surveys (Harding *et al.* 1986, p. 120; Ashford 1987, p. 144)

gender, age or marital status (Ashford 1987, p. 144; Harding *et al.* 1986, pp. 126–7). Once again, we see affection, understanding and consideration emerging as important factors for maintaining a successful marital relationship.

In the largest cross-cultural study carried out on students and co-ordinated by David Buss (Buss *et al.* 1990), 9,474 students from 37 cultures were asked to rate the importance of 18 characteristics in choosing a mate. Table 4.6 lists the 18 characteristics together with their mean ratings for women and men in each culture averaged across all culture. These characteristics were taken from a study first conducted in the United States in 1939 (Hill 1945) and which has since been repeated in 1956 (McGinnis 1958), 1967 (Hudson and Henze 1969) and 1977 (Hoyt and Hudson 1981). The characteristics were rated on a four-point scale ranging from irrelevant or unimportant (0) to indispensable (3) in mate selection. Overall the women and men ordered the characteristics in a very similar way with mutual attraction, dependability and emotional stability as most important and similar political and religious background and chastity as least important. However, for some of the characteristics there were sex and cultural differences. The biggest cultural difference was for chastity with samples from China, India, Indonesia, Iran and Taiwan placing the greatest importance on it and samples from Sweden, Finland, Norway, the Netherlands and West Germany the least. The largest sex difference (expressed as a correlation between sex and the rating of that characteristic) was for good financial prospects, followed by good looks, being a good cook and being

	Women	Men
Mutual attraction – love	2.87	2.81
Dependable character	2.69	2.50
Emotional stability and maturity	2.68	2.47
Pleasing disposition	2.52	2.44
Education and intelligence	2.45	2.27
Sociability	2.30	2.15
Good health	2.28	2.31
Desire for home and children	2.21	2.09
Ambition and industriousness	2.15	1.85
Refinement, neatness	1.98	2.03
Similar education	1.84	1.50
Good financial prospects	1.76	1.51
Good looks	1.46	1.91
Favourable social status	1.46	1.16
Good cook and housekeeper	1.28	1.80
Similar religious background	1.21	0.98
Similar political background	1.03	0.92
Chastity	0.75	1.06

Table 4.6 Mean four-point rating by female and male students in 33 countries of importance of 18 characteristics in choosing a mate (Buss *et al.* 1990)

ambitious. Women preferred good financial prospects and ambition while men preferred good looks and good cooking. David Buss also included a separate list of 13 characteristics to be rank-ordered in terms of importance in choosing a mate, the most important of which was being kind and understanding.

REASONS GIVEN FOR THE BREAK-UP OF CLOSE RELATIONSHIPS

Asking people what they would see as being sufficient grounds for divorce does not, of course, tell us whether these are the reasons that people give for the break-up of their marriages. Consequently, it is informative to find out what people see as being the causes of the break-up of their close relationships. Beginning with William Goode's (1956) research in 1948, there have been several such studies, most of which have looked at marital relationships in the United States. These studies are difficult to summarize largely because of the different ways they code the reasons given.

Gay Kitson and Marvin Sussman (1982) asked 107 women and 101 men who were filing for divorce what caused their marriage to break up. The sample comprised middle- and working-class people living in Cleveland, Ohio.

The scheme developed for coding the reasons given consisted of 52 categories, with the average number being about three per person. The most common category for both women and men was lack of communication and understanding. After that women and men tended to differ in terms of which categories were most frequent. For example, the second most common category for women was their own conflict about their gender role, while for men this category was ranked sixth. For men the second most frequent category was conflict within the relationship over the gender role of the spouse, while for women this category was ranked eighth. They also found some differences for social class, income, education and length of marriage. For instance, those with higher incomes and higher social status were more likely to cite overcommitment to work; the better educated were more likely to give change in interests and values; and those married longer were more likely to report no sense of family life and less likely to mention sexual problems due to health.

More recently Lynn Gigy and Joan Kelly (1992) asked 230 women and 207 men who were filing for divorce in Marin County, California to check any of 27 factors which were important in the breakdown of their marriage and their decision to divorce. The five most frequently checked factors for both women and men were growing apart, not feeling loved, sexual difficulties, serious differences in values and major needs not being met. They also allowed participants to add a factor not on the list and found that 20 per cent of them did so. However, 95 per cent of these factors were judged by one or both coders to fall within the 27 factors when grouped into nine areas.

A few studies have examined the reasons given for the break-up of non-marital intimate relationships. For example, Charles Hill and his colleagues (1976) presented a list of common problems that might lead to the break-up of a relationship to 77 dating couples from around Boston whose relationship had broken up. The three most common problems for both women and men were becoming bored with the relationship, having different interests and wanting to be independent. William Cupach and Sandra Metts (1986) coded the accounts of 25 female and 25 male American students for factors mentioned in describing the break-up of their relationships. The three most frequent factors for women and men taken together were the partner's behaviour, loss of intimacy and communication difficulties.

One problem with interpreting the results of research looking at the reasons people give for the break-up of their close relationships is that we do not know whether the same kinds of problems exist in relationships which have not yet broken up. For example, communication difficulties may be experienced in a close relationship but may not necessarily lead to the break-up of that relationship. Consequently, we need to find out whether the problems that are cited as bringing about the dissolution of a relationship are more common or severe in dissolved than in ongoing relationships. In addition, we may be interested in factors that distinguish happy from unhappy relationships. One of the few studies to compare the frequency of problems in happy and unhappy marriages was published by Vincent Mathews and Clement Mihanovich (1963). A checklist of 400 marital problems together with the Burgess and Wallin (1953) marital happiness scale was completed by 984 Catholic spouses who either sought help from their priest for marital problems or who were chosen by seminary students as reflecting a happy or unhappy couple. Using the marital happiness scale 64 per cent of the respondents were classified as happily married and the remaining 36 per cent as unhappily married. Significant differences between the two groups were found for 333 of the problems with the six biggest differences being: (1) not thinking alike on many things; (2) the spouse having little insight into the respondent's feelings; (3) saying things that hurt each other; (4) often feeling unloved; (5) the spouse taking the respondent for granted; and (6) needing someone to confide in. These problems are similar to the lack of understanding, love and consideration found in some of the studies previously described.

Trying to distinguish compatible from incompatible close relationships on a variety of potentially relevant variables may be very useful in helping us to determine which variables best discriminate between them. A number of such studies have been carried out. I will begin by describing those which have compared ongoing relationships with those that have broken up.

THE COMPARATIVE IMPORTANCE OF FACTORS ASSOCIATED WITH THE BREAK-UP OF CLOSE RELATIONSHIPS

Several longitudinal studies have been conducted in the United States which have investigated the extent to which various psychosocial factors can predict which relationships will break up. The results of these studies are difficult to compare or to summarize because they generally did not measure the same factors, and where they did the findings were not necessarily consistent. For example, holding dysfunctional beliefs about relationships, such as thinking that partners should not disagree, was found to predict the break-up of newly married couples (Kurdek 1993) but not that of cohabiting lesbian and gay couples (Kurdek 1992). However, for the personality measure of neuroticism results were more consistent. In three of the four studies where it was assessed the relationships of people with higher neuroticism were more likely to break up. Apart from neuroticism, however, these studies do not provide a clear indication of which factors were most reliably related to the break-up of close relationships. None the less, this research is important in showing that break-ups can be predicted.

Two studies looked at the two-year predictive validity of a relationship questionnaire called PREPARE (*Pre*-Marital *Personal and Relationship Evaluation*) which was given to two samples of 164 and 179 engaged couples (Fowers and Olson 1986; Larsen and Olson 1989). The 125-item questionnaire consisted of the following 12 scales: (1) idealistic distortion; (2) realistic expectations; (3) personality issues; (4) communication; (5) conflict resolution;

(6) financial management; (7) leisure activities; (8) sexual relationship; (9) children and marriage; (10) family and friends; (11) equalitarian roles; and (12) religious orientation. For each scale an individual score was provided. The idealistic distortion score was used to correct the scores for the other 11 scales. A positive couple agreement score was also calculated for these scales which measured the percentage of items on which couples agreed in a positive manner, such as liking the personality of their partner.

In the first study (Fowers and Olson 1986) clergy who had given the questionnaire to couples about four months before they were married were asked about two years later to select two to five couples who were satisfied with their marriages and two to five couples who were divorced, separated or dissatisfied with their marriages. Couples who were still married completed the 10-item marital satisfaction scale of the ENRICH marital inventory. The median score on this scale was used to divide the married couples into two groups comprising those who were satisfied and those who were dissatisfied based on whether both partners scored below the median or at it and above. There were 59 satisfied couples, 22 dissatisfied ones and 31 separated or divorced ones. Less premarital positive couple agreement was found for the separated/divorced group than for the satisfied group on all 11 scales apart from the children and marriage one. The most significant differences, expressed as point-biserial correlations (Cramer 1998), were for conflict resolution ($r = 0.41$), sexuality ($r = 0.35$), religion ($r = 0.34$) and communication ($r = 0.34$). Conflict resolution referred to being able to resolve conflicts satisfactorily while sexuality reflected agreement on the sexual nature of the relationship. Although there was also less premarital positive couple agreement for the separated/divorced than for the dissatisfied group, none of these differences were significant. Blaine Fowers and David Olson reported mean differences for only the couple scores and not the individual scores and consequently we do not know whether similar results would have been found for the individual scale scores. However, they showed that simply using the individual scores enabled 81 per cent of both the happily married and the separated/divorced to be correctly predicted compared with about 74 per cent using the couple scores. In other words, individual scores in this case were more predictive than couple scores.

In the second study (Larsen and Olson 1989) counsellors and clergy who had used PREPARE with premarital couples about two years earlier were asked to supply information about the current marital state of these couples. Of those still married, 156 couples completed the marital satisfaction scale of the ENRICH marital inventory. The 49 couples scoring in the upper third of this scale formed the happily married group while the 57 couples scoring in the lower third constituted the unhappily married group. In addition, there were 36 couples who had divorced or separated. The divorced/separated group had significantly less premarital positive couple agreement on all of the 11 scales apart from financial management, sexuality, and children and parenting. The most significant differences, expressed as point-biserial correlations, were for equalitarian roles ($r = 0.48$), leisure activity ($r = 0.45$), realistic expectations

($r = 0.40$) and personality issues ($r = 0.32$). Equalitarian roles referred to being flexible about work in or out of the home and being willing to share responsibilities, while leisure activities reflected spending time together enjoying similar activities. The apparent differences between the results of these two studies could have been due to the way the couples had been selected. In the first study they had been selected by the clergy while in the second they were selected by the authors of the study. None the less, the results are impressive in showing the accuracy with which marital breakdown can be predicted from information obtained prior to marriage. In the second study about 84 per cent of the couples falling into either the happily married or the separated/divorced group could be correctly predicted from the couple scores compared with 77 per cent using the individual scores, showing that the couple scores were more predictive than the individual ones.

In an earlier study on premarital predictors of divorce, Lowell Kelly and James Conley (1987) analysed data on 249 couples who were engaged in 1935–38 and who were again contacted in 1954–55 and in 1980–81. In other words, these couples were followed up over a period of about 45 years. Of these couples, 39 divorced between 1935 and 1954 and a further 11 between 1955 and 1980. Where these were known, data from 22 couples who broke off their original engagement but subsequently married were also included. The couples were white, generally well educated and came from around Connecticut. Differences between those still married and those who divorced either in or before 1954 or after 1955 were presented separately for women and men for the following 18 predictors, 14 of which were measured before marriage. Four of these were the personality traits of neuroticism, social extroversion, impulse control and agreeableness, assessed by the Personality Rating Scale which was completed by five acquaintances for each of the participants. Five measures were the early social factors of family stability, family closeness, good behaviour, religious behaviour and family tension, as reported by participants. Another five indices were the marital attitudes of companionate marriage, family conventions, spouse equality, absolute sexual fidelity and no premarital sex. The remaining four variables were retrospective reports made in 1954–55 on the extent of premarital romantic relationships, premarital sex with partner, premarital sex in general and sexual intercourse with spouse in 1935–38.

The biggest differences between those still married and those divorced will be expressed as point-biserial correlations (Cramer 1998). Compared to women still married, women who divorced prior to 1955 had higher neuroticism ($r = 0.24$), more premarital romantic experience ($r = 0.24$), more tense families ($r = 0.23$), more premarital sex with their partner ($r = 0.22$) and with others ($r = 0.17$), more unstable families ($r = 0.18$) and less close families ($r = 0.17$). Women who divorced after 1954 had more premarital sex with others ($r = 0.28$) and with their partner ($r = 0.23$). Men who were divorced before 1955 compared to those still married had lower impulse control ($r = 0.27$), higher neuroticism ($r = 0.19$) and more premarital sex with their partner

($r = 0.19$) and with others ($r = 0.19$). Men who were divorced after 1954 had more premarital sex with their partner ($r = 0.26$) and with others ($r = 0.19$) and closer families ($r = 0.18$). In general for both women and men divorce was most consistently related to premarital sex while for those who divorced before 1954, it was also related to neuroticism. Because of the likely increase in the prevalence of premarital sex since the 1930s, however, it is unlikely that premarital sex would continue to be a significant predictor of divorce at present.

Other studies have sought to predict marital breakdown in already established marriages with most of them looking at newly married couples. Peter Bentler and Michael Newcomb (1978) followed up over four years 77 newly married couples, selected from local marriage registry offices in Los Angeles. During this period 24 of the couples had separated or divorced. The following information was collected on them when they were first contacted: (1) 13 demographic background factors such as their age and whether they had cohabited prior to being married; (2) their description of themselves on 28 personality traits as assessed by the Bentler Psychological Inventory and as seen by a friend; and (3) their description of 20 sexual activities they as a couple engaged in. Four years later they were asked to rate on a three-point scale the severity of 19 potential problem areas. The following significant differences were found between the married and divorced couples. Married couples were more similar than divorced couples in terms of age, attractiveness, interest in art and extroversion but not consciousness about clothes. The discrepancy between the spouse's view of themselves and their friend's view of them was less for cheerfulness and law abidance for married than for divorced men, and for masculinity for married than for divorced women. Couples where one or both partners had been widowed were more likely to remain married than those who had divorced. The parents of both married women and men were less likely to have divorced than those of divorced women and men. Married women were more likely than divorced women to be older, to have children from their previous marriage, to have greater educational and occupational status, and to show greater clothes-consciousness and congeniality. Married men were less extroverted and orderly than divorced men but more vulnerable. Finally, on 12 of the 19 problems divorced couples had more severe problems than the married including lack of mutual affection, adultery, relationships with friends and selfishness. In terms of ill health, however, married couples were more likely to suffer from health problems than the divorced couples.

In Dayton, Ohio, Lawrence Kurdek (1993) followed up over five years 286 newly married couples during which time 64 of them broke up. He compared those who broke up with those who remained married on 36 factors measured when they were first contacted. Expressing the F ratios presented as correlations (Cramer 1998), couples who broke up compared with those who stayed together pooled their finances less ($r = 0.17$), had known each other less long ($r = 0.17$) and had a greater history of divorce ($r = 0.16$). They also differed more in having extrinsic reasons for being married ($r = 0.21$) such as parental approval, in being independent ($r = 0.14$), in having social support from others ($r = 0.14$) and in being neurotic ($r = 0.12$). Separated or divorced women relative to still married women were less educated ($r = 0.37$), were less satisfied with their marriage ($r = 0.20$), were more neurotic ($r = 0.18$), had lower personal income ($r = 0.17$), had less faith in their marriage ($r = 0.15$), were less conscientious ($r = 0.15$), had lower social support ($r = 0.15$), had fewer intrinsic reasons for being married ($r = 0.15$) and had more dysfunctional beliefs about relationships ($r = 0.14$) such as that partners should not disagree. Separated or divorced men in comparison to those still married were less satisfied with their marriage ($r = 0.23$), were less educated ($r = 0.22$), had lower personal income ($r = 0.22$), were more neurotic ($r = 0.17$), were more likely to be a stepfather ($r = 0.16$), had more dysfunctional beliefs about relationships ($r = 0.14$) and had more external reasons for being married ($r = 0.12$).

In an earlier study Lawrence Kurdek (1992) followed up over four years in North America 31 lesbian and 61 gay cohabiting couples of whom 22 couples separated during that period. At the start of the study the lesbian couples had lived together on average for about five years and the gay couples for about seven years. Although it would have been sufficient to compare partners in ongoing relationships with those in dissolved relationships, partners within a relationship were randomly ascribed as Partner 1 and Partner 2. Partner 1's who had stayed together were compared with Partner 1's who had broken up and Partner 2's who had remained together were compared with Partner 2's who had split up. They were compared on 24 variables measured when they were first contacted, many of which were the same as those in the previous study. Choosing the lowest F ratio where both ratios were significant for Partners 1 and 2 and expressing it as a correlation, those who split up relative to those who stayed together were less satisfied with their relationship ($r = 0.30$), were more independent ($r = 0.22$), were younger ($r = 0.22$), had less faith in the relationship ($r = 0.21$), pooled their finances less ($r = 0.20$), were more neurotic ($r = 0.17$) and had lived less long together ($r = 0.16$).

THE COMPARATIVE IMPORTANCE OF FACTORS ASSOCIATED WITH THE QUALITY OF CLOSE RELATIONSHIPS

Not everyone who is unhappy with a close relationship ends it. For example, Tim Heaton and Stan Albrecht (1991) in a nationally representative sample of 13,017 American households found that about seven per cent of those who were married said that they were unhappy with their marriage but thought that their chances of separating or divorcing were low or very low. Consequently, it is important to determine what distinguishes those who are satisfied with their relationship from those who are dissatisfied. Two of the longitudinal studies I previously described that attempted to predict the break-up of close relationships also tried to predict whether the individuals would be happy with their relationship.

Blaine Fowers and David Olson (1986) found that those who were subsequently less satisfied with their marriage showed less premarital positive couple agreement on six of the 11 scales. The four most significant differences, expressed as correlations, were for sexuality ($r = 0.19$), conflict resolution ($r = 0.18$), leisure activity ($r = 0.17$) and communication ($r = 0.17$). This study found that the differences between the happily and the unhappily married were less than those between the happily married and those who broke up. Peter Bentler and Michael Newcomb (1978) determined the minimum number of the variables they measured that predicted the greatest proportion of marital satisfaction in 68 of their newly married couples. Marital satisfaction was a composite score consisting of the relative lack of marital problems and the Locke–Wallace Marital Adjustment Test for the couple. They found that 10 of their variables predicted about 55 per cent of the variation in marital satisfaction four years later. Happily married couples were more likely than unhappily married couples to consist of wives who were more conscious about their clothes, were more objective, had more masculine interests, were less intelligent, were less ambitious and had children from their previous marriage, and husbands who were less orderly, were less flexible, were less impulsive and were more thrifty. These results seem to suggest that couples where the woman fulfilled the traditional wifely role of being more concerned about their attractiveness and being less ambitious and intelligent were more happily married than those where the woman did not meet this role.

Beginning with the studies by Lewis Terman and his colleagues (1935, 1938), several cross-sectional studies have compared on various variables individuals who were satisfied with a close relationship with those who were not. As part of the development of his Marital Satisfaction Inventory, Douglas Snyder (1979) in the United States gave this 280-item questionnaire to 111 couples from the general population and 30 couples undergoing marital therapy. This questionnaire consists of a 43-item global marital distress scale (e.g. 'My marriage has been disappointing in several ways' and 'The future of our marriage is too uncertain to make any serious plans'), a 21-item idealization or conventionalization scale (e.g. 'There is never a moment that I do not feel "head over heels" in love with my mate' and 'My mate completely understands and sympathizes with my every mood'), and nine other scales measuring specific aspects of marital interaction such as affective communication (e.g 'My spouse doesn't take me seriously enough sometimes' and 'I'm not sure my spouse has ever really loved me') and problem-solving communication (e.g. 'Minor disagreements with my spouse often end up in big arguments' and 'My spouse and I seem able to go for days sometimes without settling our differences'). Six of these specific scales were significantly correlated with global marital distress for the whole sample when conventionalization was partialled out. Maritally satisfied individuals had more problem-solving communication ($r = 0.57$), more and better leisure time together ($r = 0.57$), more affective communication ($r = 0.56$), less conflict over child-rearing ($r = 0.35$), less sexual dissatisfaction ($r = 0.33$) and fewer financial disagreements ($r = 0.31$).

Kathryn Rettig and Margaret Bubolz (1983) investigated the association between marital quality (as assessed by a simple seven-point scale ranging from 'terrible' to 'delighted') and the evaluation and frequency of resources received within marriage. The seven resources chosen were love, status, services, information, goods, money and shared time which were evaluated on the same seven-point scale as marital quality and whose frequency was rated on an eight-point scale from 'never' to 'about two to three times each day'. The sample consisted of 224 married couples randomly selected from a county in Michigan and who had been married on average for about 16 years. Marital quality was more highly correlated with the evaluation of resources received than with their frequency. For wives the five items that were most highly correlated with marital quality were the love and affection they experienced ($r = 0.78$), the closeness and sense of belonging they felt ($r = 0.77$), how comfortable they felt at home ($r = 0.74$), their sexual relationship ($r = 0.71$) and the amount of respect they received ($r = 0.70$). For husbands they were: how comfortable they felt at home ($r = 0.69$), the love and affection they experienced ($r = 0.69$), their sexual relationship ($r = 0.67$), how openly and honestly they could express their feelings ($r = 0.62$) and the closeness and sense of belonging they felt ($r = 0.62$). For wives about 74 per cent of the variation in their assessment of marital quality was accounted for by the following five evaluative factors: (1) the love and affection they experienced; (2) the time they spent with their husband; (3) the respect they received from their husband; (4) the sexual relationship they had; and (5) the open and honest expression of their feelings. For husbands about 56 per cent of marital quality was explained by the following four evaluative factors: (1) the love and affection they experienced; (2) the sexual relationship they had; (3) the respect they received from their wife; and (4) the kind of marital communication they had.

Using a stratified sample of 459 ever-married wives from the Detroit area and focusing on the 302 women who were only married once, Martin Whyte (1990) looked at the relationship between his seven-item marriage quality scale and about 70 diverse factors. In terms of the seven variables that were most highly correlated with marital satisfaction, happily married wives spent more time as a couple with friends ($r = 0.32$), had closer relationships with their parents ($r = 0.31$), had less control over their earnings ($r = 0.31$), were more in love when they were married ($r = 0.30$), shared more personal traits with their husband ($r = 0.30$), shared more child and marriage values ($r = 0.28$) and shared more leisure activities ($r = 0.27$). About 50 per cent of the variation in the wives' marital satisfaction could be explained by 12 of the factors. With respect to the seven variables that were most highly related to whether the couples had split up, couples who were still together were white ($r = 0.33$), wives had more influence in disputes with their husbands ($r = 0.31$), shared family values more ($r = 0.29$), were more in love when they married ($r = 0.29$), had a more elaborate wedding (r = 0.26), were raised as Catholics (r = 0.22) and had less parental opposition to the relationship (r = 0.22).

Including homosexual as well as heterosexual couples, Lawrence Kurdek and Patrick Schmitt (1986) investigated the association between relationship satisfaction and various mainly psychological factors in 44 married couples, 35 heterosexual cohabiting couples, 50 gay cohabiting couples and 56 lesbian cohabiting couples. Relationship satisfaction was a composite score consisting of the four scales of the 32-item Dyadic Adjustment Scale (Spanier 1976) and the 48-item Marital Satisfaction Scale (Roach *et al.* 1981). Certain variables were significantly correlated with relationship satisfaction in all four relationships. Individuals satisfied with their relationships shared decision-making more (r's ranged from 0.40 in gay couples to 0.57 in cohabiting heterosexual couples), found the relationship more attractive (r's ranged from 0.29 in married couples to 0.56 in cohabiting heterosexual couples), believed less that couples should not disagree (r's ranged from 0.44 in lesbian couples to 0.46 in married and cohabiting heterosexual couples), were more attached (r's ranged from 0.24 in gay couples to 0.47 in lesbian couples) and had less attractive alternatives to the relationship (r's ranged from 0.28 in married couples to 0.47 in lesbian couples). The maximum percentage of the variation in relationship satisfaction explained by some of the variables measured ranged from about 58 for married and gay couples to about 77 for cohabiting heterosexual couples.

In Britain Hans Eysenck and James Wakefield (1981) correlated marital satisfaction with a number of other variables for the wives and husbands of 566 couples who had been married on average for about eight and a half years. Marital satisfaction was measured with the 15-item Marital Adjustment Test (Locke and Wallace 1959) to which six items were added. In terms of the seven variables that were most significantly correlated with marital satisfaction, maritally satisfied wives had more maritally satisfied husbands (r = 0.73), were more sexually satisfied (r = 0.58 for Eysenck's scale, r = 0.48 for Terman's item), refused intercourse less (r = 0.45), had husbands who were less irritable when refused intercourse (r = 0.44), had less desire for sexual intercourse with someone else (r = 0.43), had more sexually satisfied husbands (r = 0.40 for Eysenck's scale, r = 0.37 for Terman's item) and had husbands having less desire for sexual intercourse with someone else (r = 0.37). Maritally satisfied husbands had more maritally satisfied wives (r = 0.73), were more sexually satisfied (r = 0.51 for Eysenck's scale, r = 0.44 for Terman's item), had more sexually satisfied wives (r = 0.45 for Eysenck's scale, r = 0.37 for Terman's item), had less desire for sexual intercourse with someone else (r = 0.43) and had fewer sexual complaints about their partner (r = 0.37). Sexual satisfaction was assessed with a 16-item scale developed by Eysenck (1976, p. 143) and again with the single item 'How much release or satisfaction do you usually get from sexual intercourse with your partner?' taken from Terman's (1938) study. The correlation between marital satisfaction and the single-item measure was always the lower of the two correlations presented but the difference was not marked.

SUMMARY

A number of studies have sought to find out which of a range of factors distinguish most clearly people who are satisfied with a close relationship or remain in it and those who are dissatisfied or leave it. These studies differ in various ways making it difficult to compare them and to summarize their findings. Impressively, a couple of studies have shown that it is possible to predict about 80 per cent of those who are either happily married or separated/divorced about two years later from information collected on the relationship a few months prior to marriage. Furthermore, other studies have demonstrated that at least 50 per cent of the variation in marital satisfaction can be explained by other factors either measured at the same time as marital satisfaction or some time before. In general psychosocial variables have been more strongly associated with marital compatibility than sociodemographic variables. Being loving, sexually satisfied, communicative and emotionally stable have all been found to be related to greater marital compatibility. Not feeling loved, sexual difficulties and lack of communication have also been cited as reasons for divorcing someone, in either hypothetical or real circumstances.

5

Personal Similarity and Complementarity

There has been a longstanding interest in whether friends and spouses tend to be similar to or different from one another. The first study of this kind was published in an anonymous paper attributed to Karl Pearson (Anonymous 1903) in which the degree of similarity in how long wives and their husbands had lived was measured in four different samples. Karl Pearson and Alice Lee (1903) had already noted the similarity between wives and husbands in terms of their height, the span of their arms and the length of their left forearm. Pearson used the term *assortative mating* to refer to sexual selection where males are attracted to and mate with females with certain characteristics. *Homogamy* assortative mating is where males and females are similar in some respect. If this generally occurred and if the characteristics were genetically determined, then this sort of mating would lead to offspring who were similar and who in turn would be attracted to and mate with similar individuals. For three of his samples he found that the correlation between the length of life of wife and husband was 0.22 on average. In the other sample he found the correlation to be much higher at 0.42, which he thought was due to the greater likelihood in large urban areas of the wife and husband only being buried in the same grave when they had died within a short time of each other. With respect to research on mortality Robert Myers (1963) has suggested that part of the association in longevity between spouses may be due to using samples which are biased in favour of couples who may have died within a relatively short period of one another. Similarity in psychological characteristics such as intelligence, personality and interests in wives and husbands as well as friends was found in subsequent research by others (Richardson 1939). Similarity of characteristics in friends is sometimes referred to as *homophily* (Lazarsfeld and Merton 1954).

Similarity between two groups of people such as wives and husbands can be measured in two ways for non-categorical variables such as length of life and intelligence. First the scores of the wives and husbands can be correlated. A positive correlation means that wives and husbands are similar, in that high scores in the wives go together with high scores in the husbands. Similarly, low scores in the wives go together with low scores in the husbands. A negative correlation, on the other hand, indicates that wives and husbands are dissimilar in that high scores in the wives go together with low scores in the husbands. A correlation close to zero implies that there is no linear relationship between the two sets of scores. A disadvantage of this method is that it does not provide an index of similarity for individual couples. So to relate this correlational measure of similarity to marital compatibility, couples have to be divided into two or more groups (such as the happily and the unhappily married) and the size and direction of the correlation is compared in those groups. The second method of measuring similarity is to develop a difference or discrepancy score by subtracting the score from one partner, say the wife, from that of the other partner, the husband. If the difference is positive it means that the wife's score is lower than the husband's while if it is negative it shows that the wife's score is higher than the husband's. We can ignore the direction of this difference by ignoring negative signs. Small differences mean that wives and husbands are similar and large differences that they are dissimilar. An advantage of this difference measure is that the difference score can be correlated with, say, a marital satisfaction score.

Some studies have used the discrepancy method. For example, Lawrence Kurdek (1992, 1993) compared the discrepancies between couples who stayed together or separated. In his five-year prospective study of 286 newly married couples (Kurdek 1993), couples who remained together were more similar than those who broke up when first tested for external motives for being married, independence, social support and neuroticism. In his four-year longitudinal study of 31 lesbian and 61 gay cohabiting couples (Kurdek 1992), however, there were no differences in discrepancy between those who stayed together and those who broke up on any of his measures.

A few studies have used both methods of similarity. For instance, Hans Eysenck and James Wakefield (1981) in their cross-sectional study of 566 married British couples employed both indices. Their discrepancy measure was more complicated in that the difference was squared to eliminate the negative signs and the unsquared difference was partialled out to control for its effect. Since very few of the correlations between the unsquared difference and marital satisfaction were significant, partialling out this difference is unlikely to have had much effect. Happily married wives were more similar to their husbands in sexual satisfaction ($r = 0.25$), libido ($r = 0.20$), psychoticism ($r = 0.20$), tender-mindedness ($r = 0.14$) and neuroticism ($r = 0.08$). Personality variables such as psychoticism and neuroticism were measured with the Eysenck Personality Questionnaire (Eysenck and Eysenck 1975). Psychoticism reflects cold, selfish, aggressive and antisocial behaviour. Happily married husbands were more similar to their wives in sexual satisfaction ($r = 0.25$), libido ($r = 0.20$), psychoticism ($r = 0.17$), tender-mindedness ($r = 0.13$) and neuroticism ($r = 0.12$). For the correlation measure, married couples were most similar in terms of age ($r = 0.77$), tender-mindedness ($r = 0.56$), radicalism ($r = 0.51$), libido ($r = 0.43$), sexual satisfaction ($r = 0.41$), the number of people they had sexual intercourse with before they were first married ($r = 0.32$) and the lie scale ($r = 0.26$), which may be interpreted as a measure of conscientiousness (Cramer 1992a).

Most studies, however, have used the correlation method. For example, Peter Bentler and Michael Newcomb (1978), in their four-year longitudinal study of 77 newly married couples in Los Angeles, compared those who were still married with those who were separated/divorced in terms of the correlations between spouses for various sociodemographic and personality characteristics when first contacted. Those who were still married were significantly more similar than those who were separated/divorced in terms of age ($r = 0.84$ for still married vs $r = 0.45$ for separated/divorced), attractiveness ($r = 0.59$ for still married vs $r = 0.07$ for separated/divorced), interest in art ($r = 0.53$ for still married vs $r = 0.02$ for separated/divorced) and extroversion ($r = 0.19$ for still married vs $r = -0.29$ for separated/divorced) but not for consciousness about clothes ($r = 0.02$ for still married vs $r = 0.52$ for separated/divorced). While neither correlation for extroversion was statistically significant, the difference between them was significant and their signs were different in that the still married tended to be similar while the separated/divorced tended to be dissimilar. Charles Hill and his colleagues (1976), in their two-year follow-up of 231 premarital relationships, reported the correlations for 117 of the couples who were still together and the 103 who had broken up. The only significant difference between the correlations was for age ($r = 0.38$ for still together vs $r = 0.13$ for separated). In other words, those still together were more similar in age than those who broke up.

The correlations between wives and husbands for a number of variables are presented in Table 5.1 for selected studies. The correlations are highest for age, followed by physical attractiveness as rated by others, various social attitudes, intelligence and several personality measures where some of them are non-significant and close to zero. Note that the correlations differ for the same variable even when measured in the same way. So, for example, for physical attractiveness the correlations range from 0.24 to 0.60 (for a meta-analytic review of such studies see Feingold 1988).

Various explanations have been suggested for some of these findings. Some sociologists have argued that couples who are dissimilar with respect to sociodemographic variables such as age are more likely to differ in terms of interests, values and role expectations, which in turn is more likely to lead to marital conflict, unhappiness and dissolution. The evidence on age heterogamy and marital compatibility is conflicting, with some studies finding no relationship and others showing marital compatibility to be less where the age differences are bigger. Stephen Jorgensen and David Klein (1979) looked at the relationship between age similarity and five measures of marital compatibility in 120 white couples in the American midwest. Age similarity was classified into three categories according to whether the age of the wife and husband

Measure	r	n	Relationship status	Sample	Study
Age	0.87	555	Married	Hawaii	Johnson *et al.* 1976
	0.84	53	Newly married	US middle class	Bentler & Newcomb 1978
	0.77	566	Married 8.5 years	UK magazine	Eysenck & Wakefield 1981
	0.69	216	Married	Chad, Africa	Crognier 1977
Physical	0.60	22	Married 15 years	US middle class	Murstein & Christy 1976
attractiveness	0.59	53	Newly married	US middle class	Bentler & Newcomb 1978
(other-rated)	0.48	39	Committed	US students	McKillip & Riedel 1983
	0.38	129	Wedding day	US newspaper	Stevens *et al.* 1990
	0.38	98	Dating	US students	Murstein 1972
	0.25	72	Married	Hawaii	Price & Vandenberg 1979
	0.24	174	Dating	US students	Hill *et al.* 1976
Attitudes					
Religious values	0.58	161	Married	US	Caspi *et al.* 1992
Tender-mindedness	0.56	566	Married 8.5 years	UK magazine	Eysenck & Wakefield 1981
Art interest	0.53	53	Newly married	US middle class	Bentler & Newcomb 1978
Radicalism	0.51	566	Married 8.5 years	UK magazine	Eysenck & Wakefield 1981
Religiousness	0.48	53	Newly married	US middle class	Bentler & Newcomb 1978
Sex-role	0.47	174	Dating	US students	Hill *et al.* 1976
Liberalism	0.44	53	Newly married	US middle class	Bentler & Newcomb 1978
Travel interest	0.35	53	Newly married	US middle class	Bentler & Newcomb 1978
Intelligence					
WAIS Verbal	0.34	397	Married	UK villages	Harrison *et al.* 1976
	0.34	193	Married	UK	Mascie-Taylor & Vandenberg 1988
Verbal factor	0.40	215	Newly married	US	Watkins & Meredith 1981
	0.23	555	Married	Hawaii	Johnson *et al.* 1976
General factor	0.20	862	Married	US Caucasians	Phillips *et al.* 1988
WAIS Performance	0.28	193	Married	UK	Mascie-Taylor & Vandenberg 1988
	0.14	397	Married	UK villages	Harrison *et al.* 1976
Self-acceptance					
Semantic Differential Questionnaire	0.37	48	Engaged	Haifa Jews	Solomon 1986
Personality					
Extroversion (EPQ)	0.16	93	Married	US adverts	Buss 1984
	−0.01	566	Married 8.5 years	UK magazine	Eysenck & Wakefield 1981
	−0.07	134	Married	US random	Price & Vandenberg 1980
Extroversion (EPI)	0.23	193	Married	UK	Mascie-Taylor & Vandenberg 1988
	−0.05	397	Married	UK villages	Harrison *et al.* 1976

Table 5.1 *cont.*

Neuroticism (EPQ)	0.13	566	Married 8.5 years	UK magazine	Eysenck & Wakefield 1981
	0.02	134	Married	US random	Price & Vandenberg 1980
	0.00	93	Married	US adverts	Buss 1984
Neuroticism (EPI)	0.07	193	Married	UK	Mascie-Taylor & Vandenberg 1988
	0.01	397	Married	UK villages	Harrison *et al.* 1976
Lie (EPQ)	0.26	566	Married 8.5 years	UK magazine	Eysenck & Wakefield 1981
	0.16	93	Married	US adverts	Buss 1984
Lie (EPI)	0.23	193	Married	UK	Mascie-Taylor & Vandenberg 1988
	0.16	397	Married	UK villages	Harrison *et al.* 1976
Psychoticism (EPQ)	0.16	93	Married	US adverts	Buss 1984
	0.14	566	Married 8.5 years	UK magazine	Eysenck & Wakefield 1981

Note: EPQ = Eysenck Personality Questionnaire; EPI = Eysenck Personality Inventory

Table 5.1 Some studies of correlational similarity between heterosexual partners on various characteristics

were within 1, 2–3 or more than 3 years of each other. The five indices of marital compatibility were: (1) similarity in 16 marital values such as the husband earning a high income; (2) similarity in 13 marital task roles such as disciplining the children; (3) similarity in marital power roles such as deciding what car to buy; (4) frequency of marital conflict in 23 areas; and (5) three levels of increasing intensity of marital conflict. Only value similarity was related to age similarity with similarly aged partners holding more similar marital values ($r = 0.17$).

Hernan Vera and his colleagues (1985) found no relationship between age similarity and either a five-point rating of getting along with one's spouse or a list of 22 marital problems in 998 married individuals in Florida. Age similarity was categorized into the following four groups: (1) wife more than three years older; (2) an age difference of up to three years for both wife and husband; (3) husband four to ten years older; and (4) husband more than 10 years older. Larry Bumpass and James Sweet (1972), on the other hand, using a US national representative sample of 5,442 white married women under the age of 45 noted that first marriages were more likely to end in divorce or separation when the age difference between wife and husband was large or when the wife was older than the husband. Meei-Shenn Tzeng (1992), in a large sample of first-married Americans, found that couples where the husband was more than three years older than the wife were about 32 per cent more likely to break up than couples where the wife was the same age as the husband or less than three years younger. Couples where the wife was older than the husband, on the other hand, were not more likely to separate.

In studies where the couples have known each other for some time, similarity in psychological characteristics such as attitudes and personality may be due to the influence that spouses have on each other. However, Hans Eysenck and James Wakefield (1981) observed that the duration of marriage was not associated with increased similarity in terms of their measures of social attitudes, sexual satisfaction, libido and personality.

SIMILARITY AS EXCHANGING VALUABLE ASSETS

Similarity in terms of such valued qualities as emotional stability, intelligence, sociability and good looks may result from a process in which individuals with these qualities are able to attract others with the same qualities whereas people without these qualities are left to associate with those who also do not have them. Take, for example, the quality of physical attractiveness. If everyone values physical attractiveness we will all seek others who are physically attractive. However, unless we are physically attractive ourselves we will be unable to attract others who are physically attractive and so we will have to associate with others who are similar to us in physical attractiveness. In other words, pairing off will take place between individuals who are similar in physical attractiveness.

This idea was initially tested by Elaine Walster and her colleagues (1966) at the University of Minnesota who predicted that individuals will prefer dating partners who are similar to them in physical attractiveness. They examined this by organizing a dance in which newly arrived first-year students were invited to take part and where they were told they would be matched by computer with someone according to their interests and personality. In reality they were randomly matched with the exception that the man was always taller than the woman. When applying for the dance the physical attractiveness of each participant was rated on an eight-point scale by four judges and the ratings averaged. During a break in the dance participants were asked to rate the physical attractiveness of their date, how much they liked their date and whether they would like to date them again. Contrary to their predictions Walster and her colleagues found that how much both women and men liked their date and wanted to go out with them again was most strongly related to their physical attractiveness, as rated by themselves or the judges. For example, the correlation between their liking of their date and their rating of their physical attractiveness was 0.69 for women and 0.78 for men. Since subsequent research has found couples to be similar in physical attractiveness, presumably attractive individuals are more likely to reject those who are unattractive. Walster and her colleagues found some evidence for this in that more attractive individuals expected their dates to be more physically attractive, personable and considerate in both women ($r = 0.23$) and men ($r = 0.18$) when these three characteristics were combined into an overall index. However, we do not know the actual correlation between the individual's own physical attractiveness and how physically attractive they expected their partner to be because they did not present this correlation separately.

Walster and her colleagues thought that one reason for their failure to find that individuals preferred partners similar in physical attractiveness to themselves may have been that participants were not aware that they would be rejected by someone more attractive than them. For example, these 'freshers' may have thought that physical attractiveness played a less important role in dating among college students. Consequently, Walster and her colleagues carried out two further studies (Berscheid *et al.* 1971) on students whose physical attractiveness had been rated. Students were asked in the first study to indicate how attractive their date should be and in the second to choose on the basis of photos one of six partners varying in attractiveness. In both studies the possibility of being rejected by the person they chose was varied. In the first study this was done by telling students in one condition that 50 per cent of dates had already turned down their partner, and in the other condition that everyone had agreed to stay with their partner for the dance. In the second study students in one condition were told that a date would only be arranged if it was a mutual choice, and in the second condition that the person selected had agreed to go for the date. In both studies and regardless of which condition they were in, the more attractive students chose the more attractive date. In other words, individuals selected dates similar in attractiveness to themselves.

Originally Walster and her colleagues (1966) were interested in testing the idea that individuals would be attracted to others who were similar to them in terms of how socially desirable they were overall, rather than specifically how physically attractive they were. They chose physical attractiveness as the indicator of a person's social desirability because it could be quickly assessed. This idea that we form relationships in terms of their value to us is generally known as social exchange theory and had earlier been applied to mate selection and marital choice (e.g. Davis 1941). It will be discussed in more detail in Chapter 6. What this theory implies is that someone who, for example, is attractive but poor may be attracted to someone who is rich but unattractive provided that the trade-off is acceptable. Several studies have sought to test this idea. One of the first was by Glen Elder (1969) who looked at physical attractiveness, educational attainment and marriage mobility in a longitudinal sample of 35 middle- and 43 working-class women born in the 1920s in Oakland, California and followed up until 1958. In both groups women who were rated at 16 as having a good physique, sex appeal and good general appearance were more likely to marry a man who had higher status than their own father at the same age. In other words, they were more likely to show upward marriage mobility or *hypergamy*. Overall attractiveness was more strongly related to the husband's occupational status in women of working-class origin ($r = 0.46$) than middle-class origin ($r = 0.35$), implying that the asset or reward of attractiveness compensated to some extent for the liability of coming from the lower social class. The difference in the size of these two correlations, however, was not significant.

In a representative sample of 300 American wives aged between 25 and 40, Patricia Taylor and Norval Glenn (1976) also found that physical attractiveness was related to their husband's occupational status in women whose fathers came from a working-class background ($r = 0.31$) rather than a middle-class background ($r = 0.13$). Once again, the difference in the size of these two correlations was not significant. However, Richard Udry (1977), in a sample of 1,243 white and 733 black American women aged between 25 and 40, noted that physical attractiveness was higher in upwardly mobile women who married men of higher status than their father in two of the three categories of origin of status for black women but in only one of these four categories for white women. Physical attractiveness was significantly related to husband's occupational status in two and three of the four regression analyses for black and white women respectively.

None of these three studies, however, measured the husband's physical attractiveness. If husbands were generally similar in physical attractiveness to their wives, then the woman's physical attractiveness was not exchanged for the man's higher status unless the woman's physical attractiveness was more highly evaluated by the man than the man's physical attractiveness was evaluated by the woman. As we have seen in Chapter 4, male, students do rate good looks more highly in a partner than female students (Buss *et al.* 1990; for a meta-analytic review of such studies see Feingold 1990). However, the finding that, apart from age, couples show the greatest similarity in physical attractiveness implies that it is highly valued by both women and men.

Two studies have taken account of the man's physical attractiveness in examining whether women can trade good looks for occupational status in men. Alan Feingold (1981) in New York measured the five qualities of physical attractiveness, intelligence, dominance, neuroticism and humour in 75 mainly dating couples. He then selected 13 couples where the man was more attractive than the woman and 12 couples where the woman was more attractive than the man. According to exchange theory individuals who were less attractive than their partner should show more desirable psychological characteristics than individuals who were more attractive than their partner. Some support for this idea was found for women in that women who were less attractive than their partner were significantly higher in humour and lower in neuroticism than women who were more attractive than their partner. There were no significant differences on any of these four characteristics for men.

Using wedding announcements in a local American paper which contained a wedding photo and details of educational attainment, Gillian Stevens and her colleagues (1990) examined the relation between physical attractiveness and educational attainment in 129 white couples. The photos were cut in two so that the physical attractiveness of the partners could be rated independently of each other. They obtained no evidence to show that either women or men traded educational attainment for physical attractiveness, or that women were better able than men to exchange physical attractiveness for educational attainment. In terms of a characteristic such as physical attractiveness it would appear that if exchange operates in close relationships it is generally restricted to physical attractiveness itself.

SIMILARITY AS COGNITIVE BALANCE

Similarity between partners, particularly attitudes, has also been explained in terms of Theodore Newcomb's (1961) AB-X model of cognitive balance, where A and B refer to two people and X signifies their orientation or attitude towards some object or person. The individual system consists of A's attraction to B, A's attitude to X and A's perception of B's attitude to X. A will be attracted to B if A perceives that she or he has the same orientation to X as B does. For example, A will be attracted to B if A believes that A is attractive and that B thinks A is attractive too. A, on the other hand, will not be attracted to B if A believes that A is attractive but that B thinks that A is not attractive. If A likes B, then A will tend to think that A and B have the same orientation to X.

The strain to having a balanced system of cognitions is greater the more important X is to A and the more relevant A believes X is to her or his relationship with B. So, the strain on A to believe that B thinks A is attractive will be greater if A thinks that attractiveness is important and is relevant to her or his relationship with B. As strain is experienced as unpleasant A will try to reduce it. If information which is inconsistent with the system cannot be discounted, strain will be reduced in one or more of the following five ways: (1) A will change her or his attitude to X; (2) A will change her or his perception of B's attitude to X; (3) A will reduce the importance of X; (4) A will lessen the relevance of X to her or his relationship with B; and (5) A will like B less. If, for example, A hears that B finds A unattractive and A cannot discount this, A will experience strain which A may reduce by believing (1) that A is unattractive; (2) that B thinks A is unattractive; (3) that attractiveness is not important; (4) that attractiveness is not relevant to their relationship; and (5) A likes B less.

Theodore Newcomb (1961) tested this and other aspects of his theory by allowing 17 men students, who had just transferred to the University of Michigan and who did not know each other, to live rent-free in a house in exchange for acting as participants in his study. This arrangement was repeated with another 17 men students the following year. This second group had to rank-order in the second and fourteenth week of their stay the following six values or interests: (1) theoretical; (2) economic; (3) aesthetic; (4) social; (5) political; and (6) religious. They also rated on a 100-point scale how favourable they felt towards each person in the house. Men who were evaluated more favourably were seen as having more similar values. Because other people in the house were the most common and important objects for the participants, Theodore Newcomb also used the men's feelings about each other as an attitude. He called these attitudes *orientations* to distinguish them from attitudes, which he defined as orientations to non-person objects. Orientations to people are more complicated than attitudes to non-person objects because people can have feelings about other people which may or may not be reciprocated. Once again, he found that men who were valued more were seen as having similar attitudes towards specific men.

Edward Sampson and Chester Insko (1964) at Berkeley in California tested the idea derived from this theory that we will agree with those we like and disagree with those we dislike. They set up an experimental situation in which an accomplice or confederate of theirs behaved in such a way as to be liked or disliked by participants. In another part of the experiment participants, who were men, were asked to judge how far a point of light moved in a dark room and were told that making judgements similar to those of the confederate indicated they had a similar underlying personality. They found, as predicted, that participants made their judgements more similar to those of the confederate when they liked him and less similar when they disliked him. Liking and disliking was manipulated by the confederate expressing either similar or dissimilar views to participants and behaving either cooperatively or uncooperatively. Sampson and Insko also reported that participants in the two unbalanced conditions (where the confederate is liked and holds dissimilar views or where he is disliked and has similar views) reported feeling more nervous at the end of the experiment than those in the two balanced conditions (where the confederate is liked and has similar views or where he is disliked and expresses dissimilar views), implying that cognitive imbalance was experienced as strain.

SIMILARITY AS REINFORCEMENT

Donn Byrne (1961, 1971) at the University of Texas thought that we liked people with similar attitudes because these attitudes were rewarding in the sense of confirming our own opinions of the world. We disliked people with dissimilar attitudes because they disconfirmed our beliefs about the world. These effects will be stronger the more important the attitude. Byrne tested these ideas by asking students to give their opinion on 13 issues that were preselected as being important (such as racial integration in public schools) and 13 topics chosen as being less important (such as their political preference). Two weeks later they were asked to evaluate someone who had expressed their opinion on the same issues. There were four conditions. One group was given opinions that were exactly the same as their own. Another group received opinions exactly opposite to their own. A third group was presented with the same opinions on the important issues and the opposite opinions on the unimportant issues, while the fourth group received the same opinions on the unimportant issues and the opposite opinions on the important issues. Participants felt that they would like the person with the same attitudes more than the one with the opposite attitudes ($r = 0.97$) and the person who agreed with them on the important issues more than the one who agreed with them on the unimportant issues ($r = 0.51$). In a second study Donn Byrne and Don Nelson

(1965) found that attraction towards a stranger was a function of the proportion of similar attitudes held by the other person rather than the absolute number of similar attitudes they expressed. So, for example, others were liked more when they held four similar attitudes and no dissimilar ones than when they had 16 similar attitudes and eight dissimilar ones.

Various studies have sought to test the idea that similar attitudes are reinforcing while dissimilar attitudes are punishing. Gerald Clore and Donn Byrne (1974) stated that the most methodologically sound support for this idea was a study by John Lombardo and his colleagues (1972) at Oklahoma University. In this study a confederate who was sitting in a separate room chose a topic on which opinions could be exchanged with a participant through an intercom. After the topic was announced, the participant could comment on it for 20 seconds by switching on the intercom. On six of the 12 topics, the confederate either agreed or disagreed with the participant. The results showed that participants were quicker to turn on the switch when the confederate agreed rather than disagreed with them, implying that agreement was experienced as positive and disagreement as negative. One methodological advantage of this design over others that have tested the reinforcing properties of attitudes was that it was not obvious to participants that the behaviour being reinforced was the speed of responding and so they were less likely to have varied their speed of response because they thought the experimenter wanted them to.

As recognized by Byrne (1971, p. 355), support for the idea that increasing uncertainty heightens the effect of attitude similarity is mixed. For example, in the first of three experiments reported by Byrne and Clore (1967) uncertainty, or what they called the *effectance motive*, was manipulated by showing participants either a meaningless film consisting of unrelated scenes or a documentary about life in Morocco before they were asked to rate the attractiveness of a similar or dissimilar stranger. Effectance motivation was measured by the five characteristics of feeling uneasy, confused, unreal, dreamy and wanting to know what others think. In line with the manipulation participants rated the meaningless film as arousing greater effectance than the documentary. Based on their theory, Byrne and Clore expected that attitude similarity would have a greater effect in the meaningless film condition where effectance was higher. In other words, participants in the meaningless film condition would like the dissimilar stranger less and the similar stranger more than participants in the documentary condition. However, contrary to expectation, they found participants in the meaningless film condition were less negative towards a dissimilar stranger and less positive towards a similar stranger than participants in the documentary condition.

John Palmer (1969), a doctoral student of Byrne, suggested that the *need for vindication* should be distinguished from the *need for evaluation*. The need for vindication is the need to defend one's position regardless of whether it is correct, while the need for evaluation is the need to be correct regardless of one's current opinion. To test the value of this distinction Palmer varied the competence of the stranger. If the need for evaluation was paramount, competent strangers should be liked more than incompetent ones, regardless of whether they held similar or dissimilar views. On the other hand, if the need for vindication was greater, a competent stranger with similar attitudes should be liked more than an incompetent stranger with similar attitudes, while a competent stranger with dissimilar attitudes should be liked less than an incompetent stranger with dissimilar attitudes. Palmer found some support for the vindication need in that the competent stranger with similar attitudes was liked more than the incompetent one with similar attitudes, but there was little difference in liking between the competent and the incompetent stranger with dissimilar attitudes. This distinction could be further tested by trying to manipulate these two needs and seeing whether the predicted effects occur.

Donn Byrne and Ray Rhamey (1965) thought that personal evaluations from others would have a stronger effect on liking for a stranger than other attitudes because of people's need to think well of themselves. That is what they found. For example, participants preferred a stranger who rated them favourably but who had no similar attitudes to one who evaluated them unfavourably but whose attitudes were all similar.

Other evidence on the importance to relationships of similarity of attitudes comes from measures of relationship adjustment which have assumed that agreement or similarity over issues is an important aspect of relationship adjustment, by including it as part of the measure. For example, eight of the 15 items of the widely used Marital Adjustment Test (Locke and Wallace 1959) assess agreement over various issues. In the Dyadic Adjustment Scale (Spanier 1976) 15 of the 32 items concern agreement over issues. Factor analyses of these tests have shown that the agreement items emerge together on one factor and that this factor is closely related to the other factors. Graham Spanier (1976) factor-analysed the correlations of the 32 items comprising his test and found four factors which he called dyadic consensus, affectional expression, dyadic satisfaction and dyadic cohesion. Thirteen of the 15 agreement items correlated most highly with the dyadic consensus factor, ranging from 0.34 for agreement on amount of time spent together to 0.73 for agreement over philosophy of life. The other two agreement items, demonstrations of affection and sex relations, correlated more strongly with the affectional expression factor than the dyadic consensus one. The internal consistency of the 13-item dyadic consensus scale was high, indicating that if there was agreement on one item, there was likely to be agreement on all the other items. Unfortunately, Graham Spanier did not report the correlation between the dyadic consensus scale and the other scales but simply gave the average intercorrelation between the four scales, which was 0.68. In their study of 666 newlywed couples from Chicago, Ernest Burgess and Paul Wallin (1953, p. 504) found that greater marital consensus was associated with greater marital happiness ($r = 0.49$) and satisfaction ($r = 0.53$).

Hans Eysenck and James Wakefield (1981) factor-analysed the 15 items of the Marital Adjustment Test together with the six items they added. Four main factors emerged for both women and men which were orthogonally rotated and which they called agreement, to marry or divorce, sex and affection, and time together. For women four of the eight agreement issues correlated most highly with the agreement factor compared with six in the men. Like Spanier, Eysenck and Wakefield did not give the correlation between the agreement factor and the other three factors but they reported that the average correlation between the first three oblique factors was greater than 0.50.

However, it should be noted that although Eysenck and Wakefield found spouses to be similar in terms of the attitudes of tender-mindedness ($r = 0.56$) and radicalism ($r = 0.51$), only similarity in tender-mindedness was significantly correlated with marital satisfaction of both wives ($r = 0.14$) and husbands ($r = 0.13$). Bernard Murstein and Gary Beck (1972) found that actual and perceived similarity of personality as measured by Norman's (1963) 20-item bipolar adjective checklist was generally positively and significantly correlated with the Locke–Wallace (1959) Marital Adjustment Test in 60 couples married for an average of three years. Actual similarity was significantly correlated with the husband's marital adjustment ($r = 0.29$) but not with that of the wife ($r = 0.13$). Similarity in personality as perceived by the husband was significantly correlated with his own marital happiness ($r = 0.41$) and similarity as seen by the wife was significantly correlated with her own marital satisfaction ($r = 0.29$).

LOW SELF-ESTEEM AND EVALUATIONS OF OTHERS

Interestingly, Newcomb's and Byrne's theories make opposing predictions concerning how people who dislike themselves will feel about others who either like or dislike them. Newcomb's theory and other consistency theories predict that people who dislike themselves will like those who dislike them and dislike those who like them. This theory, for example, may help explain why some people are attracted to those who reject or abuse them and why some reject or abuse those who like them, although these cases may be explained in other ways. Byrne's theory, on the other hand, states that people will like those who like them regardless of whether they like themselves or not. A third theory, put forward by James Dittes (1959) and usually known as self-enhancement or self-esteem theory (Jones 1973), assumes that being evaluated will have a greater effect for those who dislike themselves than for those who like themselves. According to Dittes, people with low self-esteem will have a greater need for being accepted than people with high self-esteem. Consequently, when someone accepts them they will like that person more than would people with high self-esteem because they will be more grateful to that individual. Conversely, they will dislike someone who rejects them more than would people with high self-esteem because they will feel more frustrated. The predictions from these three theories are shown in Table 5.2.

Newcomb's and Dittes's opposing predictions concerning the effects of low self-esteem on evaluating others who evaluate them has generated considerable

Theories	Evaluation from others	Self-evaluation +	−
Newcomb	+	+	−
	−	−	+
Byrne	+	+	+
	−	−	−
Dittes	+	+	++
	−	−	−−

Table 5.2 Predicted evaluation of others as a result of self-evaluation and evaluations from others

and ongoing research with somewhat inconsistent findings. Only a few of these studies will be described to give an indication of this work. In this context Newcomb's theory is usually referred to as self-consistency theory. The first study to support it was reported by Morton Deutsch and Leonard Solomon (1959). This study was initially carried out on 132 American women telephone operators and repeated on 70 American craftsmen with essentially the same results. To manipulate self-esteem participants were basically told that compared to eight other people they had performed either the best or the worst on two separate tasks. They then received a note purportedly from a team member that was either positive or negative in terms of whether they were still wanted on the team. The note-sender was evaluated most favourably by participants who had done well and who had received a positive note, and least favourably by participants who had done well and who had received a negative note. In line with consistency theory, however, there was little difference in how the note-sender was evaluated by participants who had either done well and received a positive note or done badly and received a negative note. Similarly, there was little difference between those who had either done well and received a negative note or done badly and received a positive note. Consequently, these results were interpreted as showing a consistency as well as a positivity bias for positive evaluation. In what were essentially two further replications of this study, Paul Skolnick (1971) failed to obtain a consistency effect while Donald Dutton (1972) found one.

The first study to support the esteem position was reported by James Dittes (1959) at Yale University. Male students met in small discussion groups. Self-esteem was measured rather than manipulated. Some members were presented with feedback that they were accepted by the group while others were given feedback that they were not accepted. The group was most favourably evaluated by participants who were accepted and had low self-esteem and least favourably by participants who were rejected and also had low self-esteem. However, although in the predicted direction, participants who were accepted and had low self-esteem did not evaluate the group significantly more favourably than those who were accepted and had high self-esteem.

Manipulating both self-esteem and acceptance, Larry Jacobs and his colleagues (1971) found that a woman was liked most by male students who were favourably evaluated by that woman regardless of their self-esteem, and was liked least by those students who were unfavourably evaluated and whose self-esteem had been lowered. For those participants who had been unfavourably evaluated, the woman was liked less by those with lowered than raised self-esteem. Self-esteem was manipulated by giving participants positive or negative feedback about their personality on the basis of personality tests, while acceptance was varied by providing a favourable or unfavourable evaluation by the woman based on what the men had said in five awkward social situations, four of which involved a date.

More recently William Swann and his colleagues (1992) reported two studies which supported the self-consistency, or what they refer to as the self-verification, position. Both studies used mildly depressed students who had a negative view of themselves. In the first study mildly and non-depressed students were told that they had been evaluated either positively or negatively by someone, and they were then given the opportunity of either meeting this person or taking part in another experiment. More of the mildly depressed than the non-depressed students wanted to meet the person who had evaluated them unfavourably than to participate in another experiment, whereas more of the non-depressed students wished to meet the person who had evaluated them favourably than to take part in another experiment. In addition, the mildly depressed students were more likely to think that the evaluations described themselves but were not more likely to want to change the evaluator's opinion. In other words, the depressed participants did not appear to want to meet the person who had evaluated them unfavourably because they thought their description of them was inappropriate and wanted to change their opinion. In the second study mildly and non-depressed students were presented with evaluations that were either favourable or unfavourable and were then asked to rank how much they wanted to see information about their strengths or limitations in two other areas. Mildly depressed students preferred to seek information about their limitations when they had been evaluated favourably while non-depressed students were less inclined to seek information about their limitations when they had been unfavourably evaluated. Thomas Joiner and Gerald Metalsky (1995) also found that depressed students sought more negative feedback than non-depressed students ($r = 0.15$).

SIMILARITY AND EMOTIONAL INSECURITY

Joel Goldstein and Howard Rosenfeld (1969) suggested that dissimilar people will be liked less by emotionally insecure than by emotionally secure individuals because the former will feel more threatened by people who differ from them. They obtained partial support for this idea in two studies. In the first they found that female students who were less frightened of being rejected were more likely to say that they would approach people described as having different opinions ($r = 0.61$) or interests ($r = 0.58$) than were those who were frightened of being rejected. In the second study, emotional insecurity was manipulated by providing participants with no feedback or feedback indicating they were of either average or high acceptability to their peers. Participants were presented with information about three of their peers who varied in how similar they were to them in interests and traits. They were asked to rank-order the three people in terms of how much they would like to meet them and to rate how much they would like them. There was no evidence to suggest that dissimilar others were liked more by those receiving feedback of high acceptability than by those receiving either no feedback or feedback of average acceptability. However, the results of other correlational studies have been mixed. Russell Leonard (1975) found that high self-esteem participants were less attracted to a dissimilar stranger and more attracted to a similar stranger than were low self-esteem participants, while Marti Hope Gonzales and her colleagues (1983) found no relationship between self-esteem and attraction to a stranger.

COMPLEMENTARITY

There are several theories which propose that partners or friends will differ rather than be similar to one another in certain ways. Of these, the theory that has stimulated most research is Robert Winch's theory of complementary needs which was first applied to mate selection (e.g. Winch *et al.* 1954; Winch 1958) and later extended to marital adjustment (Katz *et al.* 1960) and friendship (Izard 1960). While recognizing that people who marry each other are similar in terms of various characteristics such as social class and interests, Winch believed that within this field of eligible people we were most attracted to people who would satisfy our needs most and/or who possessed qualities we valued highly. He distinguished two types of need gratification or complementarity. Type I was where one person was high on a need and the other person was low on that same need: for example, one person was dominant and the other was submissive. Type II was where one person was high on one need and the other person was high on a different but complementary need: for instance, one person may be nurturant (i.e. wants to look after others) while the other person may be succorant (i.e. wants to be looked after by others). Based on common sense and ideas derived from Sigmund Freud, Winch formulated 44 Type I and 344 Type II complementary relationships in terms of 12 needs taken from Henry Murray (1938), such as dominance and nurturance, and the three traits of anxiety, emotionality and vicariousness (i.e. a need being gratified by seeing it being gratified in others). Some of these qualities were assessed in terms of whether they were satisfied within or outside the marriage and whether they were expressed at an overt or a covert level, making 44 variables altogether (Winch 1958, pp. 81–3, 90).

Winch tested his ideas on 25 young, recently married, middle-class American couples using three ways of assessing needs. The main method was a two- to three-hour need interview consisting of 45 open-ended questions designed to measure the strength of the needs and traits and how they were gratified or expressed. The interviews were independently rated for these qualities by two people. The second method was a case history interview to find out about the person's relationships with their family and friends and how this affected their own development. The third method was what individuals saw as happening in eight of the 31 Thematic Apperception Test (TAT) cards developed by Henry Murray (1943) to assess needs. The data from these methods were analysed as a whole by one person and rated by a group of five people at a case conference. Winch found mixed support for his theory. The need interview, holistic analysis and case conference ratings provided only weak support for the theory while the case history interview and the TAT did not support it. Of the 44 Type I correlations predicted to be negative, only eight of them were significantly so, while of the 344 Type II correlations expected to be positive only 63 were significantly so (Winch 1958, pp. 113–14).

Various other analyses of the data were carried out. Winch (1955a), concentrating on Type I complementarity only and using the need interview, found that the mean of the 44 correlations for the married couples ($r = 0.10$) was significantly lower than that for randomly paired couples ($r = 0.23$). However, the difference in mean correlations was not significant using the case conference ratings. Thomas Ktsanes (1955), factor-analysing individuals using the need interview data, found negative correlations for his four factors which were significant for hostile dominance ($r = -0.43$) and mature nurturance ($r = -0.29$) but not for yielding dependency ($r = -0.22$) or neurotic self-deprecation ($r = -0.10$). In a complex and crude cluster analysis based on the need interview, holistic analysis and case conference ratings, Winch and his colleagues (1955) suggested there was one bipolar assertive–receptive dimension underlying needs in married couples. Finally, Winch (1958, pp. 117–18) was able to correctly match 13 of the 25 couples when given the case conference data on six to seven couples at a time with all identifying material apart from gender removed. This rate of matching was considerably greater than that expected by chance.

Both Irving Rosow (1957) and George Levinger (1964) raised several conceptual criticisms of Winch's theory. Perhaps Rosow's most important criticism of the theory seemingly acknowledged by Winch (1967), is that there are no explicit criteria for determining what constitutes complementarity. Rosow pointed out that since it is unlikely that every need a person has will be met in their marriage, it is necessary to have some index of overall fit. Yet this would be difficult to devise since individuals differ in terms of which of their needs are the most important. In addition two or more needs may conflict, which Rosow illustrated with Winch's own example of a dominant, socially ambitious woman having to choose between a dependent spouse to complement her dominance and a dominant husband to complement her status needs.

George Levinger (1964) also questioned the grounds for three of Winch's examples of complementary needs, which were Type I achievement and Type II abasement–hostility and abasement–nurturance. He suggested that it may be preferable for both wife and husband to be similar in their need for achievement so as to coordinate their efforts better. In addition Levinger raised the issue of people who had moderate rather than high or low levels of needs. In these cases complementarity may be achieved by someone having moderate rather than high or low levels of needs such as dominance. Finally, Roland Tharp (1964) argued that the concept of needs may be too general and abstract to be of predictive value and that it might be more fruitful to first specify what the role requirements of being a spouse are before deciding in what ways, if any, they may be complementary.

Though it provoked considerable research (for a review see Murstein 1976), only a few studies have found any support for Winch's general idea. Two such studies were that of Milton Lipetz and his colleagues (1970) and that of Richard Wagner (1975). Lipetz and his colleagues gave the Edwards (1953) Personal Preference Schedule (EPPS), consisting of 210 pairs of items for measuring 15 of Murray's personality needs, to 50 couples not seeming to have marital difficulties and to 50 couples seeking professional therapy for marital problems. In addition, they gave these couples the Locke–Wallace (1959) Marital Adjustment Test and a shortened 60-item version of the EPPS which they had modified to refer specifically to marriage. They selected 11 pairs of complementary needs, five of which reflected need similarity such as similarity in the need for affiliation. Support for complementarity was found for the modified version of the EPPS but not, with one exception, for the original version. For both wives and husbands marital adjustment was significantly correlated with similarity in affiliation (wives $r = -0.42$, husbands $r = -0.54$), autonomy (wives $r = -0.34$, husbands $r = -0.43$), male nurturance–female succorance (wives $r = -0.30$, husbands $r = -0.45$), heterosexuality (wives $r = -0.27$, husbands $r = -0.34$), male succorance–female nurturance (wives $r = -0.22$, husbands $r = -0.26$) and male abasement–female aggression (wives $r = -0.21$, husbands $r = -0.20$). In other words, complementarity in the sense of being similar on different needs such as abasement and aggression was only found in three of the six such pairs. Complementarity in terms of being similar on the same need such as affiliation was shown for three of the five such pairs.

Richard Wagner (1975) asked 70 male counsellors working in three American summer camps to indicate which counsellors they found cooperative. This resulted in 105 cooperative pairs of counsellors and 61 uncooperative pairs. Eleven needs were chosen as being relevant to their working relationships and these formed six combinations such as high succorance and nurturance. Needs were assessed by interviews with the counsellors and the senior staff and a couple of rating scales completed by the counsellors on other counsellors. Two of the six combinations (succorance–nurturance and aggression–abasement) were significantly related to cooperativeness in all three camps, and another three of them (dominance–autonomy, exhibitionism–deference and responsibility–nurturance) in two of the camps. Only affiliation–dissociation was not related to cooperativeness.

Most studies, however, have noted that, if the needs of people in close relationships are related, they tend to be similar rather than different. For example, Bernard Murstein (1967) gave a modified version of the Edwards Personal Preference Schedule (EPPS) to 99 young couples who were engaged or going steady and most of whom were students in Connecticut. The EPPS was modified to consist of 135 items answered on a five-point scale of importance or frequency. On none of the 15 needs was there a significant negative correlation but on six of them there was a significant positive correlation of about 0.20. Jan Trost (1967) found no significant correlations on either of the two major dimensions of dominance–submissiveness and nurturance–receptiveness in 258 Swedish couples who were newly married or were about to be married.

Robert Pierce (1970) gave the Jackson (1967) Personality Research Form A, which measures 20 of Murray's needs, to a group of male students new to university. Towards the end of their first academic year, students sharing with another student were asked to name two first-year men they particularly liked. There were 39 pairs of men who chose each other. Not one of the 20 needs was significantly negatively correlated while four of them were significantly positively correlated.

John Meyer and Susan Pepper (1977) gave a revised and shortened version of the Jackson Personality Research Form to 66 Canadian couples who had been married for not more than five years. The questionnaire was shortened by using only 10 of the 20 items for each scale and measuring only 12 of the 20 needs. Wherever possible items were reworded to refer to marital situations. Couples also completed a slightly revised version of the Locke–Wallace (1959) Marital Adjustment Test which was used to divide them into a high and low adjustment group. They found no evidence for the 12 Type I and the 14 Type II complementary needs combinations they had hypothesized.

Barbara Seyfried and Clyde Hendrick (1973) suggested that people would be attracted to members of the opposite sex who were complementary in terms of attitudes characterizing their sex roles, such as 'If I marry, I would enjoy preparing meals for my family'. They found that while female students preferred a male stranger with a masculine rather than a feminine attitude, male students showed no preference for a female stranger with a feminine as opposed to a masculine attitude. John Antill (1983) thought that marital happiness would be greater in married couples with complementary sex roles. He gave the Spanier (1976) Dyadic Adjustment Scale and a shortened form of the Bem (1974) Sex-Role Inventory to 108 couples living in Sydney, Australia who had been married for about 11 years. Items assessing masculinity included being 'forceful' and 'assertive', and those measuring femininity being 'affectionate' and 'understanding'. There was no evidence for couples to be complementary in terms of their sex roles or for marital happiness to be associated with complementary sex roles. Couples tended to be similar for femininity ($r = 0.20$) but not for masculinity ($r = 0.07$). In addition, the wife's marital happiness was associated with the husband's ($r = 0.31$) and her own ($r = 0.33$) feminity, while the husband's marital happiness was associated with the wife's ($r = 0.28$) and his own ($r = 0.42$) feminity. Lawrence Kurdek and Patrick Schmitt (1986) also found relationship satisfaction to be associated with feminity in 88 married individuals ($r = 0.29$) and 112 cohabiting lesbians ($r = 0.25$) but not in 70 cohabiting heterosexuals ($r = 0.18$) or 100 cohabiting gays ($r = 0.04$).

SUMMARY

There is considerable evidence that romantic couples in particular are similar in characteristics such as age, physical attractiveness, intelligence and interests, although there is less research showing that relationship satisfaction is related to such similarity. Three explanations for similarity are social exchange, consistency and reinforcement-affect theory. There has been little attempt to test social exchange theory as applied to similarity. Consistency and reinforcement-affect theory generally make similar predictions apart from the situation in which those with low self-esteem evaluate others who evaluate them negatively: consistency theory predicts that low self-esteem individuals will make a favourable evaluation of such people while both reinforcement-affect and self-enhancement theory predict that their evaluation will be unfavourable. Recent evidence supports the consistency or self-verification position. While problems remain in defining what constitutes complementarity of needs, little support has been found for complementarity as hypothesized.

6

Social Exchange

Several theories have sought to explain human social behaviour in terms of the expected overall value or outcome of the social interaction or exchange that takes place between individuals. These theories are generally called social exchange theories. Two of them in particular have been applied to understanding close relationships and have led to increasing attempts to test the validity of some of their assumptions. These two theories are interdependence theory put forward by John Thibaut and Harold Kelley (1959, Kelley and Thibaut 1978) and equity theory as developed by Elaine Walster and her colleagues (1973, 1978a).

INTERDEPENDENCE THEORY

According to interdependence theory people try to maximize their outcomes. An outcome can be thought of as the difference between the rewards and costs of some action.

$$Outcome = Rewards - Costs$$

Thus actions with high rewards and low costs will have positive outcomes while those with low rewards and high costs will have negative outcomes. Rewards are pleasurable acts such as being helped or being agreed with. Costs, on the other hand, refer to factors that inhibit or deter behaviour; they include physical and mental effort, embarrassment and anxiety, and conflict.

Interdependence theory makes a distinction between how attractive or satisfactory we find a relationship and how dependent we are on it. Relationship attractiveness or satisfaction is the difference between the outcome level of that relationship and the outcome that we expect for other relationships in general.

$$Satisfaction = Outcome - Expected outcome$$

This expected outcome is called the *comparison level* and is based on the outcome we expect for a relationship based on our experience and knowledge of other relationships. We will be satisfied with a relationship if the outcome for it lies above our comparison level, whereas we will be dissatisfied with the relationship if the outcome for it is below our comparison level.

Our dependence on a relationship, on the other hand, is the difference between the outcome of that relationship and the best alternative outcome that is available to us.

Dependence = Outcome − Best alternative outcome

The best alternative outcome is known as the *comparison level for alternatives* and may include being alone (Thibaut and Kelley 1959, p. 100). We will be dependent on a relationship if the outcome for it is above the comparison level for alternatives. If the outcome is below the comparison level for alternatives we will generally not stay in the relationship unless our choice of alternatives is restricted, as it may be in a marital relationship (Thibaut and Kelley 1959, p. 67). When we leave a relationship our comparison level for alternatives becomes our next best alternative. Note that power may be seen as the converse of dependency: we will have power over the other person if their outcome in this relationship is greater than their best alternative outcome.

Although there is more to interdependence theory than that outlined, these are some of the main ideas that have been used in applying and testing the theory. Caryl Rusbult (1980, 1983) refers to dependence as commitment which is the tendency to stay in the relationship and to feel psychologically attached to it. Her investment model assumes that commitment is a function not only of alternative outcomes but also of non-recoverable investments made in the relationship.

Commitment = Outcome − Alternative outcome + Investment

Investments refer to extrinsic factors such as mutual friends and shared experiences and to intrinsic ones such as time and emotional effort. Investments are distinguished from rewards and costs in that they can be less readily removed from the relationship. In terms of this model, we would stay in an unsatisfactory relationship even if there were more attractive alternatives if we had heavily invested in it.

Caryl Rusbult (1983) tested some of these ideas in a seven-month longitudinal study on the romantic relationships of 17 female and 17 male American students. Rewards, costs, satisfaction, alternatives, investment and commitment were measured with several general items on 13 occasions or until the relationship ended and were averaged across occasions. However, only one item was selected to assess each measure although which item was chosen was not stated. The general concepts were explained before the items were completed. The items included such questions as 'How rewarding is this relationship?', 'How do your alternatives compare to this relationship?', 'What is the size of your investment in this relationship?' and so on. About 88 per cent of relationship satisfaction was explained by rewards, with costs not making a significant contribution. When the measures were looked at according to whether they were collected in the first stage (months 1–2) or the second stage (months 3–7) of the study, costs made a significant contribution to satisfaction in the second but not the first stage, although the size of this contribution was not given. One reason for this finding may be that costs are less apparent initially because people generally display their best behaviour first.

About 89 per cent of commitment was accounted for by relationship satisfaction, alternative outcomes and investment. Relationship satisfaction and investment were positively and most strongly related to commitment to a similar extent while alternative outcomes were negatively and less strongly related to commitment. In other words, investment in the relationship appeared to be more highly related to commitment than the attractiveness of alternative outcomes. However, whether people stayed in the relationship, were left or left the relationship was most strongly related to the alternatives, followed by their investment and satisfaction. The amount of variance explained by these three factors was not given. For those whose relationships continued rather than broke up, there were increases over time in rewards, satisfaction, investment and commitment and decreases in costs and alternatives. For those whose decision was to end the relationship, there were increases in costs and alternatives and decreases in investment and commitment with little change in rewards and satisfaction. For those whose partners ended the relationship, the changes were generally intermediate between those for the other two groups, apart from investment which increased the most.

Caryl Rusbult and her colleagues (1986) further examined the generalizability of some of these findings in a cross-sectional study of 130 adults selected from the community who were involved in relationships, of whom 74 per cent were married. Two general items were used to assess rewards (e.g. 'How rewarding is your relationship?'), costs (e.g. 'In general how do the costs you get out of the relationship compare with those of other people's?') and investment (e.g. 'All things considered, how much have you "put into" your relationship?'); three items measured alternatives (e.g. 'Generally speaking, how appealing are your alternatives – a different relationship or spending time without a romantic relationship?') and satisfaction (e.g. 'All things considered, how satisfied are you with your relationship?'); and four items assessed commitment (e.g. 'How committed are you to maintaining your relationship?'). In women 53 per cent of relationship satisfaction was explained by rewards with costs not making a significant contribution, whereas in men 38 per cent was explained with rewards and costs providing a similar contribution. Less of relationship satisfaction was explained by subtracting costs from rewards, as implied by Thibaut and Kelley's (1959) formulation, than by using rewards alone or rewards and costs together. About 50 and 42 per cent of commitment in women and men respectively was explained by satisfaction, investments and alternatives, with satisfaction being more important for women than for men.

However, Susan Sprecher (1988) in a sample of 197 American student couples found that while commitment was related to satisfaction and alternatives, it was not related to investment when social support for the relationship was taken into account. About 35 per cent of commitment was explained by alternatives and a further 10 per cent by relationship satisfaction. Commitment was measured with four items while alternative outcomes, satisfaction, investment and relationship support were each assessed with one item. It is possible, therefore, that the aspect of investment which is most strongly related to commitment is having people who would disapprove of the relationship breaking up, and which may override other aspects such as shared memories and experiences.

Richard Udry (1981) also found alternative outcomes to be a stronger predictor than relationship satisfaction of marital stability in some 400 young, middle-class urban American couples. Alternative outcomes was assessed with two three- or four-item scales of spouse replacement and economic maintenance; marital satisfaction with a single global marital happiness item; and marital stability in terms of the couples who separated or divorced between 1977 and 1979. Eight per cent of marital stability was explained by the three variables of the wife's happiness, the husband's economic alternatives and the wife's spouse alternatives. More of the variance may have been explained if marital break-ups had been analysed in terms of the person who most wanted to leave the relationship. Presumably those wanting to leave the relationship should have more attractive alternatives than those wishing to maintain the relationship.

Stephen Drigotas and Caryl Rusbult (1992) tried to test Thibaut and Kelley's (1959) dependence model more directly in two longitudinal samples of 60 and 57 American student dating relationships, by comparing two derived measures of need dependence with the two separate measures of current relationship need satisfaction and alternative relationship need satisfaction used to derive them. The results generally seemed to show that more of relationship break-up (partners categorized as stayers, abandoned and leavers) was explained by the derived measures than by current relationship need satisfaction or by both current relationship need satisfaction and alternative relationship need satisfaction. For example, a maximum of 12 and 33 per cent of relationship breakdown was explained by one of the derived measures in the first and second study respectively, compared with 8 and 26 per cent by the two separate measures together. Although the differences in the amount of relationship breakdown explained were generally significant, the differences appear small for practical purposes. Furthermore, the two separate measures may have been somewhat less sensitive since they do not seem to have taken account of the relative importance of the five needs assessed, as did the derived measure. The alternative outcomes measures did not allow for the possibility that satisfaction may not have depended on an alternative relationship.

The causal relationship between these social exchange variables have not, however, been addressed by this research. For example, it is possible that commitment is a cause rather than a consequence of alternative outcomes in that people who are committed to their relationship may be more likely to see alternatives as less attractive than would individuals not so committed to their relationship. In an attempt to determine whether commitment can affect the evaluation of an attractive alternative, Dennis Johnson and Caryl Rusbult (1989) asked students to imagine that they were either highly or lowly committed to a current relationship and then to judge how attracted they were to a stranger described as being extremely attractive. They found that the participants in the high commitment condition evaluated the stranger less favourably than those in the low commitment condition, implying that commitment can influence the evaluation of alternatives. Whether the attractiveness of alternatives also determines the commitment shown to a current relationship appears not to have been investigated yet.

EQUITY AND EQUALITY

Equity theory as propounded by Elaine Walster and her colleagues (1973, 1978a) consists of four related propositions. First, individuals will try to maximize their outcomes. Second, to discourage individual greed and to maximize the possibility that everyone benefits, groups will generally reward members who treat other members equitably and will generally punish those members who treat other members inequitably. Equity is defined as the ratio of the difference between outcomes and inputs to inputs for one person compared to another.

$$\frac{A\text{'s outcomes} - A\text{'s inputs}}{A\text{'s inputs}} = \frac{B\text{'s outcomes} - B\text{'s inputs}}{B\text{'s inputs}}$$

In other words, if one person receives relatively more or less from the relationship than the other person does, given their inputs, that relationship will be inequitable. Third, appropriately socialized individuals will generally experience greater distress the more inequitable the relationship. However, under-benefited individuals will experience more distress than over-benefited ones. More specifically, the over-benefited will feel guilty and anxious while the under-benefited will feel angry and resentful. And fourth, the more inequitable the relationship the more individuals will attempt to reduce their distress by restoring either actual or psychological equity to the relationship. Restoring actual equity refers to changing the outcomes and/or inputs in a relationship, while restoring psychological equity concerns changing one's perception of its outcomes and/or inputs.

To test this theory Elaine Walster and her colleagues (1978b) asked 310 female and 227 male American undergraduates who were in a casual or steady relationship to rate on an eight-point bipolar scale how much they and their partner put into and got out of this relationship and how content, happy, angry and guilty they felt about this. They divided their sample into the five categories of the equitably treated and the slightly or greatly under- or over-benefited. The greatly under- or over-benefited felt less content and happy than the other three groups. The greatly over-benefited felt most guilty while the greatly under-benefited felt most angry. In terms of all four moods taken together, the under-benefited did not appear more distressed than the over-benefited.

Various studies have been published subsequently which have compared the extent to which equity may be a more potent correlate of relationship compatibility than related variables such as equality or simple outcome. Although the studies have measured equity differently, the results generally agree in showing that equity is not the strongest correlate. Three studies, for example, were carried out by Rodney Cate and his colleagues (1982, 1985, 1988). All three studies included the same measures of equity, equality, reward level and relationship satisfaction and were based on exclusive dating relationships of American students. Equity and relationship satisfaction were assessed as done by Elaine Walster and her colleagues (1978b). Equality was measured in terms of how participants evaluated their own and their partner's outcome in the relationship which was obtained from the equity assessment. Equality existed where the two outcomes were the same. Reward level was measured in terms of how rewarding the relationship was in seven areas such as love and status.

The first study was a cross-sectional design involving 246 women and 91 men (Cate *et al.* 1982). Of the three variables, reward level accounted for the greatest part of relationship satisfaction (14 per cent), followed by equality (9 per cent) and then equity (4 per cent) when each of these variables was entered last in the regression equation. The other two studies were longitudinal designs. In the first one (Cate *et al.* 1985), only reward level (dichotomized at the median) of the three variables predicted the break-up either three or seven months later in 95 women and 36 men. In the second study, which did not assess the role of equality (Cate *et al.* 1988), reward level but not equity predicted relationship satisfaction three months later in 72 women and 18 men. The results of these studies, however, may have been biased towards reward level which was based on the evaluation of specific content areas. Furthermore, reward level had greater variance than the comparison variables in the third study and may have had it in the first study, which may have enabled it to explain more of the variance in relationship satisfaction. In response to this latter point Cate and his colleagues (1988) in the last study repeated the analysis using a dichotomized measure of reward level but found essentially the same results.

James Michaels and his colleagues (1984, 1986) examined whether equity was a stronger correlate of relationship satisfaction or commitment than simple outcomes in 150 female and 123 male American student exclusive dating relationships in two separate papers. Equity, equality and outcomes were initially assessed with the global indices used by Elaine Walster and her colleagues (1978b) and a measure in which participants' own and their partner's contributions and outcomes were evaluated in terms of five specific areas such as love and status. However, the latter measures were used since they showed more variation. Relationship satisfaction was assessed with the single item of satisfaction also taken from the measure used by Elaine Walster and her colleagues (1978b). Relationship commitment was measured with a single item indicating the likelihood that they would break off their present relationship in the near future.

In addition, there were various measures of Thibaut and Kelley's (1959) concept of outcomes relative to comparison level for alternatives, of which one was common to both papers. This index was a single item which asked participants to rate the extent to which their own outcomes from the relationship were above or below what they could reasonably expect from the best alternative to their present relationship. In the first paper, the other index was the single comparison level item subtracted from the outcomes measure based on the five specific areas. In the second paper there were two other indices. The first index consisted of the single comparison level item subtracted from another single outcome item which asked participants to rate their outcomes from their present relationship, while the second index treated these two items separately, as was generally done by Caryl Rusbult (1983).

Of the variables compared in explaining relationship satisfaction, outcome level explained the greatest proportion (42 per cent), followed by either measure of outcome relative to comparison level (38 per cent), equity (18 per cent) and equality (16 per cent). The analyses of relationship commitment were somewhat different. The amounts of commitment explained by the three different indices of outcomes relative to comparison level for alternatives were essentially the same with inequity not making a significant contribution. Outcomes were more highly correlated ($r = 0.57$) with commitment than either the single ($r = 0.53$) or the difference ($r = 0.39$) index of outcomes relative to comparison level, and inequity ($r = -0.32$).

Furthermore, there is some evidence to suggest that men in particular who believe that there should be a fair reciprocal exchange between partners tend to be less satisfied with their marriages. Bernard Murstein and his colleagues (1977) developed a 23-item questionnaire to measure an exchange orientation which included such items as 'If I do dishes three times a week, I expect my spouse to do them three times a week' and 'It does not matter if the people I love do less for me than I do for them'. They gave this questionnaire to 34 married American couples together with the Locke–Wallace Marital Adjustment Test and found that marital adjustment was more highly correlated with exchange orientation in husbands ($r = -0.63$) than in wives ($r = -0.27$). A spouse's own exchange orientation was also correlated with the marital adjustment of their wife ($r = -0.31$) or husband ($r = -0.39$). In another study Joan Broderick and Daniel O'Leary (1986) looked at the relationship between these two measures in 55 couples living in the state of New York and found that the correlation was similar in wives ($r = 0.47$) and husbands ($r = 0.48$). It is possible that this association may depend on the perceived equitableness of the relationship although this does not appear to have been tested.

SUMMARY

The social exchange theories of interdependence and equity both assume that people try to maximize their outcomes, which is defined as the difference between rewards and costs. Interdependence theory distinguishes relationship attraction or satisfaction from relationship dependence. We will be attracted to and satisfied with a relationship if its outcome exceeds our expected outcome for relationships in general. We will be dependent on a relationship if its outcome is greater than that of the alternatives, which may include not being in a relationship. Investment theory, which refers to dependence as commitment, assumes that staying within a relationship also depends on our non-recoverable investment in it. There is some evidence to indicate that commitment is related to the outcome of or satisfaction with that relationship, alternative outcomes and investment, and that it may influence alternative outcomes. Equity theory postulates that people try to maintain equity in their relationship and will feel distressed if they benefit more or benefit less than the other person, although under-benefiting is more distressing than over-benefiting. Equality refers to similarity of outcomes whereas equity may be most simply thought of as similarity in the ratio of outcomes to input. Relationship satisfaction and stability have been generally found to be more strongly related to reward and equality of outcome than to equity. There is also evidence to suggest that those who believe in reciprocity in marital relationships are less happily married.

7

Social Interaction

Most studies on close relationships are based on individuals reporting on how they behave and not on observations on how they actually behave. Consequently, it is important to establish whether people who are dissatisfied with their relationship behave differently from those who are satisfied and, if so, how their behaviour differs. For example, do people who are dissatisfied with their relationship have more negative interactions, in terms of either their frequency or intensity than those who are satisfied? One of the first studies to compare the behaviour of maritally distressed and non-distressed couples was reported by Gary Birchler and his colleagues (1975). An idea that they indirectly tested was that put forward by Gerald Patterson and Hyman Hops (1972) who suggested that people living together are increasingly likely to want to change some of the behaviour of the other person, and that they are more likely to do this through aversive control than positive reinforcement. The person asking for change is likely to do so in increasingly negative ways if their partner does not comply with their request. If the partner eventually does comply, then this negative demanding behaviour will have been reinforced. If the partner, however, agrees to comply, for example by saying they will carry out the request later, which temporarily satisfies the other person's immediate demands, then this avoidance or procrastination response will have been reinforced. Alternatively or at the same time, the partner may respond in a negative way out of annoyance and/or to try to prevent the other person from making demands.

Birchler and his colleagues proposed first that distressed couples would show more negative and less positive behaviour in their interaction than non-distressed couples, and second that married couples would show more negative and less positive behaviour in their interaction than opposite-sex couples who did not know each other. They tested these two propositions on 12 maritally distressed and 12 non-maritally distressed couples selected from the community. Couples were categorized according to the Marital Adjustment Test (Locke and Wallace 1959), a marital problems checklist (Weiss *et al.* 1973; Margolin *et al.* 1983) and a standardized half-hour interview. Couples completed the Inventory of Marital Conflicts (Olson and Ryder 1970) which consists of 18 short vignettes describing marital conflicts, 12 of which are written to make husbands reading them think that the wife is primarily responsible for the problem and wives reading them believe that the husband is responsible.

Couples were videotaped while they first had a four-minute conversation about anything but the vignettes, followed by a 10-minute discussion in which they were asked to resolve their difference of opinion on five of the items on which they disagreed and which had been selected for them. Each partner was paired with an opposite-sex member of both a distressed and a non-distressed couple to form two pairs of opposite-sex strangers. Two trained observers coded the videotapes in 30-second segments using the Marital Interaction Coding System (MICS, pronounced MIX; see Weiss and Summers 1983 for details). Note that learning to use this system is time-consuming. Weiss and Summers (1983) stated that training typically requires two to three months of weekly instruction and practice. The data were grouped and analysed in terms of the two broad categories of positive and negative social reinforcement. Examples of positive social reinforcement were agreement, humour, laughter and smiling while those of negative social reinforcement were complaints, criticism, denial of responsibility, interruptions and inattention.

Both of the hypotheses of Birchler and his colleagues were generally supported. Distressed couples showed significantly more negative behaviour than non-distressed couples in both the conversation and the problem-solving discussion, and less positive behaviour in the problem-solving discussion. Married individuals showed more negative and less positive behaviour towards their partner than the stranger. The extent to which individuals behaved consistently towards different people was also examined. In terms of positive behaviour, individuals tended to behave consistently towards the two strangers but there was little consistency in their behaviour towards their spouse and the stranger. With respect to negative behaviour, consistency was only found for the behaviour of distressed individuals towards strangers. These results generally imply that the more negative behaviour of distressed couples was a function of the specific relationship and was not a general characteristic of the individuals making up that relationship.

Three related limitations of this study should be mentioned. First, Birchler and his colleagues did not define reinforcement behaviours in terms of the way they are usually defined, which is whether they are observed to increase the frequency of certain responses; consequently, the behaviours chosen may not have been reinforcers as traditionally defined. Second, they did not show whether negative behaviour generally led to a negative response as implied by Patterson and Hops. And third, they did not demonstrate that the reinforcement of a demand brought about further demands or that the temporary cessation of a demand through, for example, a delaying response reinforced that delaying response.

CONTINGENT AND RECIPROCAL INTERACTIONS

At about the same time Harold Raush and his colleagues (1974) analysed the extent to which the consequent act of one spouse was related to the antecedent act of the other spouse for six categories of behaviour used in resolving four conflicts in seven harmonious and six discordant newly married American couples. These couples were those who scored at the extreme ends of a bipolar factor which appeared to represent an evaluation of the marriage and which emerged from a factor analysis of data from interviews and questionnaires collected from the original 46 married couples taking part (Goodrich *et al.* 1968). The first two conflicts dealt with the specific issues of how to celebrate the first wedding anniversary and which television programme to watch, while the second two conflicts concerned the relationship in which the husband and then the wife was more distant than the other partner wanted. The six categories of acts or behaviour were described as follows: (1) cognitive (e.g. seeking, giving and withholding information); (2) resolving (e.g. humour, acceptance, compromising); (3) reconciling (e.g. accepting blame, showing concern, reassurance); (4) appealing (e.g. to fairness, love, other motives); (5) rejecting (e.g. the other, giving up); and (6) coercive (e.g. commanding, disparaging, threatening).

When the four conflicts were analysed together discordant wives did not differ from harmonious wives in terms of how contingent their behaviour was on that of their husbands. However, discordant husbands were more likely to react in a more coercive and less cognitive way to all six categories of behaviour than harmonious husbands. Further differences emerged when the specific and relationship conflicts were examined separately. For the two specific issues (i.e. the wedding anniversary and television programme), discordant wives were more coercive to every category than discordant husbands and the harmonious wives. Discordant husbands were more likely to respond in a resolving and reconciling way than their wives to all categories. On the other hand, when husbands were asked to maintain their emotional distance, discordant husbands were more likely to use coercion than their wives and the harmonious husbands. When wives were asked to remain emotionally distant, discordant husbands were also more coercive than their wives and the harmonious husbands while the discordant wives were less rejecting and more reconciling than their husbands and the harmonious wives.

John Gottman and his colleagues (1976) were also interested in whether maritally distressed and non-distressed couples differed in the extent to which the behaviour of one partner was contingent on that of the other. In particular, they wished to determine whether distressed couples showed fewer positive and more negative reciprocal interactions in resolving conflicts than non-distressed couples. In addition, they wanted to find out if distressed and non-distressed couples differed in their evaluation of messages from their spouse and in their intention of how their messages to their spouse were to be evaluated. More specifically, they wished to test the idea that distressed couples may be less skilled than non-distressed couples in communicating accurately with their spouse and that these couples intended their messages to be more positive than they were received.

Two studies were reported which were very similar in design. Ten distressed and six non-distressed couples took part in the first study and 12 distressed and eight non-distressed couples in the second study. Couples were recruited from the community. Distressed couples were defined as having at least one partner scoring below 85 on the 22-item Marital Relationship Inventory (Burgess *et al.* 1971) as well as seeking help for marital problems. Both partners of non-distressed couples scored above 102 and had not sought marital help. In the first study couples discussed three low and two high conflict tasks while in the second study they discussed one of each. These discussions were videotaped. Couples could only talk one at a time. After one partner had said something they had to rate the intended impact of their message on a five-point scale from 'super negative' to 'super positive'. Before replying, the other partner had to rate the actual impact of the message on the same scale. Neither partner could see the ratings of the other person.

Non-distressed couples rated the impact of their partner's messages as more positive and super positive, and less negative, than distressed couples in the first study, and only as more positive in the second study. In neither study did the evaluation of the intended impact of the messages differ between distressed and non-distressed couples, implying that distressed couples did not intend their messages to be less positive. Reciprocal exchanges were analysed simply in terms of the two categories of positive and negative actual impact, because the super positive and super negative categories were relatively uncommon. In the second study there was no evidence for reciprocity, while in the first study non-distressed husbands were more likely than distressed husbands to behave positively following a positive response from their wives.

In a third study Gottman and his colleagues (1977) sought to determine whether there were differences in sequences of observed behaviour between 14 maritally distressed and 14 non-distressed couples when trying to reach a mutually satisfactory resolution to their most serious marital problem (Gottman 1979, p. 106). The discussions were videotaped and the videotapes were transcribed verbatim and coded according to the Couples Interaction Scoring System (CISS, pronounced KISS). In this system each behavioural unit is coded for the speaker's verbal content, the speaker's non-verbal affect and the listener's non-verbal affect or context. A new behavioural unit is formed by a change in either content, affect or context. There are 27 content codes which are grouped into the following eight summary codes: (1) expressing information or feelings about a problem; (2) mindreading or attributing thoughts, feelings, motives and behaviours to the other person; (3) proposing solutions; (4) talking about the communication or discussion; (5) agreeing; (6) disagreeing; (7) summarizing the conversation or what the other person has said; and (8) summarizing what one has said. Affect or context is coded as positive, negative or neutral and is based on facial, vocal and bodily cues. Note that this coding procedure is very time-consuming in that it takes about 28 hours to transcribe and code one hour of videotape.

Gottman and his colleagues looked at sequences of behaviour containing up to six exchanges or lags for affect and content. Maritally distressed couples appeared to show more reciprocity of negative affect, more reciprocity of positive affect at early lags and less at later lags than maritally non-distressed couples. Sequences in content were organized in terms of the probable three sequential stages of problem-solving comprising problem description, problem exploration and problem solution. Subsequently Gottman (1979) devised a slightly different sequence consisting of agenda building, arguing and negotiating. In the first phase of problem description, maritally non-distressed couples were likely to respond to a request for information with agreement, resulting in short sequences called validation. Maritally distressed couples, on the other hand, were more likely to respond with information of their own, in longer sequences known as cross-complaining. In the second phase of problem exploration, all but the maritally distressed wives tended to engage in mindreading leading to agreement, a sequence known as a feeling probe. Maritally distressed couples also engaged in negative exchanges in which a criticism (mindreading with negative affect) was more likely to be followed by information with negative affect. In the third phase of problem solution, proposals for solving problems were more likely to be followed with agreement in maritally non-distressed couples, a sequence called a contract. In maritally distressed wives, however, these proposals tended to be followed by another proposal, a sequence known as a counterproposal.

Several later studies have also found evidence that distressed couples may have more frequent negative reciprocal exchanges when discussing problems than non-distressed couples (Billings 1979; Revenstorf *et al.* 1980; Margolin and Wampold 1981; Pike and Sillars 1985; Levenson and Gottman 1983; Roberts and Krokoff 1990; Halford *et al.* 1990).

NON-VERBAL AND VERBAL COMMUNICATION

Gottman and his colleagues (1977) in their third study also looked at whether the verbal or the non-verbal codes were better at discriminating the maritally distressed from the maritally non-distressed couples. They did this on the five couples with the highest or the lowest scores on the Marital Relationship Inventory, finding that the affect codes were better discriminators than the content codes (as judged by the size of the F ratios). The only content code that differentiated the two groups was agreement by wives ($r = 0.87$). Distressed wives agreed less than non-distressed wives: about 6 per cent of the communication of distressed wives was agreement compared with 26 per cent for the non-distressed wives. Distressed couples showed less neutral affect and more negative affect than non-distressed couples. In terms of both content and affect codes, the two best discriminators were expressing information ($r = 0.82$) and mindreading ($r = 0.80$) with negative affect, both of which were more characteristic of distressed couples.

Using the Marital Interaction Coding System Gayla Margolin and Bruce Wampold (1981) found that the two categories that best discriminated 22 distressed couples from 17 non-distressed couples were interruptions ($r = 0.63$) and verbal agreement ($r = 0.63$) when discussing two problems for 10 minutes. Distressed couples interrupted and agreed less than non-distressed couples. The three non-verbal positive categories of assent ($r = 0.36$), smiles/laughter ($r = 0.32$) and positive physical contact ($r = 0.32$) also discriminated between the two groups, although to a lesser extent. Distressed couples showed less of these behaviours than non-distressed couples. Unlike the previous study by Gottman and his colleagues (1977) there were no significant differences in verbal and non-verbal negative behaviour between the two groups. However, it is not clear to what extent some of these differences may have been due to the distressed group being less well educated and coming from a different location (Oregon rather than California) than the non-distressed group.

DYSFUNCTION IN SENDING OR RECEIVING MESSAGES

In their earlier study Gottman and his colleagues (1976) found that distressed couples did not differ from non-distressed couples in intending their messages to be less positive. A couple of studies have sought to determine whether non-verbal miscommunication is due to difficulties the sender has in encoding messages, the receiver has in decoding them or both processes. The first study, by Patricia Noller (1980), suggested that marital dissatisfaction in couples was related to the husband's difficulty in both sending and receiving messages, while the second study, by John Gottman and Albert Porterfield (1981), indicated that the wife's marital dissatisfaction was related to the husband's difficulty in receiving messages.

Although the unit of analysis in Gottman and Porterfield's study was the individual and not the couple as in Noller's study, marital satisfaction in wives and husbands was strongly correlated ($r = 0.72$) in their study, indicating that if the wife was dissatisfied the husband was also likely to be dissatisfied. Both studies used a modified version of the Marital Communication Scale developed by Malcolm Kahn (1970) in which an individual sends eight verbal messages (e.g. 'I'm cold, aren't you?') to their partner, each having three possible meanings (e.g. 'are you cold also?'; 'I want physical affection'; 'I want you to turn up the heat'), one of which has been previously selected by the experimenter as the one to send. The partner must guess which of the three alternative meanings was the intended one. Husbands and wives send different verbal messages.

Noller (1980) in Australia modified this task by adding a ninth item and ensuring that each item had a positive, neutral and negative alternative. Partners were videotaped sending the nine items with each of the alternatives to their spouses. The videotapes were shown to groups of 8–12 psychology students to determine the accuracy with which the messages were sent. If two-thirds of the judges correctly interpreted a message, that message was categorized as a good communication that had been clearly sent; otherwise it was classified as a bad communication. Errors made by spouses of their partners' communications were classified as either encoding or decoding errors. A decoding error was recorded when a spouse did not correctly interpret a good communication made by their partner; an encoding error was noted when a spouse did not correctly interpret a bad communication sent by their partner. There were 48 married couples who were categorized as high, moderate or low according to their scores on the Locke–Wallace Marital Adjustment Test with 16 couples in each group.

Noller hypothesized that wives and husbands in the low marital adjustment group would send fewer clear messages and make more errors in decoding their spouses' clearly sent messages than wives and husbands in the high marital adjustment group. In addition, the decoding errors of wives and husbands in the low group would be more negative, while those of wives and husbands in the high group would be more positive. The results supported the first two hypotheses for the husbands but not the wives, while there was no support for the third hypothesis. The percentage of communications judged to be good communications was significantly smaller in the low than in the high marital adjustment group for husbands and wives combined ($r = 0.36$) and for husbands separately ($r = 0.40$), while the percentage of good communications decoded incorrectly was larger in the low than the high marital adjustment group for husbands and wives combined ($r = 0.38$) and for husbands separately ($r = 0.40$). In addition, there was no evidence to support the idea that couples in the high more than in the low maritally adjusted group were better able to communicate in an idiosyncratic manner in that the percentage of bad communications correctly decoded by the spouse did not appear to differ between the two groups.

Gottman and Porterfield (1981) modified the Marital Communication Scale so that participants did not show a bias towards choosing any of the three alternatives. For example, the statement 'Didn't we have chicken for dinner a few nights ago?' is more easily sent with irritation than with delight or as checking one's memory. An item with such a bias is less likely to discriminate between individuals because most people will choose the biased alternative as the intended message. They suggested that it is possible to determine if marital dissatisfaction was associated with difficulties in sending or receiving messages by looking at the correlations between marital satisfaction and the accuracy with which the partner and a stranger decoded the messages. A difficulty in receiving messages would be indicated by a positive correlation between the sender's marital satisfaction and the partner's but not the stranger's accuracy. This pattern of results suggests that the stranger's ability to decode messages was not affected by the spouse's marital adjustment but that the partner's ability to do so was affected, presumably because the distressed partner was less able to decode the message. A difficulty in sending messages, on the other hand, would be evidenced by the sender's marital satisfaction being positively correlated with both the partner's and the stranger's accuracy at decoding messages. Such a pattern of correlations would suggest that both the partner and the stranger were less accurate in decoding messages from a distressed than a non-distressed spouse, presumably as a result of the greater inability of the distressed spouse to correctly encode messages. A difficulty in both sending and receiving messages would be shown if the correlations between the sender's marital satisfaction and both the spouse's and the stranger's ability to decode messages were positive, with the former correlation being higher than the latter. In this case both the spouse and the stranger would be less accurate in decoding the messages of a distressed than a non-distressed spouse, but this difficulty would be greater for the spouse than for the stranger.

To test their ideas Gottman and Porterfield recruited 42 married couples whose marital satisfaction was assessed with the Marital Relationship Inventory. The first 21 couples formed the spouse group and the remaining 21 couples the stranger group. In the spouse group one partner watched the other partner send messages via a videotape monitor. In the stranger group couples were paired with couples in the spouse group. The wife of one of the stranger group couples watched the previously recorded videotape of the husband of the spouse group couple and her husband viewed the videotape of the wife of that couple. The wife's marital satisfaction was positively correlated ($r = 0.68$) with her husband's ability to decode her messages but the husband's marital satisfaction was not correlated ($r = 0.06$) with his wife's ability to decode his messages. The correlation between the wife's marital satisfaction and the stranger's ability to decode messages was also non-significant (although this correlation of 0.31 would have been significant if the sample had consisted of 40 or more pairs), indicating that the husband's ability to decode his wife's messages was related to his own ability to receive messages and not his wife's ability to send them. In other words, maritally dissatisfied wives had husbands who were less accurate at decoding their wife's messages.

INDIVIDUAL OR COUPLE DYSFUNCTION

Gary Birchler and his colleagues (1975) found no consistency between how maritally distressed individuals behaved towards their partner and towards two opposite-sex strangers, implying that the more negative behaviour of distressed couples was a function of their relationship and not their personality. To determine whether low maritally adjusted husbands had difficulties in decoding messages from strangers as well as their wives, Patricia Noller (1981) showed the married couples she used in her previous study a videotape consisting of 27 messages each sent by wives and husbands not known to them. There was no difference between high and low maritally adjusted wives and husbands in their ability to decode messages from either husbands or wives whom they did not know. This result suggests that the difficulties that low maritally adjusted husbands had in decoding their wives' messages was related to their relationship and was not a general personality characteristic. However, neither of these studies rules out the possibility that the problems of distressed couples may be due to the way they behave in romantic relationships rather than in relationships in general. This suggestion would be more difficult to test as it would entail examining the way they behaved in more than one romantic relationship.

PREDICTION OF RELATIONSHIP SATISFACTION

Several studies have shown that measures of couples interacting are also related to subsequent marital satisfaction, although the results do not provide a coherent view of the way in which these variables may be operating. In the first of these studies Howard Markman (1979) found that the way couples planning to marry evaluated the impact of their messages on each other while discussing how to resolve five tasks was related to relationship satisfaction one and then again 2½ years later. Relationship satisfaction was measured with the Marital Relationship Inventory while the impact ratings were carried out using the procedure developed by John Gottman and his colleagues (1976). Fourteen American student couples provided data on both measures on all three occasions. Initial relationship satisfaction was related to relationship satisfaction one year ($r = 0.82$) but not 2½ years ($r = -0.02$) later, while impact ratings were related to relationship satisfaction 2½ years ($r = 0.67$) but not one year ($r = 0.06$) later. The results were essentially the same for individuals as for couples.

In a further follow-up study Markman (1981) reported that relationship satisfaction for nine of these 14 couples 5½ years later was correlated with initial impact ratings ($r = 0.59$) but not relationship satisfaction ($r = -0.18$), implying that these ratings may be a better predictor of relationship satisfaction than the satisfaction measure itself. Surprisingly, considering the change in the sample, the correlations he presented for the other two times were exactly the same as those in his previous study. Presumably these correlations were those of the original 14 couples (Markman 1984). In neither paper did he report the correlation between initial relationship satisfaction and impact ratings which Gottman and his colleagues (1976) had found to be related to some extent. However, Markman (1984) subsequently disclosed that these two variables were not initially related ($r = 0.06$) in his sample, suggesting that the correlations for variables which are measured at the same time as relationship satisfaction may not be similar to those obtained when these same variables are used to predict subsequent relationship satisfaction.

A similar point was made by John Gottman and Lowell Krokoff (1989). One of their findings was that engaging in conflict was associated with marital dissatisfaction in both husbands and wives when these variables were measured concurrently but that conflict was generally related to increased marital satisfaction three years later, implying that while conflict engagement may be distressing it may prove subsequently beneficial. This finding was based on 25 married American couples who had the lowest or highest scores on the Marital Adjustment Test Inventory and Marital Relationship Tests. They were videotaped for 15 minutes discussing a serious marital problem and the videotapes were coded with the Marital Interaction Coding System. The category of conflict engagement contained the two codes of disagreement and criticism, the latter of which included hostility. Erik Woody and Philip Costanzo (1990) suggested that this reversal in the direction of the association of these variables may have been a statistical artifact resulting from using extreme groups and a change index consisting of the difference between marital satisfaction at the two points, which Gottman and Krokoff (1990) have disputed. Subsequently John Gottman (1993) found that couples who broke up were more likely to have engaged in earlier hostile conflict, which appears to be inconsistent with his earlier finding although this criterion was different in that it was relationship stability rather than relationship satisfaction.

Using a different method David Smith and his colleagues (1990) also found that conflict disengagement measured six weeks before marriage was not significantly related to relationship satisfaction at that time ($r = -0.11$) or six months after marriage ($r = -0.18$) but was significantly related to marital satisfaction 18 ($r = -0.27$) and 30 ($r = -0.33$) months after marriage in 91 American couples. While negativity was associated with initial relationship dissatisfaction ($r = -0.31$), it was not related to subsequent increased dissatisfaction. Couples were audiotaped for 10 minutes discussing a relationship problem and the audiotapes (divided into two five-minute segments) were globally coded for positive, negative and disengagement affect. Disengagement affect consisted of terms such as quiet, sluggish and silent which seemed to indicate a lack of involvement, while negativity included items such as dissatisfied, upset and distressed. Relationship satisfaction was assessed with the Marital Adjustment Test. Change in relationship adjustment was measured by partialling out initial relationship satisfaction.

Finally, Erik Filsinger and Stephen Thoma (1988) videotaped 21 American premarital couples discussing a moderately severe relationship problem for 15 minutes and followed up these couples at six months, 1½ years, 2½ years and five years later, by which time eight of the couples had split up. The interaction was coded with the Dyadic Interaction Scoring Code (Filsinger 1983) and relationship satisfaction was assessed with the Dyadic Adjustment Scale (Spanier 1976). The most consistent predictor of relationship stability was positive reciprocity (a positive response from one partner followed by a positive response from the other) which discriminated those who stayed together from those who broke up at 1½ years ($r = 0.42$), 2½ years ($r = 0.40$) and five years ($r = 0.44$). On the other hand, the only predictor of relationship satisfaction was the number of female interruptions, which was negatively related to relationship satisfaction in men at 1½ years ($r = -0.67$), 2½ years ($r = -0.56$) and five years ($r = -0.71$).

DEMAND/WITHDRAW BEHAVIOUR

Although it is important to observe how couples interact, doing so has four main disadvantages as pointed out by Andrew Christensen (1988). First, the data are time-consuming to collect and analyse. Second, people may behave differently when they know they are being observed. Third, exchanges which take place over a longer period of time or which involve considerably delayed reactions may not be observed: for example, a spouse may respond to a criticism not immediately but some time later. And fourth, the statistical techniques for analysing such data require that the behaviour in question should occur frequently, which may not be the case. Consequently, Megan Sullaway and Andrew Christensen (1983) began by trying to develop a simple self-report measure of repetitive asymmetrical exchanges in which couples take different but mutually complementary roles in the interaction. They presented 22 descriptions of such interactions to 46 psychology undergraduates in Los Angeles and asked them whether they had occurred in their relationship. Twelve of them had happened in over 50 per cent of the relationships and these formed the first version of the Interaction Patterns Questionnaire. These 12 patterns can be summarized as follows: (1) introvert/extrovert; (2) flirtatious/jealous; (3) assertive/non-assertive; (4) more/less involved; (5) repress/express emotions; (6) less/more devoted to partner; (7) dependent/independent; (8) relationship-/work-oriented; (9) emotional/rational; (10) demand/withdraw; (11) leader/follower; and (12) cautious/committed. Note that if asymmetrical patterns are thought to be more characteristic of distressed than non-distressed couples, it would seem more appropriate to select patterns that differentiated the two groups the most rather than select the most common patterns. In a second sample of 55 undergraduate dating couples the three patterns of relationship-/work-oriented, emotional/rational and demand/withdraw were found to be significantly more common in the distressed couples as measured by the Dyadic Adjustment Scale.

The final version of the questionnaire, called the Communication Patterns Questionnaire (Christensen 1988), consists of symmetrical as well as asymmetrical patterns and specifies the context of the interaction as one of three stages of conflict. The three stages are when a problem arose, and during and following a discussion of a problem. There are four patterns in the first stage about discussing or avoiding issues, 18 patterns in the second stage concerned with behaviours such as blaming and negotiating, and 13 patterns in the third stage involving behaviours such as withholding and reconciliation as well as reactions such as guilt and understanding. Respondents are required to rate the likelihood of each pattern on a nine-point scale from 'very unlikely' to 'very likely'. An example of two items are 'During a discussion of a relationship problem: (1) Husband nags and demands while wife withdraws, becomes silent or refuses to discuss the matter further. (2) Wife nags and demands while husband withdraws, becomes silent or refuses to discuss the matter further.' Three sub-scales were created: a six-item Demand/Withdraw Communication sub-scale; a Demand/Withdraw Roles sub-scale where the husband's ratings of the previous scale were subtracted from the wife's ratings; and a five-item Mutual Constructive Communication sub-scale. In a sample of 142 married or cohabitating couples, satisfied couples (as assessed by the Dyadic Adjustment Scale) had higher Mutual Constructive Communication ($r = 0.79$) and lower Demand/Withdraw Communication ($r = -0.55$). It is not known whether these two sub-scales were more strongly related to the Dyadic Consensus than to the Dyadic Satisfaction Sub-scale, and if so whether these correlations primarily reflect lack of disagreement rather than the way disagreements are resolved. Patricia Noller and Angela White (1990) found that a factor analysis of the questionnaire completed by 96 married Australian couples resulted in four oblique factors which they called Coercion (e.g. verbal and physical aggression), Mutuality (e.g. mutual understanding and resolution), Post-Conflict Distress (e.g. one tries to reconcile while the other withdraws) and Destructive Process (e.g. one criticizes and the other withdraws).

In an important later study Christopher Heavey and his colleagues (1993) examined the extent to which demand/withdraw interactions in 29 married American couples were related to marital satisfaction concurrently and one year later. Demand/withdraw behaviour was assessed with both a shortened version of the Communication Patterns Questionnaire and coding two seven-minute videotaped interactions. Marital satisfaction was measured with the Dyadic Adjustment Scale. Unfortunately, the relationship between the two demand/withdraw measures was not reported in this study or a previous one where the two measures were used (Christensen and Heavey 1990). The short form of the Communication Patterns Questionnaire consists of five items assessing symmetrical patterns (mutual avoidance of discussion, mutual discussion, mutual expression of feelings, mutual blame and mutual negotiation) and three pairs of items measuring complementary patterns (discussion/avoidance, demand/withdraw and criticize/defend). It has four sub-scales: (1) wife demands/husband withdraws; (2) husband demands/wife withdraws; (3) total demand/withdraw; and (4) positive communication. The first three sub-scales are based on the appropriate asymmetrical patterns while the fourth sub-scale consists of mutual discussion, expression and negotiation.

To ensure that there was no gender bias in the issues discussed, wives and husbands talked about two different issues: in one of them it was the husband's behaviour that the wife wanted to change, in the other it was the wife's behaviour that the husband wanted to change, and the extent of change for both issues was similar and as high as possible. The behaviours were chosen from a list of 20. After each discussion couples completed a six-item scale assessing how satisfied they were with the discussion. For each discussion wives and husbands were independently rated on the 15 dimensions of the Conflict Rating System which were grouped into four sub-scales: (1) demand (discusses, blames and pressures for change); (2) withdraw (avoids and withdraws); (3) positive communication (negotiates, backchannels, validates partner, expresses positive feelings and communicates clearly); and (4) negative communication (expresses critical feelings, interrupts, dominates discussion and expresses negative feelings). Also created were the three additional sub-scales of wife demands/husband withdraws, husband demands/wife withdraws and total demand/withdraw.

Only a few of the major findings of this study will be summarized. The results for satisfaction with the two discussions were presented only for the observer ratings and not for the questionnaire. The spouse's satisfaction with the discussion of either issue was generally most highly and consistently related to the positiveness of the other spouse. So, for example, the positiveness of the husband's behaviour was related to the wife's satisfaction with discussing her own ($r = 0.48$) and her husband's ($r = 0.36$) issue. Greater satisfaction with the discussion was also related to greater marital satisfaction in both wives ($r = 0.42$) and husbands ($r = 0.61$). Marital satisfaction did not reflect satisfaction with the discussion because marital satisfaction was measured before the discussion began. More positive behaviour in the wife was related to her own ($r = 0.40$) and her husband's ($r = 0.46$) greater marital satisfaction measured then but not one year later. Increased marital satisfaction in wives one year later but not concurrently was associated with greater demandingness ($r = 0.92$) and negativity ($r = 0.91$) in the husband, although these very high correlations may have partly reflected a statistical artifact. In terms of self-reported behaviour, demanding husband/withdrawing wife was associated with decreased current marital satisfaction ($r = -0.45$ for wives and -0.59 for husbands) but increased marital satisfaction one year later ($r = 0.40$ for wives and 0.47 for husbands). The results of this study may be consistent with those of John Gottman and Lowell Krokoff (1989) and of David Smith and his colleagues (1990) in suggesting that subsequent relationship satisfaction may be higher in couples where husbands engage in conflict.

However, a later longitudinal study by Patricia Noller and her colleagues (1994) found no relationship between the total demand/withdraw sub-scale of the Communication Patterns Questionnaire and marital satisfaction as measured by the Quality Marriage Index (Norton 1983) 12 and 21 months later in 33 newly married Australian couples. With concurrent relationship satisfaction partialled out, only marital satisfaction in wives 12 months after marriage was related to self-reported communication assessed four to six weeks before marriage. Less satisfied wives showed more disengagement ($r = -0.43$), destructiveness ($r = -0.41$) and negativity ($r = -0.40$). These three communication variables were derived from a factor analysis of the questionnaire.

CAUSALITY

Research on how maritally distressed and non-distressed couples interact is non-experimental in design. Consequently, the causal nature of any observed findings cannot be ascertained. For example, it is possible that any observed interaction differences are the result rather than the cause of differences in relationship satisfaction. The most appropriate way of determining whether interaction affects relationship satisfaction may be to select individuals or couples who are dissatisfied and to randomly assign them to, say, one of two treatments. One of the treatments would aim to teach participants the interaction behaviour which is thought to result in greater relationship satisfaction, while the other treatment would act as the control condition. One control would be to have couples interact without teaching them the behaviour considered to be necessary. This kind of research has been carried out by Neil Jacobson (1978) in empirically evaluating the effectiveness of marital behaviour therapy. Although this study is described in Chapter 11 on relationship counselling, it is worthwhile describing here those aspects that are relevant for examining the effects of interaction on relationship satisfaction.

Jacobson (1978) compared the effectiveness of eight weekly 1–1½ hour sessions of two forms of marital behaviour therapy with a non-specific and a waiting-list control condition in 32 American couples experiencing marital problems. Behavioural marital therapy consisted of communication and problem-solving training with contingency contracting. The two behavioural groups differed in terms of the type of contracting. One group used good faith or parallel contracts, in which partners agree to actions which are not dependent on whether the other person carries out their obligation. The other group used 'quid pro quo' contracts in which one person only carries out their agreed action if the other person has already performed theirs. In the non-specific control condition a couple discussed a marital problem until they reached some agreement. The therapist only participated in these discussions by asking factual questions, by primarily restating the apparent feelings underlying what was said, by interpreting the couple's interaction and by disclosing relevant personal information. The couples' expectations about the effectiveness of this non-specific control treatment were reported as being similar to those of the couples receiving the behavioural treatment although details of which items were used were not given. In other words, in two of the conditions couples received communication and problem-solving training while in a third condition an attempt was made to treat them in the same way but without giving them this training. Couples were randomly assigned to the four conditions.

Outcome was measured before and after treatment. One of the marital satisfaction measures was the Marital Adjustment Test (Locke and Wallace 1959). The interaction measure was based on a five- to ten-minute videotape of couples trying to resolve a hypothetical problem from the Inventory of Marital Conflicts (Olson and Ryder 1970) and a minor problem of their own. The measure was the number of positive and negative responses made per minute during this discussion using the Marital Interaction Coding System (Weiss and Summers 1983). Prior to treatment, the four groups were similar in terms of marital satisfaction and the rate of positive and negative responses. After treatment the two behavioural groups showed a significant increase in marital satisfaction and positive behaviour and a significant decrease in negative behaviour. Since the main difference between the two behavioural groups and the non-specific control group was the presence or absence of communication and problem-solving training, these results suggest that increased positive and decreased negative behaviour may have been responsible for the increased marital satisfaction. However, since the treatments were lengthy and contained many different components, it remains possible that the increased marital satisfaction may have been due to factors other than changes in these behaviours. Consequently, it is preferable, if one is primarily concerned with determining causality, for the intervention to be much shorter and restricted as much as possible to the behaviours under investigation. A more limited intervention, however, is unlikely to affect marital satisfaction and a more sensitive measure may have to be used, such as the individuals' current feelings towards one another.

As well as determining whether interaction affects relationship satisfaction, it is also important to establish whether relationship satisfaction influences interaction. One way of doing this is to compare couples behaving as they normally do with the way they do when asked to act as if they were happy or unhappy. This procedure was used by John Vincent and his colleagues (1979) who rated the behaviour of 20 maritally distressed and 20 maritally non-distressed couples trying to resolve five problems from the Inventory of Marital Conflicts (Olson and Ryder 1970) acting normally and as if they were either happily or unhappily married. Their behaviour was coded according to the Marital Interaction Coding System. Couples acting happy showed more positive problem-solving, verbal and non-verbal behaviour and less negative verbal behaviour than those acting unhappy, indicating that relationship satisfaction affects interaction.

SUMMARY

There have been a considerable number of studies which have observed the behaviour of couples who were satisfied or dissatisfied with their relationship to determine how their behaviour differs. The task most commonly used involved resolving disagreements, and most of the couples studied have been married. Distressed couples have generally been found to have more frequent negative reciprocal exchanges than non-distressed couples. Other findings are more tentative in being based on a few studies which often used different measures and in some cases involved relatively small samples. There is some evidence to suggest that distressed couples did not intend their behaviour to be perceived by their partner as being less positive, that the behaviour was more characteristic of the relationship than of the individual, and that distressed husbands had difficulty in understanding their wife's messages.

Some longitudinal studies have shown behavioural measures to be related to subsequent relationship compatibility, and that these measures were not necessarily the same as those that were related to concurrent relationship satisfaction. In particular, engaging in conflict may be associated with decreased concurrent but increased subsequent relationship satisfaction. Where the husband engaged in conflict while the wife withdrew (as measured by self-report) has also been found to be related to lower concurrent but higher subsequent relationship satisfaction. There is little evidence on the causal relationship between behaviour and relationship satisfaction, which may be reciprocal. Marital behavioural therapy involving training in communication and problem-solving has led to increased marital satisfaction which may have been brought about by an improvement in these skills. More positive problem-solving behaviour was shown by couples when asked to act as if they were happily married, implying that this behaviour was determined by their enacted attitude.

8

Conflict Resolution, Power and Violence

Studies which have observed how couples interact when discussing problems are implicitly and ostensibly concerned with ways or styles of resolving conflict. However, they have generally not been concerned with trying to develop schemes for classifying conflict resolution, which have been left to other investigators. Furthermore, because couples are required to try to resolve disagreements in these studies it is not known to what extent they may otherwise typically avoid trying to do this when not asked to do so, and how this avoidance might be associated with relationship compatibility. The outcome of the observed discussion has also not usually been determined, and whether this outcome might be more closely associated with relationship compatibility than the manner in which these decisions were reached. Moreover, more extreme forms of coercion such as physical violence are less likely to be observed because of the constraints of the situation and because they are less common. Therefore, before devoting considerable resources to observing how couples interact, it seems important to try initially to establish what aspects may be most worthwhile observing – although there is, of course, no guarantee that this object is more likely to be achieved through the more convenient and less time-consuming method of self-report of either one's own or one's partner's behaviour.

STYLES OF CONFLICT RESOLUTION

Several studies have related styles of conflict resolution to relationship compatibility. Marlyn Rands and her colleagues (1981) constructed a 15-item scale assessing the spouse's perception of their partner's style of conflict resolution and a 14-item scale measuring their perception of the outcome of those conflicts. These scales and a seven-item index of marital satisfaction were separately completed by 244 young wives and husbands living in San Francisco.

The two scales were independently factor-analysed. The conflict style scale consisted of three orthogonal factors called attack (e.g. 'S/he says or does something to hurt my feelings' and 'S/he gets really mad and starts yelling'), avoidance (e.g. 'S/he clams up, holds in her/his feelings' and 'S/he tries to avoid talking about it') and compromise (e.g. 'S/he tries to work out a compromise' and 'S/he tries to smooth things over'). The conflict outcome scale had two orthogonal factors called escalation (e.g. 'We start out disagreeing about one thing and end up arguing about lots of things' and 'S/he agrees to change but never does it') and intimacy (e.g. 'Afterwards I feel closer to her/him and more loving than before' and 'Afterwards I feel I understand her/him better than before'). Marital satisfaction was more strongly related to the outcome factors of intimacy ($r = 0.48$) and escalation ($r = -0.47$) than to the style factors of compromise ($r = 0.41$), attack ($r = -0.37$) and avoidance ($r = -0.28$). Satisfied couples felt more intimate afterwards, compromised more and showed less escalation, attack and avoidance. Conflict style was also associated with conflict outcome. Attack was correlated with escalation ($r = 0.56$) and low intimacy ($r = -0.32$); compromise with intimacy ($r = 0.46$) and low escalation ($r = -0.34$); and avoidance with escalation ($r = 0.31$) and intimacy ($r = 0.46$). It would have been of interest to know whether these associations differed according to gender and whether style and outcome were also related to extent of conflict, which was not measured.

Caryl Rusbult and her colleagues (1986) suggested the following four ways of responding to problems in a close relationship: exit (ending the relationship); voice (trying to solve the problem); loyalty (wait and hope for improvement); and neglect (being negative). Each response was assessed by seven items: for example, for exit, 'When I'm unhappy with my partner, I consider breaking up' and 'When we have problems, I discuss ending our relationship'; for voice, 'When my partner and I have problems, I discuss things with her/him' and 'When I'm unhappy with my partner, I tell her/him what's bothering me'; for loyalty; 'When we have problems in our relationship, I patiently wait for things to improve' and 'When my partner hurts me, I say nothing and simply forgive her/him'; and for neglect, 'When I'm upset with my partner I sulk rather than confront the issue' and 'When I'm upset with my partner, I ignore her/him for a while'. Relationship satisfaction was assessed by combining various measures including Zick Rubin's (1970) Love and Liking Scales. These questionnaires were completed by 68 young American dating couples. Relationship satisfaction was most strongly related to the exit scale in a multiple regression analysis followed by the neglect scale. The other two scales were not significantly related to satisfaction. These results may be due to the fact that the exit items represented the most extreme dissatisfaction with the relationship and hence were most strongly related to the relationship satisfaction index.

Katherine McGonagle and her colleagues (1993) looked at marital disruption over three years as a function of five conflict styles, as well as frequency of conflict and four outcomes, in a community sample from Detroit of 691 non-black married couples. Each of these variables was assessed by a single question. One of the questions on conflict style asked about avoiding disagreements ('How much do you avoid talking about certain things with your spouse because of how s/he might react?'), while the other four asked how they reacted when they disagreed ('How often do you discuss your differences calmly?'; 'How often do you try to appreciate your spouse's point of view?'; 'How often do things become tense or unpleasant?'; and 'How often does your spouse say cruel or angry things to you?'). The outcome questions were also phrased in terms of frequency ('How often do you work things out so that both of you are satisfied?'; 'How often do you both refuse to compromise?'; 'How often do you give in to your spouse?'; and 'How often does your spouse give in to you?'). Conflict was referred to as 'unpleasant disagreement' in the question on frequency of conflict which means that it is not possible to disentangle disagreements from unpleasantness. The answers of wives and husbands were combined as they differed little. Of these ten variables, frequency of conflict was most strongly related to subsequent separation or divorce. Couples who stayed together had fewer unpleasant disagreements, compromised more, were less cruel and tense, avoided disagreements less, were more calm and were more satisfied with the outcome than couples who parted.

Lawrence Kurdek (1994) developed the 16-item Conflict Resolution Styles Inventory which measured the four styles of positive problem-solving (e.g. 'Focusing on the problem at hand'), conflict engagement (e.g. 'Launching personal attacks'), withdrawal (e.g. 'Reaching a limit, shutting down, and refusing to talk any further') and compliance (e.g. 'Giving in with little attempt to present my side of the issue'). Individuals completed this questionnaire in terms of their own style and that of their partner. Conflict style was related to the three-item Kansas Marital Satisfaction Scale (Schumm *et al.* 1986) and to the subsequent dissolution of the relationship. The first study involved 75 gay and 51 lesbian couples in North America assessed twice over three years and 207 married couples from Dayton, Ohio assessed twice over one year (Kurdek 1994). The data for gay and lesbian couples were combined and presented for the two partners (randomly assigned) separately. Because of space limitations, only some findings are reported here for self-reported conflict style. For gay and lesbian couples withdrawal was related to subsequent dissolution (point-biserial $r = 0.27$ and 0.18) and decreased relationship satisfaction (r partialling out initial satisfaction = -0.19 and -0.14). For heterosexual couples conflict engagement was related to subsequent dissolution (point-biserial $r = 0.25$ for wives and 0.15 for husbands) and positive problem-solving was related to subsequent increased relationship satisfaction (r partialling out initial satisfaction = 0.14 for wives and 0.16 for husbands).

Kurdek's (1995) second study involved 155 married couples assessed twice over two years. An individual's conflict style was based on their own and their partner's report. Positive problem-solving was omitted from the analyses because essentially it was found to load on the same factor as conflict engagement. One major finding was that for husbands the relationship between initial conflict styles and subsequent marital satisfaction was stronger than the relationship between initial marital satisfaction and subsequent conflict styles, implying that conflict styles affected rather than were affected by marital satisfaction. Increased marital satisfaction in husbands was related to wives not withdrawing when their husbands engaged in conflict and to husbands complying when their wives withdrew. Another finding was that decreased marital satisfaction in both husbands and wives was associated with husbands withdrawing when wives engaged in conflict. Of course, it should be emphasized that the behavioural sequence in both these latter findings could not be determined by the wording of the items used to assess conflict style: for example, wives may engage in conflict when their husbands withdraw.

It should be noted that relationship satisfaction as measured by the Marital Adjustment Test and the related Dyadic Adjustment Scale includes items which assess the extent of agreement on various topics. In other words, agreement has been found to be an index of relationship satisfaction. In looking at the role that conflict resolution plays in relationship satisfaction, two questions merit further attention. Both questions need to be examined with a measure of relationship satisfaction that excludes agreement as part of it. First, is relationship satisfaction associated with agreement that has had to be reached in some way as well as with agreement that has always appeared to be there? Second, is relationship satisfaction more strongly associated with unpleasant disagreement than with disagreement without unpleasantness?

POWER

It is somewhat surprising that research which has observed the way couples resolve disagreements has generally not analysed the outcome of those discussions or coded the behaviour to reflect the attempt by one person to influence the other, since both these phenomena have been interpreted as indicative of the power relationship within the couple. Indeed, resolving disagreement through mutual give and take is included in the Marital Adjustment Test as an index of marital satisfaction, presumably because it was found to be so, although possibly not strongly enough to have remained part of the subsequently developed Dyadic Adjustment Scale. In reviewing research on family power David Olson and Robert Cromwell (1975) suggested that this work can be organized according to the three domains of power bases (such as the resources for rewarding and punishing others), power processes (such as being assertive and controlling) and power outcomes (such as making the final decision). There have been a number of studies on the relationship between marital power, measured in various ways, and marital compatibility. In their review of this research based largely on American couples, Bernadette Gray-Little and Nancy Burks (1983) concluded that these studies were fairly consistent in showing that egalitarian couples were the most satisfied, while couples where the wife was dominant were least satisfied. They suggested that the latter finding may be because in these couples the husband had effectively withdrawn from the marriage leaving the wife to make the decisions. A few of these studies are described below to illustrate the nature of some of this work.

Robert Blood and Donald Wolfe (1960), in their study of 731 wives living in Detroit, examined the relationship between marital satisfaction and a decision-making index of power. Decisions in eight areas were chosen because they were relatively important and had to be made by all couples. They included what job the husband should take, what house or apartment the couple or family should live in and how much money they could afford to spend on food. Wives were asked who usually made the final decision in each of these areas, on a five-point scale from 'husbands always' to 'wife always'. A 10-point index was created where a score of four indicated that decisions were taken equally and a score above four signified decisions taken more often by the husband. Marriages were divided into four groups according to this score. Of these, 22 per cent had scores of seven or more and formed the husband-dominant group; 22 per cent had scores of three or less and formed the wife-dominant group; and 46 per cent had scores of four to six and formed the egalitarian group, which was further subdivided into a 'syncratic' group who make most of their decisions jointly and an 'autonomic' group who have equal but separate areas of influence (Herbst 1952). The remaining 10 per cent were excluded as they failed to answer one or more of the eight decision-making questions. The egalitarian and husband-dominant group were more heavily biased towards husband dominance because of the higher scores used to create these categories. The percentages of the 731 families falling into these four groups were respectively 16, 12, 16 and 26 for the analysis involving marital satisfaction. Marital satisfaction was measured with five items on satisfaction with standard of living, understanding of problems and feelings, love and affection, companionship and number of children weighted according to their importance. It was highest for syncratic marriages, followed by autonomic, husband-dominant and wife-dominant, although whether any of these differences were statistically significant was not reported. Blood and Wolfe stated that the reason for wife-dominance was the absence of the husband from the marriage.

A later study by Richard Centers and his colleagues (1971) on a representative sample of 410 wives and 337 husbands in Los Angeles gave essentially similar results using an additional six decisions and interviewing husbands as well as wives. The additional decisions were those more likely to be taken by wives and included decorating the house, viewing TV programmes and buying clothes. Adding these items reduced the decision-making power of husbands in the marriage. Unlike the previous study, the two egalitarian groups did not contain marriages where there were some husbands who were somewhat more dominant than their wives. Using the 14-item decision-making scale, 9 per cent of the Los Angeles marriages were husband-dominant, 5 per cent wife-dominant, 18 per cent syncratic and 68 per cent autonomic. Marital satisfaction was assessed with a single three-point item of very, fairly or not at all satisfied. The percentage of very satisfied spouses was greatest for autonomic marriages (79), followed by the husband-dominant (73), syncratic (70) and wife-dominant (20). Although Centers and his colleagues did not determine which of these groups differed, a chi-square test carried out by myself was statistically significant, indicating that there were more very satisfied autonomic marriages and fewer very satisfied wife-dominant marriages than expected by chance.

Included in this study but reported later by Bertram Raven and his colleagues (1975) were questions on five of the six bases of power previously identified by John French and Bertram Raven (1959). The six bases were called coercion, reward, expert, legitimate, referent and informational. The last of these was not included in this study because it was found it could not be asked in a way which excluded the others. To assess these five bases, spouses were presented with five reasons for doing something for their partner, even though they might not be clear as to why they should perform this request, and were asked to say how likely each of these reasons were for carrying out the request. The five reasons were: (1) because if you did, s/he would do or say something nice for you in return (reward); (2) because if you did not do so, s/he might do or say something unpleasant for you in return (coercion); (3) because s/he knew what was best in this case (expert); (4) because you felt that s/he had a right to ask you to do this and you felt obliged to do as s/he asked (legitimate); and (5) because you felt that you were both part of the same family and should see eye-to-eye on these matters (referent). Although not mentioned as having been tried, saying that you carried out the request because s/he clearly and carefully explained why you should do it might have been an appropriate way of assessing informational power. After rating the likelihood of the five power bases, spouses chose the type that predominated in their marriage. Significantly more of the dissatisfied couples (42 per cent) used coercion power than the satisfied couples (2 per cent), although no details are given of the statistical test applied or its value. Fewer of the dissatisfied couples (21 per cent) used referent power than the satisfied couples (47 per cent).

Ramon Corrales (1975) found that marital satisfaction, as measured by the Marital Adjustment Balance Scale (Orden and Bradburn 1968) in 203 Catholic and 191 Lutheran married couples in Minnesota, did not differ significantly between the three major kinds of marital couples as defined by either Blood and Wolfe's (1960) decision-making scale or a decision-making task. In this task spouses were given a list of 10 words concerned with family-related values such as housing, communication and career and asked individually to rank-order the five most important. After doing this spouses were asked as a couple to agree on a joint ranking. The extent to which the joint list reflected the wife's or the husband's initial choice was used as the index of relative power.

Using a single six-response item on egalitarianism of decision-making, Marie Osmond and Patricia Martin (1978) found that out of nine variables this characteristic was the most strongly related to whether individuals were divorced or married in 561 low income and predominantly disabled American individuals. This item explained 18 per cent of the variance, followed by the item on willingness to give in which accounted for a further 7 per cent. The number of topics on which spouses disagreed often or most often was not related to marital dissolution.

Using a stratified sample of 459 ever-married wives from the Detroit area and selecting the women who had only married once, Martin Whyte (1990, p. 197) found that women who had more influence in disputes with their husband were less likely to split up ($r = 0.31$), had fewer marital problems ($r = 0.19$) but were not more satisfied with their marriage than women who had less influence. Marital power was measured with five items assessing the degree of disagreement over five issues, which was multiplied by who usually got their way on these issues (p. 306). The correlation between marital power and marital problems may have been due to the fact that five of the 11 items that made up the marital problems index were the same as those used in the marital power index for assessing the extent of disagreement. Marital quality or satisfaction was measured with seven items such as the degree of overall satisfaction with the marriage and the amount of affection shown.

John Gottman (1979, ch. 10) looked at the relationship between dominance and marital satisfaction in 19 distressed and 19 non-distressed married couples who were videotaped discussing for 15 minutes activities they enjoyed doing, followed by improvising six scenes that caused them the greatest conflict. The videotapes were coded with the Couple Interaction Scoring System. Dominance or power was conceptualized as asymmetry in the predictability of affective behaviour. For instance, if a wife's response to her husband's behaviour was more predictable than his response to her behaviour, the husband would be seen as being dominant. The three most conflictful improvisations were treated separately from the three least conflictful improvisations which were combined with the enjoyable activities, creating a high and a low conflict condition. In the low conflict condition both distressed and non-distressed couples were found to be egalitarian. However, in the high conflict condition non-distressed couples tended to be egalitarian while distressed couples were husband-dominant. Because of the way in which it was measured, this dominance could be interpreted either as the husband determining the wife's emotional expressiveness more than vice versa or the husband being less emotionally responsive to the wife than she was to him.

Frank Millar and Edna Rogers (1988) related marital satisfaction to measures of domineeringness and dominance based on the coding of verbatim transcripts of 132 American married couples discussing their relationship for about 40 minutes. Domineeringness was an individual or monadic index consisting of the number of one-up moves made by the spouse during the conversation whereas dominance was a dyadic index made up of the number of one-up moves responded to with a one-down move by the spouse. A one-up move is an attempt to assert one's definition of the relationship while a one-down move is a request or an acceptance of the other person's definition of the relationship. For example, 'Let's eat' is a one-up move characteristic of domineeringness which if followed by 'OK' reflects dominance. Millar and Rogers found that wives and husbands were less satisfied when the wife was domineering and husbands were more satisfied when husbands were dominant. Neither husband domineeringness nor wife dominance were consistently related to marital satisfaction in either spouse. However, the marital satisfaction measure used and the statistical details of the analyses were not presented. More recently Valentin Escudero and his colleagues (1997) in Spain found that domineeringness, based on a 20-minute discussion of a marital conflict, was significantly higher in 18 couples seeking marital help than in 12 non-distressed couples.

PHYSICAL VIOLENCE

Physical violence may be seen as an extreme reaction to disagreement and was to a large extent measured as such by Murray Straus (1979, 1990a) with his Conflict Tactics Scale, which lists various acts that a partner may carry out when involved in an argument with their spouse. These acts are ordered in increasing coerciveness and are grouped together in the three categories of reasoning ('discussed an issue calmly' to 'tried to bring in someone to help settle things'), verbal aggression ('insulted or swore at her/him' to 'threw or smashed or hit or kicked something' and excluding 'cried') and physical aggression or violence ('threw something at her/him' to 'used a knife or fired a gun'). Minor violence ('threw something at her/him' to 'slapped her/him') may be distinguished from severe violence ('kicked, bit, or hit her/him with a fist' to 'used a knife or fired a gun'). The items are answered in terms of how frequently they occurred over the last 12 months. There have been three versions of this scale: (1) Form A, the original version; (2) Form N, used in the 1975 National Family Violence survey of 2,143 American families; and (3) Form R, used in the 1985 National Family Violence survey of 6,002 families. Form R differs from Form N in including the additional violence item of 'choked her/him' for partners and 'burned or scalded her/him' for parents, and excluding 'never' as a presented response. In the 1985 telephone survey of a representative sample of American households, in the 18- to 24-year age range severe violence against wives was reported by 13.9 per cent of wives and 1.3 per cent of husbands while severe violence against husbands was mentioned by 16.7 per cent of wives and 8.0 per cent of husbands (Straus 1990b, p. 553). In the 25 and older age range severe violence against wives was reported by 4.2 per cent of wives and 1.4 per cent of husbands while severe violence against husbands was mentioned by 3.5 per cent of wives and 4.8 per cent of husbands.

Agreement between partners on the extent of physical violence during the past year was examined by Maximiliane Szinovacz (1983) in 103

Pennsylvanian couples. Excluding the two most severe and least frequent acts of violence of threatening with or using a knife or gun, similar levels of total physical violence were reported by both wives (17 per cent) and husbands (16 per cent) for the husband's behaviour while for the wife's behaviour higher levels were expressed by wives (26 per cent) than by husbands (16 per cent).

There have been only a few studies which have related violence to relationship satisfaction. Daniel O'Leary and his colleagues (1989) looked at physical aggression as measured by Form N of the Conflict Tactics Scale in a longitudinal sample of 272 couples from New York State who were assessed one month before marriage and 18 and 30 months after marriage. Couples had not been previously married. Women reported being significantly more violent to their partner than did men at all three times. Overall violence from premarriage to 30 months after marriage decreased significantly for women but the decrease for men was not significant. Partners of individuals who said they were violent at all three times were less satisfied with their relationship as measured by the Marital Adjustment Test than partners of individuals who said they had not been violent at all three periods. In a later paper Daniel O'Leary and his colleagues (1994) reported that marital satisfaction at 18 months was related to less physical violence at 30 months in both wives ($r = 0.31$) and husbands ($r = 0.22$).

Ileana Arias and her colleagues (1987) examined the relationship of various measures of attraction to both violence to and violence from one's partner in current dating relationships of 104 female and 40 male psychology undergraduates from New York. The measures of attraction were the 17-item Positive Feelings Questionnaire (O'Leary *et al.* 1983), a commitment item and Rubin's (1970) Love and Liking Scales. Because the sample of men was considerably smaller than that of the women, the number of significant correlations for men is likely to be less than that for women, which it was. For men the only significant relationship was that men who were the victims of violence liked their partner less ($r = -0.29$). Women who were violent towards their partner had less liking ($r = -0.28$) and less positive feelings ($r = -0.19$) for them. Similarly women with partners who had been violent to them had less liking ($r = -0.29$) and less positive feelings ($r = -0.16$) for them.

SUMMARY

Although several studies have developed questionnaires for assessing styles of conflict resolution, there appears to be little consensus on what these styles are. There is some evidence to suggest that satisfied couples tend to discuss their disagreements and to compromise more than dissatisfied couples. The outcome of a decision-making process such as resolving disagreement is one indication of power within a relationship. Other indications include the resources available to a partner and the extent to which one partner tries to influence the other. These three aspects have been called power outcomes, power bases and power processes. Power outcomes have been most frequently studied with respect to relationship compatibility. Satisfied couples tend to be more egalitarian in their decision-making than dissatisfied couples. Physical violence may be seen as an extreme form of coercion. The few studies that have looked at this issue have found satisfied couples to be less violent.

9

Sexuality

In western culture at least, many people believe that sexual behaviour should mainly take place within a loving or married relationship and should be confined to that relationship. In a nationally representative survey of 18- to 59-year-olds carried out in the United States in 1992 by Edward Laumann and his colleagues (1994, p. 514), about 66 per cent of 2,843 respondents said that they would not have sex with someone unless they were in love with them. About 77 per cent of them thought that extramarital sex was always wrong. In a similar survey conducted in the United Kingdom in 1990/91 by Anne Johnson and her colleagues (1994, p. 237), about 80 per cent of over 10,000 women and about 69 per cent of over 8,000 men thought that having sexual relationships outside a regular relationship was always or mostly wrong. About 84 per cent of the women and 79 per cent of the men considered that sex outside marriage was always or mostly wrong. Taken together, the answers to these two questions suggest that most people believe that sexual relationships should take place within a regular relationship.

Similar findings have been obtained in young people although the samples have been smaller and less representative. For instance, a nationally representative survey of 181 female and 212 male 13- to 19-year-olds undertaken in the United States in 1972 by Robert Sorensen (1973, p. 412) found that about 55 per cent of the females and 50 per cent of the males agreed that sex is immoral unless it is between two people who love each other, while 38 per cent of the females and 40 per cent of the males believed that sex is immoral unless it is between two people who like each other and have something in common (p. 414), implying that liking someone in many cases is sufficient reason for having sex. In representative samples of 431 female and 432 male students at the University of Wisconsin-Madison and 293 female and 220 male non-students in Madison in the United States, John DeLamater and Patricia MacCorquodale (1979) investigated the acceptability to young women and men of having sexual intercourse. The percentage of respondents who thought that sexual intercourse was acceptable if both wanted it but did not feel love or affection for the other person (p. 90) varied from 22 (in student women for females) to 46 (in non-student men for males).

Furthermore, many people also report behaving according to these beliefs. Laumann and his colleagues (1994, p. 208) found in their American survey that, of those born between 1933 and 1942 and who married without previously cohabiting, about 8 per cent of the women and 13 per cent of the men had had extramarital sex. Johnson and her colleagues (1994, p. 121) noted in their British survey that about 2 per cent of the women and 6 per cent of the men had had extramarital sex in the last year. DeLamater and MacCorquodale (1979, pp. 160–3) in their survey of young adults in Madison, Wisconsin noted that, of 12 psychosocial correlates of premarital sexual behaviour, the emotional intimacy of the current relationship was the variable most highly correlated with current sexual behaviour in student women ($r = 0.61$) and men ($r = 0.62$) and the third most strongly correlated variable in non-student women ($r = 0.59$) and men ($r = 0.55$). Current sexual behaviour was measured with a nine-stage inventory of sexual behaviour, ranging from necking to female oral contact with male genitals (p. 59), while emotional intimacy was classified in six categories, varying from only one or two dates to being engaged (p. 153). A number of other studies have found that sexual behaviour was more likely to occur with either greater affective commitment or in the later stages of premarital relationships. For example, Robert Lewis and Wesley Burr (1975) found that, of 1,565 female and 837 male American students questioned in 1967–68, 2 per cent of the women and 30 per cent of the men had had sexual intercourse on a first date whereas 19 per cent of the women and 48 per cent of the men had had sexual intercourse while going steady with someone.

RELATIONSHIP SATISFACTION AND VARIOUS ASPECTS OF SEXUALITY

Beginning with the work of Katherine Davis (1929) and Gilbert Hamilton (1929), a substantial number of studies have investigated the association between various aspects of sexuality and relationship compatibility. The most common measure of relationship compatibility has been relationship adjustment or satisfaction, although a few studies have assessed more specific aspects such as love or commitment. Similarly, the most frequent measure of sexuality has been sexual satisfaction with one's partner, although some studies have only investigated particular behaviours such as the frequency of sexual intercourse or frequency of orgasms. One of the pioneering studies in this area was carried out by Lewis Terman (1938) who looked at the relationship between marital happiness and over 40 questions on sexual behaviour in 792 married couples from California. Seventeen and 15 of these items on sexual behaviour were subsequently used by, respectively, Ernest Burgess and Paul Wallin (1953) and Hans Eysenck and James Wakefield (1981) in their research on marital satisfaction. Marital happiness was measured with a 19-item questionnaire which included questions on how happy the marriage was, the number of marital problems and whether the marriage had been unhappy for a year or more. Twelve of the items were the same as or similar to ones in the Locke–Wallace (1959) Marital Adjustment Test. Arrangements were made to ensure that the couples completed their questionnaires separately.

Eighteen of the questions on sex which were most strongly associated with marital adjustment for either wives or husbands were used to form a measure of sexual adjustment. Because the correlation between marital happiness and most of the items was not reported, the eight most heavily weighted items on this scale are presented here (with their correlation with marital happiness reported in brackets where available): (1) frequency of wife's orgasm, where orgasm was described as 'a climax of intense feeling followed by quietude and a feeling of relief'; (2) number of sexual complaints ($r = -0.46$ for wives and -0.42 for husbands); (3) frequency of refusal of intercourse; (4) degree of release or satisfaction from intercourse ($r = 0.37$ for wives and 0.45 for husbands); (5) attitude when refusing intercourse; (6) frequency of desire for extramarital intercourse ($r = -0.46$ for wives and -0.52 for husbands); (7) satisfaction with frequency of intercourse as judged by the ratio of the reported to the preferred frequency of intercourse for wives and husbands; and (8) similarity of sexual passion. Wives who had more frequent orgasms were more happily married, as were their husbands. Happily married wives and husbands had fewer sexual complaints, refused intercourse less, felt greater release or satisfaction from intercourse, were more agreeable when refusing intercourse, had less desire for extramarital intercourse, were more satisfied with the frequency of intercourse and were more similar in how sexually passionate they were.

There was close agreement between wives and husbands ($r = 0.72$) in their estimates of how many times per month they had intercourse during the last year but less agreement on how long a single act of intercourse (excluding foreplay) lasted ($r = 0.47$). The mean duration of intercourse was about 12 minutes for husbands and 13 minutes for wives. The median frequency of intercourse per month decreased with age for both wives and husbands. For wives it decreased from 7.2 for those under 25 to 1.2 for those over 55, while for husbands it decreased from 6.3 for those aged 20–29 to 1.4 for those over 59. In general wives were satisfied with their frequency of intercourse in that their preferred and reported frequency was similar, while husbands preferred having intercourse once or twice per month more.

The frequency of type of complaint mentioned was compared for 300 happily married and 150 unhappily married couples, where couples were selected on the basis of one partner having the highest or lowest marital happiness score. Furthermore, the two groups were matched for age, number of years married, number of years in education and husband's occupation. Of the 18 problems listed for wives, the four most frequently cited by unhappily married wives were: not enough foreplay (42 per cent); too quick ejaculation (39 per cent); too frequent desire for intercourse (28 per cent); and too little expression of tenderness during intercourse (27 per cent). The first three of these problems were also those most commonly mentioned by the happily married wives but were reported less often: too quick ejaculation (23 per cent); too frequent desire for intercourse (23 per cent); and not enough foreplay (9 per cent). The fourth most frequently mentioned problem for the happily married wives was their husband wanting to go to sleep or get up too soon after ejaculation (7 per cent). Of the 16 problems presented to husbands, the four most commonly cited by unhappily married husbands were: too little enthusiasm shown (54 per cent); desire for intercourse too rare (44 per cent); orgasm not always achieved (40 per cent); and orgasm too slowly achieved (40 per cent). The same problems were most often reported by happily married husbands but to a lesser extent: orgasm too slowly achieved (27 per cent); orgasm not always achieved (26 per cent); too little enthusiasm shown (21 per cent); and desire for intercourse too rare (21 per cent).

Ernest Burgess and Paul Wallin (1953) looked at how sexual adjustment was related to the four relationship measures of marital satisfaction, marital happiness, marital permanence and love in 666 young couples married for three to five years and living in Chicago in the early 1940s. Sexual adjustment was measured using 17 differentially weighted items (p. 673), all of which had been taken or modified from those developed by Terman (1938). Marital satisfaction was measured with 26 items such as 'My marriage is successful but not extraordinarily so' (pp. 488–9); marital happiness with 21 items such as 'I believe our marriage is reasonably happy' (pp. 486–7); marital permanence with eight items such as 'Have you ever considered separating from your mate?' (p. 485); and love with five items such as 'To what extent are you in love with your mate?' (p. 497). Greater sexual satisfaction was correlated with greater marital satisfaction ($r = 0.45$) and happiness ($r = 0.45$). The relationships between sexual satisfaction and marital happiness, marital permanence and love were presented in 3×3 contingency tables for 629 wives and 600 husbands (pp. 690–3). When these data are calculated as Pearson correlations as done here, greater sexual satisfaction was associated with greater marital happiness ($r = 0.27$ for wives and $r = 0.34$ for husbands), greater marital permanence ($r = 0.19$ for wives and $r = 0.24$ for husbands) and greater love ($r = 0.30$ for both wives and husbands).

Four hundred and twenty-eight of these married couples were re-interviewed between 1956 and 1958. Robert Dentler and Peter Pineo (1960) examined the relationship between marital and sexual adjustment in the 397 husbands who provided this information on both occasions. Sexual adjustment was measured in the same way as in the original study, as was marital adjustment which consisted of a 26-item scale largely concerned with consensus and marital satisfaction (Burgess and Wallin 1953, p. 479; Burgess and Cottrell 1939). Scores on the two scales were dichotomized with those in the top two-thirds categorized as high and those in the bottom third as low. Of the 99 husbands who were in different marital and sexual categories (e.g. high marital but low sexual adjustment), 23 achieved subsequent consistency by a change in sexual adjustment and 25 by a change in marital adjustment. Because the numbers of husbands who achieved consistency by changing either marital or sexual adjustment were similar, Dentler and Pineo concluded that marital and sexual adjustment interact. This kind of analysis is similar to cross-lagged panel correlation analysis as described in Chapter 3 and its interpretation is limited by the same constraints.

Also using the same study, Alexander Clark and Paul Wallin (1965) looked at how changes in marital satisfaction were related to changes in the frequency of orgasms in the women who provided this information on both occasions. This figure was reported as 397 in the text of the paper (p. 193) but totalled to 426 in Table 2. Marital satisfaction was dichotomized as positive or negative according to the median score of the sample. Women who always, usually or mostly had orgasms were categorized as responsive whereas those who had orgasms less frequently were categorized as unresponsive. About 68 per cent of the wives were classified as responsive. In general, the evidence seemed to suggest that responsiveness increased in marriages that remained positive and decreased in those that remained negative. Furthermore, responsiveness tended to increase in marriages that improved from being negative in the earlier years to positive in the later years and to decrease in those that deteriorated from being positive in the early years to negative in the middle years. These results seem to suggest that marital happiness leads to increased sexual responsiveness in women, although the design of this study does not enable the causal direction of this relationship to be inferred.

In Britain Hans Eysenck and James Wakefield (1981) examined how marital satisfaction was related to sexual attitudes and behaviour in 566 married couples. Fifteen of the 18 questions on sexual behaviour were taken from those used by Terman (1938). Sexual attitudes were assessed with a 36-item sexual libido scale (e.g. 'The thought of an illicit relationship excites me' and 'It is better not to have sex relations until you are married') and a 16-item sexual satisfaction scale (e.g. 'Something is lacking in my sex life' and 'All in all I am satisfied with my sex life') previously developed by Eysenck (1976, p. 143). The sexual satisfaction scale was more a measure of general sexual satisfaction than sexual satisfaction with one's partner, as only one of its items refers to a partner ('108. My sex partner satisfies all my physical needs completely'). However, one of the items taken from Terman (1938) was a measure of satisfaction with sexual intercourse with one's partner ('How much release or satisfaction do you usually get from sexual intercourse with your partner?'). As the number of possible responses to one item is less than that to more than one item, the correlation with marital satisfaction is likely to be less for a single-than a multiple-item scale of sexual satisfaction, as was the case, although this may have been for other reasons. Marital satisfaction was measured with the Locke–Wallace (1959) Marital Adjustment Test to which six items were mentioned as having been added. It is not clear what all these items were, since only four are cited as having been added and there were 23 items altogether (pp. 153–4). Many of the variables on sexual behaviour were related to marital satisfaction. However, it is not known to what extent these associations were due to at least two of the items in the marital satisfaction questionnaire also referring to sexual behaviour.

In terms of the eight sex variables that were most significantly correlated with marital satisfaction, maritally satisfied wives were more sexually satisfied ($r = 0.58$ for Eysenck's scale, $r = 0.48$ for Terman's item), refused intercourse less ($r = 0.45$), had husbands who seemed less irritable when the wives refused intercourse ($r = 0.44$), had less desire for sexual intercourse with someone else ($r = 0.43$), had more sexually satisfied husbands ($r = 0.40$ for Eysenck's scale, $r = 0.37$ for Terman's item), had fewer sexual complaints about their husbands ($r = 0.36$), and had husbands who expressed less desire for someone else ($r = 0.37$) and who had fewer sexual complaints about them ($r = 0.34$). Maritally satisfied husbands were more sexually satisfied ($r = 0.51$ for Eysenck's scale, $r = 0.44$ for Terman's item), had more sexually satisfied wives ($r = 0.45$ for Eysenck's scale, $r = 0.37$ for Terman's item), had less desire for sexual intercourse with someone else ($r = 0.43$), had fewer sexual complaints about their wives ($r = 0.37$), had wives who expressed less desire for someone else ($r = 0.34$), had wives who thought their husbands were less irritable when the wives refused intercourse ($r = 0.34$), had wives who said they refused intercourse less often ($r = 0.33$) and thought their wives were not over modest or prudish in their attitude towards sex ($r = 0.30$). Unlike Terman's (1938) study, there was less agreement between wives and husbands on the frequency of intercourse ($r = 0.27$) but more agreement on its usual duration ($r = 0.61$). The mean duration of intercourse (excluding foreplay) was about 12 minutes for both wives and husbands while the mean frequency was about 13 times per month for wives and 15 times per month for husbands.

RELATIONSHIP SATISFACTION AND SEXUAL SATISFACTION

When measuring sexual satisfaction not all studies have made it clear whether they were referring to general sexual satisfaction, sexual satisfaction with one's partner or both aspects. For example, Josef Schenk and his colleagues (1983) reported that a 20-item measure of partner appreciation and support was related to an eight-item measure of sexual satisfaction in the wives ($r = 0.53$) and husbands ($r = 0.49$) of 631 German couples. Although one of the items was described as agreeing with one's partner's wishes about sex, the context of the other items was not reported. Of course, even if the items do not specify the context of sexual activity it is possible that individuals may answer them in terms of their main sexual relationship, but this needs to be demonstrated.

In other studies it is evident that sexual satisfaction with the partner was being assessed. Douglas Snyder (1979) noted that the Global Distress Scale of his Marital Satisfaction Inventory was correlated with his Sexual Dissatisfaction Scale ($r = 0.53$) in his sample of 141 American couples even when an individual's tendency to idealize their marriage was controlled ($r = 0.33$). The Sexual Dissatisfaction Scale consisted of 29 items such as 'My spouse sometimes shows too little enthusiasm for sex' and 'My spouse has too little regard sometimes for my sexual satisfaction'. Darla Rhyne (1981) found that a four-item Index of Marital Quality was associated with a single four-point item of the extent to which marital sexual needs were met in a Canadian national sample of 1,188 wives ($r = 0.54$) and 1,002 husbands ($r = 0.47$). Kathryn Rettig and Margaret Bubolz (1983) reported a moderately strong correlation between marital sexual relations and marital love and affection, both rated on a seven-point 'Delighted–Terrible' scale, in the wives ($r = 0.65$) and husbands ($r = 0.69$) of 224 Michigan couples.

Edward Laumann and his colleagues (1994) in their national survey of sexual behaviour asked their American respondents how satisfied and loved they felt after having sex (oral, vaginal and/or anal) with their primary partner, and a secondary one if they had one, during the last 12 months. The primary partner was considered to be the spouse or person they lived with, if there was one: otherwise it was who the respondent thought had been the most important or primary sex partner during the past year. The secondary partner was the person with whom the respondent had most recently had sex other than the primary partner. Satisfaction with sex was related to feeling loved in the 1,288 women ($r = 0.45$) and the 931 men ($r = 0.41$) who had only had sex with their primary partner (p. 366).

There is also some evidence to suggest that greater sexual satisfaction with one's partner is related to greater relationship satisfaction in gay and lesbian relationships. Lawrence Kurdek (1991b) assessed these aspects together with the importance of sexual fidelity, the importance of new sexual techniques and the irrational belief of sexual perfection in 77 gay, 58 lesbian, 49 married and 36 heterosexual American couples, all of whom cohabited and none of whom had children living with them. Relationship satisfaction was measured with four items from Spanier's (1976) Dyadic Satisfaction Subscale (e.g. 'Do you ever regret that you lived together?'); sexual satisfaction with one's partner with four items (e.g. 'An unhappy sexual relationship is a drawback in my relationship'); the importance of sexual fidelity with three items (e.g. 'If my relationship with my partner were to end, I would enjoy being with another sexual partner'); the importance of new sexual techniques with one item ('Trying new sexual activities and techniques with my partner' rated on a nine-point scale of importance); and sexual perfection beliefs with Epstein and Eidelson's (1981) eight-item scale (e.g. 'I get upset if I think I have not completely satisfied my partner sexually'). Controlling for income and the number of months couples had lived together, relationship satisfaction was generally most strongly correlated with sexual satisfaction in gay ($r = 0.44$), lesbian ($r = 0.59$), married ($r = 0.51$ for wives and $r = 0.40$ for husbands) and heterosexual cohabiting couples ($r = 0.76$ for women and $r = 0.54$ for men).

Finally, Elise Pinney and her colleagues (1987) found that general sexual satisfaction could be distinguished from sexual satisfaction with one's partner in her factor analysis of the Pinney Sexual Satisfaction Inventory, although these orthogonally rotated factors were moderately strongly correlated ($r = 0.57$). Relationship commitment as measured with a single item was slightly more strongly correlated with general sexual satisfaction ($r = 0.49$) than with sexual satisfaction with partner ($r = 0.43$) in 275 American female undergraduates studying introductory psychology, although the internal reliability of the two scales was not reported. General sexual satisfaction was measured with 14 items (e.g. 'I feel that nothing is lacking in my sex life' and 'I am satisfied that my physical needs are completely met during lovemaking') whereas satisfaction with partner was assessed with 10 items (e.g. 'I wish my partner(s) were more loving and caring when we make love' and 'I wish my partner(s) were more romantic when we make love'). The slightly higher correlation for general satisfaction may have been due to the potentially greater response variation or reliability of this scale.

RELATIONSHIP SATISFACTION AND FREQUENCY OF SPECIFIC SEXUAL BEHAVIOURS

Several studies have found relationship satisfaction to be associated with the frequency of specific sexual behaviours such as intercourse and orgasms. John Edwards and Alan Booth (1976) reported the correlation between frequency of intercourse over the past four weeks and 18 other variables in 294 wives and 213 husbands in Toronto. A dichotomous variable based on two items of whether the partner was less critical and as loving as before was the strongest predictor of intercourse frequency for men ($r = 0.38$) and the third equal strongest predictor for women ($r = 0.16$). Although slightly lower, this dichotomous variable was still significantly associated with intercourse frequency when the other 17 variables were entered into the same regression equation, indicating that this association was not due to the spurious effects of these other variables, which included age.

Other studies have also found more frequent intercourse to be weakly associated with greater relationship satisfaction. Lewis Terman (1938, p. 276) noted that more frequent intercourse was related to marital happiness in wives ($r = 0.12$) and husbands ($r = 0.09$) although he considered the association to be too weak to include intercourse frequency in his measure of sexual adjustment. Hans Eysenck and James Wakefield (1981) found frequent intercourse to be weakly associated with marital satisfaction in wives ($r = 0.22$) and husbands ($r = 0.10$). Ted Huston and Anita Vangelisti (1991) reported correlations between their two-item factor of partner's sexual interest (which was based on how often during the previous 24 hours couples had sexual intercourse and the partner had initiated sex) and marital satisfaction in 106 first and newlywed couples who were interviewed about two months after their wedding and about one and two years later. The lowest correlation was for the wife's marital satisfaction and the husband's sexual interest after one year of marriage ($r = 0.00$), while the highest correlation was for the husband's marital satisfaction and the wife's sexual interest after two years of marriage ($r = 0.27$).

David Hurlbert and Karen Whittaker (1991) compared a group of 41 women who had never experienced an orgasm through self-stimulation with another group of 41 women who had experienced a masturbatory orgasm and who were matched on nine sociodemographic variables such as race and employment. The women were military wives at Fort Hood in Texas. Greater marital satisfaction, as measured by an index about which no details are given apart from a reference to Hudson (1981), was expressed by women who had had a masturbatory orgasm ($r = 0.39$). Of the seven variables on which the two groups were compared, marital satisfaction was most strongly correlated with the number of times one of the partners had experienced an orgasm with their partner as recorded in a diary over a four-week period ($r = 0.39$). Hans Eysenck and James Wakefield (1981) also noted that wives who usually or always experienced an orgasm during sexual intercourse with their partner had greater marital satisfaction ($r = 0.28$), as did their husbands ($r = 0.27$).

CAUSAL RELATIONSHIP BETWEEN SEXUAL AND RELATIONSHIP SATISFACTION

Although these studies show that relationship compatibility is associated with sexuality, they do not tell us what the causal relationship is between these two variables. There is an American study which suggests that people generally believe that sexual intercourse increases the love they feel for their partner. Eugene Kanin and Karen Davidson (1972) found that about 82 per cent of 92 female students and 80 per cent of 88 male students reported that the love they felt for someone increased after their first experience of sexual intercourse with them, and that this tendency was greater for those who were more strongly in love.

One way of exploring the causal relationship between sexual and relationship satisfaction is to compare the relative effectiveness of relationship therapy and sex therapy in treating people who have relationship and sexual difficulties which are comparable in severity. This kind of study is similar to those discussed in Chapter 3 which compared the effectiveness of relationship therapy with therapies for depression in people who had relationship difficulties as well as being depressed. If sex therapy leads to greater relationship and sexual satisfaction than relationship therapy, this finding implies that sexual satisfaction is a stronger determinant of relationship satisfaction than vice versa. Although, as we have seen, relationship dissatisfaction is associated with sexual dissatisfaction, at present there only appear to be studies which have compared the effectiveness of relationship therapy and sex therapy on individuals with sexual problems. Consequently, it is not possible to assess whether sexual satisfaction is more a consequence than a determinant of relationship satisfaction. However, where these studies include a measure of relationship satisfaction they allow us to ascertain whether increased sexual satisfaction leads to increased relationship satisfaction and whether increased relationship satisfaction produces improved

sexual satisfaction. Some of these studies have compared the relative effectiveness of relationship therapy and sex therapy on sexual and relationship
satisfaction, which enables us to find out whether increasing relationship satisfaction also enhances sexual satisfaction. Other studies have evaluated one
or more forms of treating sexual problems, which permits us to determine
whether increasing sexual satisfaction also improves relationship satisfaction.
Although the findings of these studies are mixed, they provide some evidence
for the idea that improved relationship satisfaction may lead to improved
sexual satisfaction and that improved sexual satisfaction may bring about
enhanced relationship satisfaction.

We will begin by reviewing three studies comparing the effectiveness of relationship therapy with that of sex therapy and one study evaluating the efficacy
of relationship therapy with a placebo control condition. Walter Everaerd and
Joost Dekker (1981) evaluated the efficacy of sex therapy and communication
therapy in 45 Dutch couples where the wife complained of orgasmic dysfunction, three of whom subsequently dropped out of treatment. Ten of the wives
had primary orgasmic dysfunction in that they had never experienced an
orgasm. Couples were seen by a female and male co-therapist for one hour
twice weekly for an unlimited number of sessions. The average number of sessions was 15 for sex therapy and 17 for communication therapy. The sex therapy was adapted from that developed by William Masters and Virginia
Johnson (1970) and consisted of six sensate focus and sexual stimulation exercises not involving intercourse. Although the specific exercises were not
described, sensate focus exercises require couples to alternately stimulate each
other in non-sexual areas of the body which give them pleasure, while the sexual stimulation exercises involve them doing this in the sexual areas. The communication therapy was based on the ideas of George Bach and Peter Wyden
(1969) and Bakker and Bakker-Radbau (1973) and consisted of eight exercises
concerned with active and passive listening, expressing and reflecting feelings,
conflict management and assertiveness.

The effects of these two interventions were assessed before, three weeks
after and then again six months after treatment. Sexual functioning was
assessed with Scale 3 of the Sexual Experience Scales (Schiavi *et al.* 1979) and
relationship satisfaction with an adapted form of the Marital Attitude
Evaluation Scale (Schutz 1967). Whether couples were randomly assigned to
treatments was not stated. However, there were no significant differences in
sexual functioning prior to treatment between the two groups. The wives
showed a significant improvement in sexual functioning and there was no difference between the two therapies. However, only the husbands receiving sex
therapy showed a significant improvement in sexual functioning whereas the
husbands receiving communication therapy displayed a significant decrease in
sexual satisfaction at six months follow-up. In terms of relationship satisfaction, the only significant finding was an improvement at six months follow-up
for the wives receiving sex therapy and for the husbands receiving communication therapy. The results of this study are difficult to interpret because it is

not clear to what extent the general failure of communication therapy to increase relationship satisfaction was due to factors such as pre-treatment differences in relationship satisfaction, high pre-treatment levels of relationship satisfaction, measurement insensitivity or ineffective treatment or its application. However, the findings imply that increasing sexual satisfaction may lead to increased relationship satisfaction in wives.

Lorne Hartman and Eleanor Daly (1983) compared the effectiveness of sex therapy and behavioural marital therapy in 12 Canadian couples where seven of the wives and seven of the husbands had a sexual dysfunction. Four husbands ejaculated prematurely and three wives had inhibited orgasms. Sex therapy began with talking about sexual activities and sensate focusing without genital stimulation before progressing to genital stimulation. Behavioural marital therapy was primarily concerned with communication and problem–solving skills. A cross-over design was used in which couples received five sessions of one treatment followed by five sessions of the other treatment. Sessions were weekly and lasted 90 minutes. Couples were treated in groups of three couples with a wife and husband co-therapist. The effects of therapy were measured before treatment, at the cross-over point and after treatment. Sexual satisfaction was assessed with the Sexual Interaction Inventory (LoPiccolo and Steger 1974) and relationship satisfaction with the Dyadic Adjustment Scale (Spanier 1976). Groups of couples were randomly assigned to the two orders of treatment and there were no significant differences between these two conditions at pre-treatment. The only significant effect appeared to be that during the first phase couples receiving sex therapy showed greater improvement in sexual satisfaction than those receiving behavioural marital therapy. In general, the results seemed to suggest that while sex therapy improved both sexual and relationship satisfaction, behavioural marital therapy only enhanced relationship satisfaction. Note, however, that two of the 32 items of the Dyadic Adjustment Scale are concerned with sexual activity, which therefore this measure may also assess.

Ariel Stravynski and his colleagues (1997) compared the effects of sex therapy, social skills training and the two treatments combined, with a waiting-list control condition in 69 heterosexual single Canadian men who were sexually dysfunctional. Most of the men suffered from either premature ejaculation or impotence. Patients were randomly assigned to the four conditions. Social skills training involved describing, modelling and practising global social skills that individual patients needed, such as introducing themselves or expressing appreciation. Sex therapy consisted of five components including masturbation exercises and practising disclosing fears about sexual inadequacy. Patients were treated in groups with two therapists and received 15 weekly sessions during the treatment period, followed by four six-weekly sessions during the first six months of the 12-month follow-up period. Sessions lasted 90 minutes. Patients were assessed one week before treatment began and one week, six months and 12 months after it ended. Sexual functioning was measured with the 258-item Derogatis Sexual Functioning Inventory (Derogatis and

Melisaratos 1979) and social functioning with the 28-item Social Avoidance and Distress questionnaire (Watson and Friend 1969), the 30-item Fear of Negative Evaluation questionnaire (Watson and Friend 1969) and the 58-item Social Adjustment Scale (Schooler *et al.* 1979).

Patients being treated improved on all these measures and there were no differences between the three treatments, while patients on the waiting list generally did not improve. Furthermore, while an initial criterion for selecting patients to participate in the study was that they should not have had a stable partner for at least six months, about 60 per cent had such a relationship at the end of treatment although satisfaction with this relationship was not assessed. The results suggest that improved social functioning may lead to enhanced sexual functioning and that improved sexual functioning may bring about better social functioning. These findings may be explained by assuming that both social and sexual functioning were adversely affected by anxiety, and that alleviating this anxiety produced an improvement in both social and sexual functioning.

In part of a study by Dirk Zimmer (1987) the effect of behavioural marital therapy was compared with that of a placebo control condition in 19 German couples where the woman had secondary sexual dysfunction, such as no longer being sexually aroused or having orgasms. Behavioural marital therapy was primarily concerned with communication and problem-solving skills while the placebo control condition consisted of relaxation training, a more detailed assessment of personal history and information on sexuality and sexual myths. Couples received nine sessions of either intervention, to which they were randomly assigned. The effects of treatment were assessed before and after the nine sessions. Relationship satisfaction was measured with three sub-scales of the author's Tuebingen Scales for Sex Therapy (Equality of Mutual Influence, Experienced Respect and Communication Anxiety) and sexual satisfaction with four other of its sub-scales (Symptom Severity, Sexual Aversion, Sexual Desire and Intensity of Coitus) as well as with two scales of the Sexual Interaction Inventory (Problem Sum Score and Dissatisfaction of Female Partner). Behavioural marital therapy seemed to produce greater improvement on all these measures than the placebo control condition. These results suggest that greater relationship satisfaction may lead to greater sexual satisfaction in women.

There are three studies which have examined the effect of therapy on sexual dysfunction. Roy Auerbach and Peter Kilmann (1977) compared the effects of systematic desensitization and relaxation training on secondary erectile failure in 16 men. Treatment consisted of 15 45-minute group sessions with a male therapist which took place over five weeks. The men in the two conditions were matched on various characteristics such as the severity and duration of their disorder. Systematic desensitization, which was developed by Joseph Wolpe (1958), consisted of: relaxation training; constructing a hierarchy of scenes evoking increasing anxiety about sexual performance; and then gradually progressing through the hierarchy imagining being in these situations while remaining relaxed. The effects of treatment were assessed before, immediately after and three months after treatment. The measures were the number of successful sexual intromissions divided by the number of attempts at coitus, and a questionnaire devised by the authors for assessing satisfaction with sexual and non-sexual aspects of their most frequent sexual relationship. The men receiving systematic desensitization showed significantly greater improvement on all these measures than the men receiving relaxation training on its own. These results suggest that improving sexual performance enhanced both the sexual and the non-sexual aspects of their relationship.

Walter Everaerd and Joost Dekker (1982) evaluated the effectiveness of systematic desensitization, sex therapy and a combination of these two methods, with a waiting-list control condition in 42 Dutch couples where the wife had secondary orgasmic dysfunction. Couples were randomly assigned to these four conditions. The effects of treatment were assessed after 12 twice-weekly one-hour sessions held with a female and male co-therapist. Systematic desensitization involved relaxation training, constructing an anxiety hierarchy and, while relaxed, being progressively exposed to these situations in imagination (*in vitro*) in therapy and in reality (*in vivo*) at home. Sex therapy consisted of six sensate focus and sexual stimulation exercises not involving intercourse. As in their previous study (Everaerd and Dekker 1981) sexual functioning was measured with Scale 3 of the Sexual Experiences Scales and relationship satisfaction with the Marital Attitude Evaluation Scale. In addition, sexual anxiety and inhibition were assessed with an adaptation of the Heterosexual Behaviour Assessment Scale (Bentler 1968a, b). On all three measures significant improvement was shown by the women and men receiving sex therapy and the women receiving systematic desensitization. These results indicate that improving sexual functioning also enhances relationship satisfaction.

Finally, Walter Everaerd and Joost Dekker (1985) reported the results of two studies evaluating the effectiveness of treating sexual dysfunction in Dutch men, the most common of which was erectile dysfunction. The first study compared the effectiveness of systematic desensitization with that of sex therapy in 22 couples, while the second compared the effectiveness of rational-emotive therapy with that of sex therapy in 16 couples. Patients were randomly assigned to treatments which consisted of an unlimited number of sessions held with a female and male co-therapist once or twice a week. The mean number of sessions was about 24 for both systematic desensitization and sex therapy in the first study and about 18 for rational-emotive therapy and 17 for sex therapy in the second study. Sex therapy and systematic desensitization were carried out as described in the previous study (Everaerd and Dekker 1982). Rational-emotive therapy, which was developed by Albert Ellis (1962), involved couples making rational analyses of their sexual as well as their non-sexual difficulties. The effects of treatment were assessed before, three weeks after and six to 12 months after treatment. Relationship satisfaction was measured with the Marital Attitude Evaluation Scale and sexual functioning with Scale 3 of the Sexual Experiences Scale.

In the first study women and men receiving either systematic desensitization or sex therapy showed a significant improvement in sexual functioning but not in relationship satisfaction, possibly because relationship satisfaction was relatively high and could not be further enhanced. In the second study the only significant improvements were for sexual satisfaction in men receiving sex therapy (three weeks after treatment) or rational-emotive therapy, and for relationship satisfaction in both women and men receiving rational-emotive therapy (but not 6–12 months after treatment possibly because data were only available for two couples). The interpretation of the results of this second study was made more difficult by the relatively small number of couples in either treatment and by the women assigned to sex therapy being significantly more satisfied with their relationship than those allocated to rational-emotive therapy. The findings, however, suggest that increased sexual satisfaction does not necessarily lead to increased relationship satisfaction and that improved relationship satisfaction does not necessarily lead to enhanced sexual satisfaction.

SUMMARY

Many people believe that sexual behaviour should primarily take place within a loving or married relationship and should be restricted to that relationship. Furthermore, many people report behaving in accordance with these beliefs. A substantial number of studies have investigated the association between various aspects of relationship compatibility and sexuality. The aspects most commonly measured have been relationship satisfaction and sexual satisfaction with one's partner, which have been found to be moderately strongly correlated in women and men in heterosexual, gay and lesbian relationships. Relationship satisfaction in women and men has also been found to be correlated with frequency of orgasm and frequency of sexual intercourse, although this association was less strong. One way of determining the causal relationship between relationship compatibility and sexual behaviour is to compare the relative effectiveness of relationship and sex therapy in patients having relationship and sexual problems of comparable severity. While no such study appears to have been conducted, there is research which has evaluated the effects of relationship and various forms of sex therapy on relationship and sexual satisfaction in people with sexual problems. Although the results of this research are mixed, there is evidence to suggest that relationship therapy may lead to improved sexual satisfaction and that sex therapy may bring about enhanced relationship satisfaction. These findings imply that the causal relationship between relationship and sexual satisfaction is reciprocal.

10

Love

As we have already seen, many people believe that love is one of the most highly desirable characteristics in choosing a mate or marrying someone. Several studies have shown this. For instance, in the largest cross-cultural study carried out to date on students and co-ordinated by David Buss (Buss *et al.* 1990), 9,474 students from 37 cultures were asked to rate the importance of 18 characteristics in choosing a mate. Love or mutual attraction was rated by both women and men as being the most essential of these characteristics. When Ernest Burgess and Paul Wallin (1953) asked 998 engaged couples living in Chicago in the late 1930s whether a person should ever marry someone they did not love, about 80 per cent of the women and 82 per cent of the men said they should not (p. 394). Asked further as to whether married people should continue to live together when they were no longer in love, about 84 per cent of 911 of the women and about 81 per cent of 913 of the men replied that they should not do so (p. 395). In the 1986 British Social Attitudes Survey 75 per cent of the sample said that ceasing to love one another was a sufficient reason for divorce (Ashford 1987, p. 126).

There is evidence to suggest that people report being in love when they marry. Of the 226 engaged Chicago couples who were asked this question Ernest Burgess and Paul Wallin (1953) found that only 7.1 per cent of the women and 6.2 per cent of the men said that they were 'somewhat' or 'mildly' in love (p. 170); the rest said that they were either 'head over heels' in love or 'very much' in love. Using a stratified sample of 459 ever-married wives from the Detroit area and focusing on the women who had only married once, Martin Whyte (1990) noted that only 4 per cent of them said that they had not been in love when they married (p. 53). Forty-seven per cent chose the extreme 'head-over-heels' option.

Furthermore, several studies have found that relationships characterized by love are experienced as being more satisfactory and are more likely to endure. Ernest Burgess and Paul Wallin (1953) reported that, of eight relationship qualities, love was the most strongly correlated with both marital happiness ($r = 0.65$) and marital satisfaction ($r = 0.64$) in the 666 Chicago couples who were followed up three to five years after they had married

(p. 504). Love was assessed with five items such as 'To what extent are you in love with your mate?' (p. 497), marital satisfaction with 26 items such as 'My marriage is successful but not extraordinarily so' (pp. 488–9) and marital happiness with 21 items such as 'I believe our marriage is reasonably happy' (pp. 486–7).

Measuring satisfaction with the extent to which nine characteristics were met within marriage on a four-point scale, Darla Rhyne (1981) reported that the amount of love and affection shown by the spouse was the quality that was most highly correlated with a four-item Index of Marital Quality in a Canadian national sample of 1,188 wives ($r = 0.62$) and 1,002 husbands ($r = 0.59$). Kathryn Rettig and Margaret Bubolz (1983) noted in a multiple regression analysis that marital love and affection was the variable most highly correlated with marital satisfaction in the wives ($r = 0.78$) and husbands ($r = 0.69$) of 224 Michigan couples. Both these qualities were rated on a seven-point 'Delighted–Terrible' scale. In 55 couples from the state of New York, Joan Broderick and Daniel O'Leary (1986) found that of five variables their 17-item measure of positive feelings or love was the most strongly correlated with the Locke–Wallace Marital Adjustment Test in both the wives ($r = 0.87$) and the husbands ($r = 0.89$).

In his survey of first-married wives in Detroit, Martin Whyte (1990, p. 179) noted that wives who were less in love when they married were more likely to split up ($r = -0.29$), and if they were still together to be more dissatisfied with their marriage ($r = -0.30$) and to have more marital problems ($r = -0.14$). Marital quality or satisfaction was measured with seven items such as the degree of overall satisfaction with the marriage and the amount of affection shown, while marital problems were assessed with 11 items such as the amount of disagreement on five issues (p. 306).

The degree of love has been found to predict the stability of dating relationships. Relationships characterized by greater love are more likely to endure. Charles Hill and his colleagues (1976) gave Rubin's (1970) Love and Liking Scales to 231 dating students in the Boston area. After two years 103 couples had broken up. Love Scale scores at the start of the study were significantly lower for both the women and the men who broke up subsequently. For women the Liking Scale score was also significantly lower for those whose relationships ended. Women's love for their partner was a stronger predictor ($r = 0.32$) of the state of the relationship two years later than men's love for their partner ($r = 0.18$). Mary Lund (1985) gave nine of the 13 items of the Love Scale to 129 dating students in Los Angeles and asked them about their relationship four months later, by which time 29 of the relationships had ended. Students whose relationships had ended had lower Love Scale scores at the start of the study than those whose relationships were still ongoing ($r = 0.46$). Similar results were obtained by John Berg and Ronald McQuinn (1986) with a 10-item scale developed by Harriet Braiker and Harold Kelley (1979), completed by 38 American dating couples who were followed up over four months. Items on this scale included 'To what extent did you love _____ at this stage?' and 'How sexually intimate were you with _____?'.

Although love and relationship satisfaction have been found to be closely related, little is known about the causal nature of this relationship. The fact that most people report that they did not fall in love at first sight and that their love for their partner grew over time implies that love develops as a function of particular aspects of the relationship. In a survey of 200 working-class married couples from London interviewed in 1943–46, Eliot Slater and Moya Woodside (1951) found that only about 4 per cent of the wives and 7 per cent of the husbands reported experiencing love at first sight. When Eugene Kanin and his colleagues (1970) asked 429 female and 250 male American students when they first realized they were in love with their current or most recent partner, 15 per cent of the women and 27 per cent of the men said it was within the first four dates or meetings. About 43 per cent of the women and 30 per cent of the men did so after 19 or more meetings.

Studies which evaluate the effects of therapy on love as well as relationship satisfaction would help to determine whether changes in one variable are associated with changes in the other. There appear to have been three such studies published, with mixed results. Daniel O'Leary and Hillary Turkewitz (1981) compared the effects of behavioural marital therapy, communication therapy and a waiting-list control condition in 30 American couples on relationship satisfaction as assessed by the Dyadic Adjustment Scale and love as measured by the 17-item Positive Feelings Questionnaire (O'Leary *et al.* 1983). However, the results of this study do not appear to be very informative with respect to this issue in that the only significant change for either of these two variables was the difference between pre-treatment and four-month follow-up for marital satisfaction. This finding is difficult to interpret in that it was not clear whether the initial levels of marital satisfaction and love were equivalent to enable improvement on both these measures to be shown. Kim Halford and his colleagues (1993) compared the effects of 12–15 weekly 1½-hour sessions of either behavioural marital therapy or enhanced behavioural marital therapy in 26 maritally distressed Australian couples on the Dyadic Adjustment Scale and the Positive Feelings Questionnaire. Both treatments led to significant improvements on both measures, indicating that relationship improvement may lead to increased love. Paul James (1991) compared the effects of 12 weekly one-hour sessions of emotionally focused couple therapy (on its own or combined with communication training) with a waiting-list control in 42 distressed Canadian couples on the Dyadic Adjustment Scale and the 15-item version of the Passionate Love Scale (Hatfield and Sprecher 1986). Although both forms of emotionally focused couple therapy produced significantly greater improvement in relationship satisfaction than the waiting-list control, there was no similar improvement in passionate love, suggesting that increased relationship satisfaction did not result in greater passionate love.

ATTITUDES TOWARDS LOVE AS A PHENOMENON

One of the potential difficulties in carrying out research on love is that there are different views on how it should be conceptualized and measured. One important distinction which has not always been maintained is that between one's attitudes about love and one's loving attitude towards a particular person. Although the two attitudes may be related, they are not the same. For example, we may believe that love is an intensely positive experience but we may not feel intensely positive about our partner. The first attempt to measure attitudes towards love appears to have been made by Llewellyn Gross (1944). He was interested in distinguishing romantic from realistic attitudes towards love and developed Form A and B of the Romanticism Scale, both of which consisted of 40 romantic statements and 40 realist statements. Charles Hobart (1958) developed a shortened form of this scale comprising 12 items (e.g. 'Lovers ought to expect a certain amount of disillusionment after marriage'). However, neither scale appears to have been used in subsequent published research.

A scale which has received somewhat more interest was devised by David Knox (Knox and Sporakowski 1968) and contained 85 items. The number of items used in this and his own subsequent studies was considerably less than 85 and was based on those items that best discriminated low from high scorers. A low score on each item was seen as indicative of a romantic attitude towards love, and a high score as reflecting a conjugal or realistic attitude towards love. Two items on this scale were 'When you are really in love, you just aren't interested in anyone else' and 'Love doesn't make sense. It just is'. Dennis Hinkle and Michael Sporakowski (1975) gave the 29 items that

---

Traditional Love

13 Usually there are only one or two people in the world whom you could really love and could really be happy with.

23 There are probably only a few people that any one person can fall in love with.

Love Overcomes All

9 As long as two people love each other, the religious differences they have really do not matter.

8 It doesn't matter if you marry after you have known your partner for only a short time as long as you know you are in love.

Irrationality

24 When you are in love, your judgement is usually not too clear.

11 When you are in love, you are usually in a daze.

Table 10.1 The two items correlating most highly with each of the three oblique factors of the Knox Attitudes to Love Scale (Hinkle and Sporakowski 1975)

initially significantly differentiated low from high scorers to 234 American undergraduates and factor-analysed the results. Although eight factors emerged, all but one item loaded on the first factor, indicating that the scale was unidimensional. Oblique rotation of these factors suggested to them that the scale consisted of three sub-scales which they called Traditional Love, Love Overcomes All and Irrationality. The two items that loaded most highly on each of these three sub-scales are shown in Table 10.1.

Brenda Munro and Gerald Adams (1978) questioned whether high scores on Knox's romanticism scale indicated a conjugal attitude towards love. To test this, 31 romantic and 26 conjugal items were taken from the literature on love and were answered by 302 North American university students. Oblique and orthogonal rotation of the factors that emerged resulted in three similar factors which they called Romantic Ideal, Conjugal-Rational Love and Romantic Power. The two items that correlated most highly with each of the factors comprising these scales are presented in Table 10.2.

These three New Love Attitude Scales together with the Knox Attitudes to Love Scale and the Rubin Love Scale were completed by 236 high-school-educated and 92 college-educated residents of Calgary in Canada. Of the three New Love Attitude Scales, the Romantic Power Scale in both samples correlated most highly with the Traditional ($r = 0.41$ for high-school-educated, $r = 0.50$ for college-educated), the Love Overcomes All ($r = 0.30$ for high-school-educated, $r = 0.41$ for college-educated) and the Irrational Love ($r = 0.35$ for high-school-educated, $r = 0.43$ for college educated) sub-scales of the Knox Attitudes to Love Scale. The Conjugal-Rational Love Scale was not significantly correlated in either of the two samples with any of the three

---

Romantic Ideal

8 To live in love is more pleasant than any other way of life in the world.

1 Love is the highest goal between a man and a woman.

Conjugal-Rational Love

8 Love is feeling warm, close and involved, but not necessarily sexually excited.

2 It is more important to feel calm and relaxed with the one you love, rather than excited and romantic.

Romantic Power

7 Love is an intense flame which devours the roughness in each loved person, leaving only what is pure and fine.

9 Just being together with the one you love takes away worries over the future.

Table 10.2 The two items correlating most highly with each of the three orthogonal factors reflecting the New Love Attitude Scales (Munro and Adams 1978)

sub-scales of the Knox Attitudes to Love Scale, suggesting that high scores on the Knox sub-scales indicate the absence of romantic love rather than the presence of conjugal love. The New Love Attitude Scales were also completed by 25 engaged, 25 married and 15 divorced individuals. Married and divorced people had significantly higher Conjugal-Rational Love scores and significantly lower Romantic Ideal and Romantic Power scores than engaged couples.

Kenneth and Karen Dion (1973) used an attitudes to love questionnaire which consisted of 16 items and which came from questions derived by Marvin Dunnette and his students. These questions were answered by 116 female and 127 male introductory psychology American undergraduates. Although no details were given of the kind of factor analysis undertaken, three factors emerged which were called the Idealistic, Cynical and Pragmatic Views of love. The two items that correlated most highly with each of these three factors of this questionnaire are reproduced in Table 10.3. However, in a subsequent factor analysis on the same questionnaire completed by 156 introductory psychology Canadian students, Karen and Kenneth Dion (1975) found four factors which they called Cynical (e.g. 'True love lasts forever'), Non-instrumental (e.g. 'There's no room in modern marriage for the old idea of romance'), Idealistic (e.g. 'Even if not as strong, a previous love affair may still have been real love') and Stereotypic (e.g. 'True love is known at once by the parties involved'). Once again, no information was provided about the factor analysis used and there was no discussion of why the results were not consistent with those of the previous study, as shown by the following two examples. In the first study agreement with the item 'True love lasts forever' was seen as characteristic of Idealistic Love, whereas in the second study disagreement

---

Idealistic View
True love leads to almost perfect happiness.
There is only one real love for a person.

Cynical View
Romantic love is an outmoded and unrealistic concept.
There's no room in modern marriage for the old idea of romance.

Pragmatic view
Even if not as strong, a previous love affair may still have been real love.
It is possible to love two people at the same time.

Table 10.3 The two items correlating most highly with each of the three factors of the attitude to romantic love questionnaire (Dion and Dion 1973)

with this item was considered as reflecting Cynical Love. Agreement with the statement 'Even if not as strong, a previous love affair may still have been real love' in the first study was viewed as representing Pragmatic Love whereas in the second study disagreement with this statement was thought of as indicative of Idealistic Love.

Susan Sprecher and Sandra Metts (1989) devised the 15-item Romantic Beliefs Scale based on the romantic love ideal typology put forward by Herman Lantz and his colleagues (1968, 1973). This typology consisted of the following five beliefs: (1) love at first sight occurs; (2) there is only one person we can love; (3) love overcomes all obstacles; (4) our loved one will be perfect; and (5) our choice of partner should be based on love rather than other considerations. This questionnaire was completed by 453 female and 277 male American undergraduates. Four factors were extracted and orthogonally rotated, and were called Love Finds a Way, One and Only (Love), Idealization (of Partner) and Love at First Sight. Items representing love overcomes all obstacles and love should determine choice of partner formed part of Love Finds a Way. The two items loading most strongly on each of these four factors for this scale are presented in Table 10.4.

Love Finds a Way

11 If a relationship I have was meant to be, any obstacle (e.g. lack of money, physical distance, career conflicts) can be overcome.

15 I believe if another person and I love each other we can overcome any differences and problems that may arise.

One and Only (Love)

 3 Once I experience 'true love', I could never experience it again, to the same degree, with another person.

 4 I believe that to be truly in love is to be in love forever.

Idealization (of Partner)

 7 I'm sure that every new thing I learn about the person I choose for a long-term commitment will please me.

 8 The relationship I will have with my 'true love' will be nearly perfect.

Love at First Sight

12 I am likely to fall in love almost immediately if I meet the right person.

 1 I need to know someone for a period of time before I fall in love with him or her.

Table 10.4 The two items most highly correlated with each of the four factors of the Romantic Beliefs Scale (Sprecher and Metts 1989)

ATTITUDES OF LOVE TOWARDS SOMEONE

One of the first attempts to measure important aspects of romantic love that one person may feel towards another was the 13-item Love Scale developed by Zick Rubin (1970). This scale and the 13-item Liking Scale were derived from a factor analysis of 70 items completed by 198 introductory psychology American undergraduates in terms of both a romantic and an opposite-sex platonic relationship. Examples of these items are reproduced in Table 2.2. The Loving Scale was positively correlated with a simple three-point scale of whether the respondent and their partner were in love in both the female (r = 0.59) and male (r = 0.52) partner of 158 American student dating couples. In addition, dating partners were rated more highly on this scale than a same-sex close friend. As part of another study by myself (Cramer 1992b) these two scales together with another 74 items on attraction were answered by 225 16- to 17-year-old British females with respect to someone they had been or were currently in love with. Six factors were extracted and orthogonally rotated. Seven of the 13 Love Scale items correlated above 0.44 with the first factor and two below it, providing some independent support for this scale. The 13 items loading most highly on this first factor are presented in Table 10.5.

The most detailed, thorough and complex attempt to distinguish different kinds of romantic love towards a person was made by John Lee (1973, 1976). In developing his scheme Lee constructed a Love Story Card Sort (1976, p. 221) which consisted of 1,500 cards each describing an event, idea or emotion which might occur in a romantic relationship. Initially 112 English and Canadian women and men were interviewed using this card sort

Loadings	Items
0.65	I really love _____.
0.65	I want to see _____ frequently, usually every day.
0.64	I would forgive _____ for practically anything. (Rubin's Love Scale)
0.62	I would still love _____ even if _____ no longer loved me.
0.62	I want to be looked after by _____.
0.62	I want to look after _____.
0.61	If I could never be with _____, I would feel miserable. (Rubin's Love Scale)
0.61	I would do almost anything for_____. (Rubin's Love Scale)
0.60	I often think about _____.
0.59	I would be very upset if we did not see each other again.
0.57	It would be hard for me to get along without _____. (Rubin's Love Scale)
0.56	One of my primary concerns is _____'s welfare. (Rubin's Love Scale)
0.56	I cannot control my love for _____.

Table 10.5 The 13 items most strongly loaded with the first factor of a love questionnaire (Cramer 1992b)

and a provisional typology of love styles was produced which was tested on more than 100 North Americans (1976, p. 228), including gay and lesbian individuals. The answers to the card sort were coded and eventually reduced to 32 key factors (1976, p. 231) which were sorted into the following six classes: (1) predisposing anxiety; (2) mental preoccupation; (3) sensual rapport; (4) manipulative control; (5) conflict and tension; and (6) companionship (1976, p. 233).

Based on this information and the literature on love, Lee discriminated between at least 12 types or styles of love. The three primary types were Eros, Ludus and Storge. These three primary types could be combined to form three secondary compounds and three secondary mixtures. The three secondary compounds were Mania (Eros-Ludus), Agape (Eros-Storge) and Pragma (Ludus-Storge) while the three secondary mixtures were Ludic Eros, Storgic Eros and Storgic Ludus. In addition, Lee identified the three tertiary mixtures of Manic Eros, Manic Ludus and Manic Storge. The three primary types and three secondary compounds consist of a number of characteristics. They may be summarized as follows in terms of one of their predominant features: Eros (physical attraction); Ludus (non-commitment); Storge (friendship); Mania (obsessiveness); Agape (altruism); and Pragma (practicality).

Although Lee (1976, p. 144) cautioned against taking such tests too seriously, he presented a 20-item (Lee 1976, pp. 149–58) and a 35-item (Lee 1975) questionnaire for identifying eight of these styles (omitting Agape and the three tertiary mixtures). To further evaluate the longer questionnaire I gave it to 105 female and 44 male British students to complete (Cramer 1987) and found that the items could be most meaningfully grouped together into four orthogonal factors which were called relationship satisfaction, relationship openness, relationship importance and physical intimacy. Correlating the scores on these four factors with the scores on the five love styles of Eros, Mania, Storge, Pragma and Ludus, the results suggested that the factors could differentiate the love styles. For example, physical intimacy was positively correlated with Eros ($r = 0.31$) but negatively correlated with Storge ($r = -0.34$).

Thomas and Marcia Lasswell (1976) initially distinguished six hypothetical or ideal types of love which they found were essentially similar to Lee's three primary and three secondary compound types. They developed a 50-item questionnaire to construct a SAMPLE (Storge Agape Mania Pragma Ludus Eros) profile of an individual's romantic relationship. Clyde Hendrick and his colleagues (1984) gave the Lasswells' questionnaire together with four new items to 439 female and 374 male American undergraduates and factor-analysed the results. Nine oblique factors appeared to be the most interpretable for women and men, of which the first three represented Pragma, Mania and Agape. Ludus also emerged as a factor. Subsequently Clyde and Susan Hendrick (1986) developed a revised 42-item Love Attitudes Scale consisting of seven items for assessing the six types. This questionnaire was completed by 341 female and 466 male American undergraduates and factor-analysed. The most meaningful solution comprised six orthogonal factors which generally reflected the six love styles. Six items of the questionnaire were revised and the modified questionnaire was answered by 368 female and 199 male American undergraduates. Six factors were again extracted and orthogonally rotated and seemed to correspond to the six love styles. In a third study this revised scale was completed by 202 female and 189 male American undergraduates and once again the six orthogonal factors extracted represented the six love styles (Hendrick and Hendrick 1989). The two items that loaded most strongly on each of these six factors for the latest version of this scale are reproduced in Table 10.6.

While some of the items on this questionnaire assess one's attitude of love for a person (e.g. 'My lover and I have the right physical "chemistry" between us'), others measure attitudes about love (e.g. 'I enjoy playing the "game of love" with a number of different partners') or characteristics of past relationships (e.g. 'I have sometimes had to keep two of my lovers from finding out about each other'). Consequently, this questionnaire appears to confound these three aspects.

Eros

2 My lover and I have the right physical 'chemistry' between us.

4 I feel that my lover and I were meant for each other.

Ludus

14 I enjoy playing the 'game of love' with a number of different partners.

10 I have sometimes had to keep two of my lovers from finding out about each other.

Storge

18 The best kind of love grows out of a long friendship.

21 My most satisfying love relationships have developed from good friendships.

Pragma

27 One consideration in choosing a partner is how s/he will reflect on my career.

24 A main consideration in choosing a lover is how s/he reflects on my family.

Mania

32 When my lover doesn't pay attention to me, I feel sick all over.

33 When I am in love, I have trouble concentrating on anything else.

Agape

38 I cannot be happy unless I place my lover's happiness before my own.

39 I am usually willing to sacrifice my own wishes to let my lover achieve her/his.

Table 10.6 The two items most highly correlated with each of the six factors of the Love Attitudes Scale (Hendrick and Hendrick 1989)

As part of a study by myself (Cramer 1993b), the four items that correlated most highly on the six factors of the Love Attitudes Scale (Hendrick and Hendrick 1986) and the Rubin Love Scale (Cramer 1992b) together with 36 other items on attraction were completed by 276 16- to 17-year-old British females with respect to someone they had been or were currently in love with. Twelve factors were extracted and orthogonally rotated. The Storge, Ludus and Pragma items emerged as separate factors while the Mania and Agape items formed part of the first factor together with two of the Love Scale items. The Eros items were shared between three factors. As a factor analysis of just the 24 items of the Love Attitudes Scale on their own was not carried out, it is not known to what extent the items would have emerged on their respective factors.

An attempt to measure passionate love was made by Elaine Hatfield and Susan Sprecher (1986) with their 30-item Passionate Love Scale which included such items as 'I would rather be with _____ than with anyone else' and 'I have an endless appetite for affection from _____'. However, they found this scale to be highly positively correlated with Rubin's Love Scale in 60 female ($r = 0.83$) and 60 male ($r = 0.86$) American students, which suggests that a very similar construct is being measured by these two scales. Clyde and Susan Hendrick (1989) reported that in their sample of 202 female and 189 male American undergraduates the items of this scale loaded on a single factor. This scale was most strongly correlated with the love styles of Agape ($r = 0.56$) and Eros ($r = 0.53$).

In his triangular theory of love, Robert Sternberg (1986) suggested that seven kinds of love can be distinguished by the presence or absence of the three components of intimacy, passion and decision/commitment, as shown in Table 10.7. Liking, for example, is indicated by the presence (+) of intimacy and the absence (−) of both passion and decision/commitment. There are three 15-item

| | Components | | |
| | --- | --- | --- |
Kinds of loves	Intimacy	Passion	Decision/ commitment
Nonlove	−	−	−
Liking	+	−	−
Infatuated love	−	+	−
Empty love	−	−	+
Romantic love	+	+	−
Companionate love	+	−	+
Fatuous love	−	+	+
Consummate love	+	+	+

Table 10.7 Sternberg's (1986) love taxonomy based on the presence (+) and absence (−) of the three components of intimacy, passion and decision/commitment

scales to measure intimacy (e.g. 'I communicate well with _____'), passion (e.g. 'Just seeing _____ excites me') and commitment (e.g. 'I view my relationship with _____ as permanent'). One potential problem with this scheme is that for the decision/commitment component it is not clear on what basis an individual decides to love another person, since this concept is not defined. If it is in terms of the other two components, the category of empty love disappears.

Cindy Hazan and Phillip Shaver (1987) suggested that romantic love in adults may be seen as being similar to and derived from the way in which infants become attached to their primary carers. Mary Ainsworth and her colleagues (1978) distinguished three types of parent–infant attachment which are usually referred to as secure, anxious/ambivalent and avoidant. Hazan and Shaver (1987) assessed the attachment type of an individual by asking them which one of three sets of statements best described their feelings. These three descriptions are reproduced in Table 10.8. The wording of these descriptions has been somewhat revised subsequently (Shaver and Hazan 1988).

Clyde and Susan Hendrick (1989) found, in their sample of 202 female and 189 male American undergraduates, low correlations between the Passionate Love Scale and the avoidant ($r = -0.14$), the anxious/ambivalent ($r = 0.10$) and the secure ($r = 0.08$) attachment types when each of the latter had been rated on a five-point scale of agreement, indicating that these descriptions do not appear to be measuring the degree of love felt for another person. This may not be surprising given that the descriptions refer to relationships in general and not to a specific relationship.

Attempts to develop more sensitive measures of these types and to differentiate them further have been made. Nancy Collins and Stephen Read (1990) tried to devise a more sensitive index of these three attachment types by constructing three six-item scales of dependence, anxiety and closeness which were derived from a factor analysis of 21 items completed by 206 female and 184

Secure: I find it relatively easy to get close to others and am comfortable depending on them and having them depend on me. I don't often worry about being abandoned or about someone getting too close to me.

Avoidant: I am somewhat uncomfortable being close to others; I find it difficult to trust them completely, difficult to allow myself to depend on them. I am nervous when anyone gets too close, and often, love partners want me to be more intimate than I feel comfortable being.

Anxious/Ambivalent: I find that others are reluctant to get as close as I would like. I often worry that my partner doesn't really love me or won't want to stay with me. I want to merge completely with another person, and this desire sometimes scares people away.

Table 10.8 Hazan and Shaver's (1987) three attachment types

Dependence
6 I am not sure that I can always depend on others to be there when I need them.
4 I know that others will be there when I need them.

Anxiety
8 I often worry that my partner does not really love me.
10 I often worry that my partner will not want to stay with me.

Closeness
16 I am nervous when anyone gets too close to me.
15 I am somewhat uncomfortable being close to others.

Table 10.9 The two items most highly correlated on each of the three attachment type factors (Collins and Read 1990)

male American undergraduates. The two items correlating most highly on each of the three factors are presented in Table 10.9. Most of the items on this questionnaire describe relationships in general and not one's attitude towards a particular relationship.

Unlike the Collins and Read questionnaire, which does not appear to have been related to a measure of love for a specific person, Jeffry Simpson (1990) correlated the Rubin Love Scale in 144 American dating couples with a 13-item measure of attachment types consisting of statements taken from Hazan and Shaver's (1987) descriptions (e.g. 'I find it relatively easy to get close to others'). There was no check on the factor structure of these items. For both female and male partners love was weakly correlated with the secure ($r = 0.28$ for women, $r = 0.22$ for men), the avoidant ($r = -0.28$ for women, $r = -0.22$ for men) and the anxious ($r = -0.07$ for women, $r = -0.12$ for men) attachment style, presumably because the statements referred to relationships in general and not to a specific dating relationship.

Finally, Kim Bartholomew and Leonard Horowitz (1991) suggested dividing Hazan and Shaver's (1987) avoidant type into a fearful and a dismissive type, while renaming the ambivalent type the preoccupied type. Descriptions of the four types are shown in Table 10.10 which individuals can use for rating their own attachment type. Once again these descriptions refer to relationships in general and not to a particular relationship.

ATTITUDES TO AND OF LOVE

There is some evidence to suggest that attitudes towards love are associated with the love felt for a particular individual, although the causal nature of this relationship has not been investigated. Brenda Munro and Gerald Adams (1978) found that in the smaller college-educated sample the Rubin Love Scale was positively correlated with the Romantic Idealism Scale ($r = 0.42$), the

Secure: It is easy for me to become emotionally close to others. I am comfortable depending on others and having others depend on me. I don't worry about being alone or having others not accept me.

Dismissing: I am comfortable without close emotional relationships. It is very important to me to feel independent and self-sufficient, and I prefer not to depend on others or have others depend on me.

Preoccupied: I want to be completely emotionally intimate with others, but I often find that others are reluctant to get as close as I would like. I am uncomfortable being without close relationships, but I sometimes worry that others don't value me as much as I value them.

Fearful: I am uncomfortable getting close to others. I want emotionally close relationships, but I find it difficult to trust others completely, or to depend on them. I worry that I will be hurt if I allow myself to become too close to others.

Table 10.10 Bartholomew and Horowitz's (1991) four attachment styles

Romantic Power Scale ($r = 0.36$) and the Knox Attitudes to Love Scale ($r = 0.18$). However, in the larger high-school-educated sample, while the Rubin Love Scale was positively correlated with the Romantic Power Scale ($r = 0.41$), it was negatively correlated with the Knox Attitudes to Love Scale ($r = -0.17$) and not significantly correlated with the Romantic Idealism Scale ($r = 0.05$). Possible reasons for this inconsistency were not given. Furthermore, the correlation between the Love Scale and the Conjugal-Rational Love Scale was not presented. Susan Sprecher and Sandra Metts (1989) noted that in a sample of 125 American undergraduates both Rubin's (1970) Love and Liking Scales correlated significantly and positively with their Romantic Beliefs sub-scales of Love Finds a Way ($r = 0.40$ for Love, $r = 0.38$ for Liking), One and Only Love ($r = 0.42$ for Love, $r = 0.33$ for Liking) and Idealization of Partner ($r = 0.22$ for Love, $r = 0.24$ for Liking) but not with the sub-scale of Love at First Sight ($r = 0.08$ for Love, $r = 0.07$ for Liking).

LOVE STYLES AND RELATIONSHIP COMPATIBILITY

Several studies have examined the association of relationship compatibility with love and attachment styles. However, since attachment styles do not necessarily refer to love towards a specific individual these studies will not be described. Four studies looking at love styles in American student heterosexual romantic relationships have generally found relationship satisfaction to be most highly related to Eros, Ludus and Agape. Keith Davis and Holly Latty-Mann (1987) reported that in 70 dating couples relationship satisfaction as assessed by a 10-item global relationship satisfaction scale was most highly related to Agape ($r = 0.32$) and Eros ($r = 0.31$) in the women and Eros ($r = 0.43$) and Ludus ($r = -0.28$) in the men. Marc Levy and Keith Davis (1988) noted that in 117 dating couples relationship satisfaction as measured in the previous study was most strongly associated with Agape ($r = 0.37$) and Ludus ($r = -0.36$) for the women and men analysed together. Susan Hendrick and her colleagues (1988) found that in 57 dating couples relationship satisfaction as measured by the Dyadic Adjustment Scale was most strongly correlated with Eros ($r = 0.46$) and Agape ($r = 0.39$) in the women and with Ludus ($r = -0.61$) and Eros ($r = 0.51$) in the men. Of 30 couples who were followed up two months later those with higher Eros ($r = 0.55$) and lower Ludus ($r = -0.50$) scores were more likely to be still together. Finally, Patricia Frazier and Ellen Esterly (1990) noted that relationship satisfaction as measured by four items was most strongly correlated with Eros ($r = 0.56$) and Agape ($r = 0.51$) in 158 women and with Ludus ($r = -0.48$) and Agape ($r = 0.47$) in 129 men. However, it was not stated whether this analysis included any or all of the 10 per cent of the sample who had never been in a romantic relationship, and how they were expected to answer the satisfaction measure.

SUMMARY

Many people see love as being one of the most highly desirable characteristics in choosing a marital partner and report being in love when they marry. Love has been shown to be one of the variables that is most strongly associated with relationship satisfaction and has been found to be related over a two-year period to the subsequent likelihood of couples staying together. Little research, however, has been carried out on trying to establish the causal nature of the association between love and relationship satisfaction. There have been several attempts to measure attitudes to romantic love as well as love towards a particular individual; while there is some evidence to suggest that these are linked, the causal nature of this relationship has not been investigated. Various types or styles of love have been distinguished, although some of the items making up the measures refer to attitudes to love as well as characteristic patterns in past relationships. Relationship satisfaction has been found to be most strongly related to the love styles of Eros, Agape and Ludus. Although conceived as forms of romantic love, attachment styles have generally been measured as characteristic ways of relating to others and as such have not assessed the attachment to a particular romantic partner.

11

Relationship Counselling

When people have problems with their close relationships they are likely to first discuss those problems with other people they are close to. For example, in the British Social Attitudes 1986 Survey (Brook and Witherspoon 1987), about 19 per cent of the respondents said that the first person they would turn to for help if they were upset about a problem with their partner which they had not been able to sort out with them would be their closest friend, followed by their mother (15 per cent) and then their partner (13 per cent). About 8 per cent would not approach anyone for help, and very few people would turn to a professional person such as a family doctor, priest or marriage guidance counsellor. However, more people were likely to approach one of these professional people as their second choice for help. Doctors were the most popular choice (6 per cent) followed by the combined category of psychologists, psychiatrists, marriage guidance or other professional counsellors (4 per cent), after which came religious professionals (3 per cent). In their 1976 survey of help-seeking among 2,267 American adults, Joseph Veroff and his colleagues (1981, p. 131) found that the most common personal problems people sought professional help for were problems with their spouse or marriage (40 per cent) followed by personal adjustment problems (22 per cent). Based on the figures presented in their book, we can estimate that about 11 per cent of the people who were or had been married in their sample had sought professional help for marital problems. A further 5 per cent thought that professional assistance could have helped them with their marital difficulties (p. 190). People generally found that they were helped with their marital problems by these professionals (p. 144). Only 22 per cent said that they had not been helped.

In Britain the largest voluntary organization for specifically helping people with relationship problems is Relate, formerly known as the National Marriage Guidance Council, which was first established in 1947. According to its publicity, in 1994/95 over 2,300 professionally trained counsellors worked in 126 centres in England, Wales and Northern Ireland. Some 70,000 people were initially assessed for relationship counselling, of which about 60 per cent chose or were able to begin a programme of counselling.

A further 56,000 people received relationship education and training. Counsellors are trained in an approach which includes elements from psychodynamic, attachment, object-relations, systemic and behavioural theory. Clients are asked to make a contribution to the organization according to their income.

Some idea of the most common types of problems treated by professionals may be gleaned from a study by Susan Geiss and Daniel O'Leary (1981) who asked a random sample of 116 members of the American Association of Marriage and Family Therapists to estimate the percentage of couples seen during the past year who had expressed complaints in each of 29 areas. The seven most common problems were: communication (84 per cent); unrealistic expectations of marriage or spouse (56 per cent); demonstration of affection (55 per cent); lack of loving feelings (55 per cent); sex (52 per cent); power struggles (52 per cent); and decision-making and problem-solving (49 per cent). Although the sample was small, this study also gives some indication of the most common kind of professional person who carries out marital therapy in the United States and the most frequent theoretical orientation adhered to. The largest professional group were psychologists (32 per cent), followed by social workers (23 per cent), marriage and family therapists (11 per cent), clergy (3 per cent) and psychiatrists (3 per cent). The most common theoretical orientation was eclecticism (69 per cent), followed by systems theory (11 per cent). The remaining theoretical orientations were fairly equally divided among the communication, psychoanalytic, ego-analytic and behavioural orientations.

Partners may be seen in five different ways. In *individual* therapy partners are seen separately by two different therapists. In *collaborative* therapy partners are seen separately by two different therapists who consult each other about the partners and their relationship. In *concurrent* therapy partners are seen separately by the same therapist. In *conjoint* therapy partners are seen together by one or two therapists, while in *conjoint group* therapy partners are seen together with other partners by one or two therapists.

Three kinds of relationship counselling have been distinguished. One may be generally called relationship problem prevention and relationship enhancement (or enrichment) interventions. These programmes are designed to improve the quality of the relationship and to prevent more serious problems from arising. A second kind of relationship counselling may be broadly referred to as relationship therapy, which is primarily directed at resolving more serious relationship problems, while the third kind may be generically known as separation counselling and mediation. Initially these kinds of interventions were described in terms of marital status, but nowadays they are being increasingly more commonly and more appropriately referred to as relationship or couple interventions. In addition, the terms 'therapy' and 'counselling' will not be distinguished as the theory and practice underlying a particular intervention does not generally differ according to which term is used.

RELATIONSHIP PROBLEM PREVENTION AND RELATIONSHIP ENHANCEMENT

The three main relationship enhancement programmes whose effectiveness has to some extent been empirically evaluated are the Relationship Enhancement Program, the Minnesota Couple Communication Program and the Prevention and Relationship Enhancement Program. The nature of these three programmes will be outlined before research on their effectiveness is described. These programmes are usually offered to couples planning to marry and so are sometimes referred to as premarital programmes.

Relationship Enhancement Program

Since 1962 Bernard Guerney (1977) and his colleagues have been developing highly structured programmes for enhancing various kinds of relationships including parent–child and staff relationships. The basic aim of these programmes is to enable people to express their feelings and to be aware of the feelings of others. The format of the programme includes groups of three or four couples and two co-leaders meeting weekly for 2½ hour sessions for eight or more weeks, or for two alternating eight- and four-hour sessions over a two-month period. Four basic skills or modes are taught: (1) expressing emotions, thoughts and desires accurately; (2) empathic responding to these expressions in an unconditionally accepting manner; (3) switching between expressing and empathic responding; and (4) facilitating the learning of these skills through structuring, demonstrating, modelling, covert rehearsal, behavioural rehearsal, prompting and reinforcement. More recently Guerney and his colleagues (1986) have drawn attention to the five additional skills of problem-conflict resolution, self-change, helping others change, generalization-transfer and maintenance.

Couple Communication Program (CCP)

The Couple Communication Program (CCP), formerly known as the Minnesota Couple Communication Program (MCCP) is conceptually grounded in systems and communication theory (Watzlawick *et al.* 1967) and has been described by Sherod Miller and his colleagues (1976). Five to seven couples meet in a group with two certified instructors for a three-hour session one night per week for four weeks. The programme consists of lectures, exercises, discussions, homework and the reading of the programme text (Miller *et al.* 1975). Each session focuses on a particular conceptual framework and its related skills. The first framework is the Awareness Wheel, which comprises five sections representing the following aspects about oneself which one may disclose to others: sensing, thinking, feeling, wanting and doing. Related to this framework are the six skills of generally speaking for oneself and, more specifically, of disclosing information about the five different aspects of oneself. The second framework is the Shared Meaning Process which consists of the sender sending a message, the receiver restating the message in their own words, and the sender confirming or clarifying the restated message. The aim of this framework is to ensure that the messages are accurately sent and received and the skills include the three stages of that process. The third framework is Communication Styles, which embodies four types organized according to whether they primarily reflect thinking or feeling and being low or high on disclosing or being receptive to others. Skills include identifying the types and impact of the various styles and practising skills such as being aware, active, congruent, accepting, responsible, disclosing, responsive, understanding, caring and cooperative. The fourth and final framework is the I Count/I Count You scheme, in which responsibility is encouraged for enhancing one's own and other people's esteem processes.

Prevention and Relationship Enhancement Program (PREP)

This approach, as outlined by Frank Floyd and his colleagues (1995), is generally based on social learning theory and on research which has investigated factors that best predict relationship satisfaction (e.g. Gottman 1979; Jacobson and Margolin 1979). It assumes that relationship satisfaction results from the exchange of rewarding behaviours between partners and the resolution of conflict in a mutually satisfying way, which does not lead to negative feelings and aggression or withdrawal and avoidance. Originally it was developed in 1980 (Markman and Floyd 1980) and called the Premarital Relationship Enhancement Program (PREP). Since then it has undergone various revisions as a result of ongoing research on relationships.

The programme is available in two formats. In the extended version four to ten couples attend a series of six two-hour weekly sessions. Each presentation or unit consists of a 15- to 45-minute lecture presenting a skill or relationship issue and an accompanying exercise for applying it to their own relationship (Markman et al. 1994). A consultant or coach is assigned to each couple to help them acquire and practise the skill in a private room. Couples are also given weekly homework assignments of skills practice and readings. In the second format 20 to 60 couples hear the lectures in a large group over the course of a single weekend. The programme is typically held in a hotel and couples use their private rooms to practise the skills on their own.

The programme consists of the following skills and relationship issues: (1) the listener hearing the message the speaker intends and factors that disrupt this process; (2) the speaker learning to speak about themselves and about specific aspects, and the listener learning to paraphrase and check what the speaker says; (3) destructive and constructive styles of communicating; (4) the role of expectations and beliefs about communication and relationships; (5) identifying hidden issues or agendas and their effect on communication; (6) the role of fun in relationships; (7) problem discussion and problem solution; (8) discussing issues relevant to the other partner; (9) team-building and relationship commitment; (10) the four spiritual values of honour, respect, intimacy and forgiveness; (11) sensual communication and sexual dysfunction; and (12) developing ground rules for handling differences before they arise.

EMPIRICAL EVALUATION OF ENHANCEMENT PROGRAMMES

A number of studies have tried to evaluate the effectiveness of various enrichment programmes. There are three methods for reviewing similar studies on the same issue, such as the evaluation of these interventions. The traditional method is the *narrative* review in which each study may be described and criticized and where greater weight may be given to the findings of the more methodologically sophisticated studies (e.g. Wampler 1982). The other two methods provide a quantitative index for summarizing the results, which may also consider the effect of methodological rigour on the overall results. The simpler method is a *box score* analysis in which the results of different studies are counted (e.g. Gurman and Kniskern 1977). The more complicated and increasingly used method is *meta-analysis* in which findings are standardized and summarized across studies as *effect sizes* (e.g. Giblin *et al.* 1985; Giblin 1986; Hahlweg and Markman 1988).

A study designed to evaluate the effectiveness of a treatment (such as an enrichment programme) should ideally incorporate the following features. The treatment should be compared with a group not receiving treatment to ensure that treatment is more effective than no treatment since people may improve despite not receiving treatment and it is obviously necessary to show that the improvement in the treated group is greater than that in the untreated group. This group usually consists of people waiting to be treated and so is known as a waiting-list control condition. The treatment should also be compared with another treatment to determine whether the treatment is more effective than other treatments and to control for non-specific factors which may be common to different treatments. In many ways the most appropriate comparison is with a treatment which has been shown to be the most effective, since this should generally be the treatment of choice and would also include the non-specific factors. Participants should be randomly assigned to the different conditions to control for any differences between them, and they should be similar to people typically receiving the form of treatment being evaluated. The treatments should be of the same duration. The person conducting the treatment should be experienced in providing the treatment and should carry out all the treatments being compared. Treatments should be monitored to ensure that the appropriate one is being given. The outcome of treatment should be assessed in various appropriate ways immediately before treatment (pre-test), immediately after treatment has ended (i.e. post-test) and some time later after treatment (i.e. follow-up). Pre-test assessment is important to determine how distressed individuals are and to see whether the distress being treated is similar in the different conditions. Assessment should be carried out by the participant, by someone who knows them well and by a professional assessor who is blind to the treatment the participant has received. The results should be appropriately statistically analysed, and should for each condition include the number of people dropping out and the number becoming worse. Information on other treatments being received by participants at the same time should be sought. Many of the design criteria listed here are essentially similar to those proposed by Alan Gurman and David Kniskern (1978) in their review of marital and family therapy outcome studies.

The first meta-analysis of enrichment outcome studies was reported by Paul Giblin and his colleagues (1985) who analysed the results of 85 studies, 75 per cent of which were unpublished. The effect size was the difference between the change score for the treatment and the untreated group or alternative treatment divided by the standard deviation of the pooled post-test score. Average effect sizes for particular treatments were presented for marital and family therapy but not for premarital therapy. For marital therapy the largest effect size was for Relationship Enhancement (Guerney 1977) which was 0.963 and which was based on 54 effect sizes. This effect size means that the average person treated by Relationship Enhancement was better off than 83 per cent of those not so treated. The next largest effect size was 0.445 (21 effect sizes) for a combined communication and behaviour exchange programme followed by 0.437 (124 effect sizes) for the Couple Communication Program. These latter two effect sizes indicate that the average person treated by either of these two methods was better off than 67 per cent of those not so treated.

Robert Rosenthal and Donald Rubin (1982) suggested that it may be more informative to report an effect size as a binomial effect size display which presents the percentage change attributable to the treatment. The change rate is computed as $(0.50 + r/2) \times 100$ for the treatment group and as $(0.50 - r/2) \times 100$ for the control group. Effect sizes can be transformed into correlations (r) using the formula in Cohen (1969, p. 21). So, an effect size of 0.963 for Relationship Enhancement means that the rate of improvement for the intervention group was 72 per cent compared with 28 per cent for the control group. The rate of improvement for the combined communication and behaviour exchange programme was 61 per cent compared with 39 per cent for the control group, which are the same figures for the Couple Communication Program compared with the control group.

Kurt Hahlweg and Howard Markman (1988) carried out a meta-analysis of seven premarital behavioural interventions which included the three programmes described above. None of the studies compared one programme with another but all of them compared a programme with either an attention-placebo, a waiting-list or a no-treatment control group. Comparing the intervention with a placebo or untreated control gave effect sizes of 1.12 and 0.55 respectively, which is unusual in that the placebo control would be expected to be more effective than the untreated control. The largest effect size was 1.14

for Relationship Enhancement followed by 0.71 for the Couple Communication Program and 0.61 for the Premarital Relationship Enhancement Program.

One of the studies included in the above meta-analysis was by Howard Markman and his colleagues (1988), although it did not incorporate the four- and five-year follow-up which was done subsequently (Markman *et al.* 1993). In this study 42 premarital American couples were selected from a larger sample of 135 couples taking part in research on couples planning marriage. The 42 couples had a mean age of about 24, and 60 per cent of them were engaged. Couples were matched on four criteria and were then randomly assigned to either no treatment or the Premarital Relationship Enhancement Program where they received five three-hour sessions in groups of three to five couples. The four matching criteria were confidence in getting married, engaged versus planning marriage, relationship satisfaction and the positiveness of the impact of their communication on one another. There were 21 couples in each of the two conditions. Couples not receiving treatment were unaware they were in the control condition. About 50 per cent of the 85 couples offered the programme declined to take it and nine of the 42 couples starting did not complete it, so the control group probably included couples who would not have taken the programme or completed it. It is not known what effect this factor had on the results of the study. The effect of the programme was primarily measured in terms of the Marital Adjustment Test (Locke and Wallace 1959), the Relationship Problem Inventory (Knox 1970; Markman *et al.* 1994, p. 98) and Communication Impact (Markman and Floyd 1980) immediately before and after the programme and 18 and 36 months later. Treated couples tended to have higher relationship satisfaction, less severe problems and more positive communication impact than untreated couples at post-test and follow-up, although these differences were only significant for relationship satisfaction at 18 and 36 months and for problem intensity at 36 months. The only sex difference was that men were less satisfied than women at 36 months. Perhaps the most impressive finding was that more couples in the control than in the intervention group had broken up at 18 and 36 months. However, when I re-analysed the data using a one-tailed Fisher's exact test, the difference was only almost significant at 18 months ($p = 0.053$) and 36 months ($p = 0.092$). At 18 months 19 per cent (four couples) in the control group and none in the intervention group had broken up ($r = 0.32$), while at 36 months 24 per cent (five couples) in the control group and 5 per cent (one couple) in the intervention group had split up ($r = 0.27$).

In a subsequent paper Markman and his colleagues (1993) reported the results for relationship satisfaction at four- and five-year follow-ups for 25 couples who completed the programme, 42 couples who declined to participate in the programme and 47 couples who served as untreated controls. The only significant difference in relationship satisfaction between these three groups was that at five years men in the control group had lower relationship satisfaction than men in the treatment group. It would appear, therefore, that any beneficial effect in relationship satisfaction due to the programme was not readily apparent four or five years later. More couples in the control than in the intervention group broke up before marriage at both the four- and five-year follow-ups. When I re-analysed the results for these two groups with a one-tailed Fisher's exact test the differences were significant at both follow-ups. At four years, 21 per cent (10 couples) in the control group and 4 per cent (one couple) in the intervention group had parted ($r = 0.23$), while at five years 25 per cent (12 couples) in the control group and 4 per cent (one couple) in the intervention group had split up ($r = 0.27$). However, there were no differences between the two conditions at either follow-up in the number of couples who broke up *after* they had married. At four years, 10 per cent (three couples) in the control group and 4 per cent (one couple) in the intervention group had separated ($r = 0.11$), while at five years 16 per cent (five couples) in the control group and 8 per cent (two couples) in the intervention group had split up ($r = 0.27$).

Two studies not covered in Hahlweg and Markman's (1988) meta-analysis were that of Karen Wampler and Douglas Sprenkle (1980) and that of Gregory Brock and Harvey Joanning (1983) on American couples. Wampler and Sprenkle compared the effectiveness of six 2½-hour sessions of the Couple Communication Program with an attention-placebo control condition in which enrichment programmes were outlined and discussed but training in communication skills was not provided. The 43 couples taking part had volunteered for a course in couple relationship skills training, and were married undergraduates primarily with a mean age of 25. Couples were matched for type and length of relationship and randomly assigned to the two conditions. A cross-over design was used in which couples initially assigned to one condition subsequently received the other condition. The two main measures were a behavioural measure of the openness of the couple communication style, and the Barrett-Lennard (1962) Relationship Inventory which assesses the extent to which the partner feels that the other person behaves towards them in an unconditionally accepting, empathic and congruent manner. These measures were taken immediately before and after the first phase and 23 weeks later. The cross-over design was not fully implemented in that there was no post-test immediately after the second phase. Twelve couples were not available for follow-up testing. The analysis was weakened by not including the data for all participants who had completed the first phase. None the less, participants showed a significant improvement between pre- and post-test in terms of openness of communication and level of acceptance and congruence. Comparison between the two conditions at follow-up was less meaningful as all participants had by then also received the training programme.

Brock and Joanning (1983) compared the effectiveness of 20 hours (spread over 10 weeks) of relationship enhancement (Guerney 1977) and of couple communication in married couples. The couple communication programme included an extra eight hours of treatment to make it the same duration as the relationship enhancement intervention. Six of these hours were devoted to problem-solving, which is not a standard part of the programme. One group for each of the interventions was run by the same pair of trainers. Couples were recruited from the community to take part in communication skills training to improve their marriage. Twenty-six couples were randomly assigned to each condition. Six couples withdrew from the couple communication programme, but none of these expressed dissatisfaction with the programme. The effectiveness of the two programmes was assessed by the Dyadic Adjustment Scale, Bienvenu's (1970) Marital Communication Inventory (Schumm *et al.* 1983) and a behavioural measure of communication skill at pre-test, mid-test, post-test and three months after the post-test. At pre-test the mean score of couples on the Dyadic Adjustment Scale was below average for Spanier's (1976) original sample. The standard 10-week relationship enhancement programme was compared with both the 10-week and the standard four-week couple communication programme at post-test. In both comparisons the relationship enhancement programme was more effective than the couple communication programme on all three measures. At follow-up, however, the relationship enhancement group was significantly more effective than the extended couple communication condition on only the communication measure and the consensus and satisfaction sub-scales of the Dyadic Adjustment Scale.

Although meta-analyses suggest that the relationship enhancement programme is more effective than the couple communication or the prevention and relationship enhancement programme when compared with a non-treatment control condition, too few studies have evaluated these treatments within the same design to enable a direct comparison to be made of their effectiveness.

RELATIONSHIP THERAPY

Various theoretical approaches to relationship therapy have been developed such as psychoanalytic marital therapy (Dare 1986) and Bowen's family systems marital therapy (Aylmer 1986). However, there have only been attempts to evaluate what have usually been referred to as behavioural marital therapy, cognitive-behavioural marital therapy and emotionally focused couple therapy. Consequently only these three approaches will be briefly outlined.

Behavioural Marital Therapy (BMT)

Behavioural marital therapy, as it was initially known, was largely developed by Neil Jacobson and Gayla Margolin (1979) on the basis of social learning and behaviour exchange principles. Its original therapeutic techniques included behaviour exchange procedures, communication training, problem-solving training, cognitive restructuring, contingency contracting and paradoxical directives. Behaviour exchange refers to increasing the frequency of positive exchanges in the relationship. Communication training may involve teaching general skills such as empathy and listening as well as the specific skill of problem-solving through the use of feedback, instructions and behaviour rehearsal. Guidelines for solving problems include beginning with a positive issue, being specific, discussing only one problem at a time and focusing on solutions. Cognitive restructuring includes modifying faulty attributions about the partner's behaviour, mistaken concepts about love and unrealistic expectations about intimacy. A contingency contract is a written agreement about changing relationship behaviour and the consequences of carrying out or not carrying out those changes. Paradoxical directives are instructions to the couple to engage in behaviour they want to eliminate. It is generally advocated that these latter two techniques should only be used in special circumstances.

Partly as a result of recognizing that improving relationships may be more difficult than at first envisaged, behavioural marital therapy has undergone two major shifts which have effectively broadened its conceptual basis and techniques by placing greater emphasis on cognitive and affective variables. Neil Jacobson and Amy Holtzworth-Munroe (1986) referred to the first revision as the social learning-cognitive (SLC) model while Andrew Christensen and his colleagues (1995) called the second revision integrative behavioural couple therapy (IBCT). In the social learning-cognitive model the lack of appropriate behaviour is more frequently seen as a skills deficit which commonly involves problem-solving and receiving and expressing feelings. Much of therapy, which usually consists of 20 weekly sessions of 60 to 90 minutes each, is concerned with learning these skills through the use of homework assignments. More attention is paid to maintaining and generalizing positive change by increasing the interval between sessions and having booster sessions. The technique of troubleshooting has been introduced to explore the thoughts, feelings and possible alternative behaviours that occur when negative conflict escalates. Problems may be conceived as being individual rather than relationship ones and treated as such. Recognition is given to themes underlying the relationship which may need to be explored to facilitate progress. Assessment includes the option of not proceeding with marital therapy.

Integrative behavioural couple therapy recognizes that behaviour change is not always possible or desirable, and that emotional acceptance of problems may be necessary by itself or as a prelude to change. The following four strategies have been developed to promote emotional acceptance. The problem may be reformulated in terms of how it affects the couple's feelings rather than who is responsible for it. The problem may be discussed in a more detached and objective way as if it existed outside the couple. Negative aspects of the problem may be desensitized by emphasizing their positive features and through role-playing. Couples may be encouraged to be more self-reliant.

Cognitive-Behavioural Marital Therapy (CBMT)

Cognitive-behavioural marital therapy as developed by Donald Baucom and Norman Epstein (Baucom and Epstein 1990; Baucom et al. 1995) pays attention to cognitions that appear to be related to marital distress as well as behaviour and emotions. There are at least five different types of cognition that may underlie marital distress: these include selective attention, attributions, expectancies, assumptions and standards. Distressed couples tend to focus on certain aspects of their interactions, such as perceiving them in linear causal terms rather than in more complex circular processes, which causes them to engage in destructive mutual blaming. They tend to attribute or explain past events in negative rather than positive ways. They expect future events to be negative. They are more likely to hold assumptions such as that disagreement is destructive and relationships cannot be changed. Finally, they are more likely to have standards or values about the relationship that are not being met. The aims of cognitive interventions are to enable couples to identify cognitions that are associated with marital distress, to assess their validity or appropriateness, and to change those that are invalid or inappropriate. There are various techniques for carrying out these aims. For example, couples may be helped to identify attributions and expectancies by encouraging them to ask themselves how they are interpreting their partner's behaviour.

Emotionally Focused Couples Therapy (EFT)

Emotionally focused couples therapy has been developed by Leslie Greenberg and Susan Johnson (1986, 1988) using concepts from the experiential and systemic approaches and, more recently, attachment theory (Johnson and Greenberg 1995). It assumes that relationship distress results from rigid, repetitive negative interaction patterns that prevent emotional engagement and the satisfaction of essentially healthy attachment needs of security, protection and closeness. The main problems in relationship distress are seen as the inability to respond effectively to the other, the inaccessibility of feelings and the resulting lack of engagement or contact.

Therapy essentially consists of enabling couples to become aware of and to express the feelings which underlie their negative reactions to each other, and in so doing to evoke new positive responses which satisfy their attachment needs. The therapist is active in helping couples to access their feelings, to express them within the relationship and thereby to restructure and to reframe the relationship. For example, the negative interaction of a couple may consist of the wife criticizing and blaming the husband who then withdraws. The husband comes to realize that he copes with his negative feelings, including his fear of losing his wife, by withdrawing and distancing himself from those feelings. The wife begins to acknowledge that she handles her negative feelings, including her fear of being abandoned by her husband by being angry. By experiencing each other as being vulnerable and in need of care, each partner is then able to give the love and care desired by the other partner.

Therapy usually consists of 12 to 20 sessions involving the following nine steps: (1) delineating conflict issues in the core struggle; (2) identifying the negative interaction cycle; (3) accessing unacknowledged feelings underlying the interaction positions; (4) reframing the problem in terms of underlying feelings, attachment needs and negative cycles; (5) promoting identification with disowned needs and integrating these into the relationship interactions; (6) promoting acceptance of the partner's experience and new interaction patterns; (7) facilitating the expression of needs and creating emotional engagement; (8) facilitating the emergence of new solutions; and (9) consolidating new positions. Homework assignments are also given, which are typically awareness exercises.

EMPIRICAL EVALUATION OF RELATIONSHIP THERAPY

There have been two major meta-analyses of marital therapy. The first, by Kurt Hahlweg and Howard Markman (1988), was solely concerned with studies of behavioural marital therapy, of which there were 17. The second, by Ryan Dunn and Andrew Schwebel (1995), included studies of insight-oriented marital therapy and was based on 15 studies in all. Comparing behavioural marital therapy with a waiting-list control or non-specific control condition gave effect sizes of 1.03 and 0.63 respectively, while comparing it with a behaviour exchange programme only or a programme combining behaviour exchange, communication skills and problem-solving training produced effect sizes of 0.78 and 1.00 respectively. It seems surprising that the effect size of behavioural marital therapy compared with a waiting-list control condition (1.03) was found to be similar to the effect size of behavioural marital therapy compared to three of its components (1.00), which would be expected to be more effective than a waiting-list control condition. It was not clear whether the same form of behavioural marital therapy was being evaluated in these four comparisons. Dunn and Schwebel (1995) presented their analyses in terms of whether the outcome measure used assessed behaviour, irrational beliefs, feelings or relationship quality and whether the outcome was assessed immediately after the intervention or some time later. To simplify matters, the results are presented here for only one of the measures at one time. Because relationship quality was the most common measure and because time of follow-up varied markedly from one to 48 months, relationship quality at post-test was chosen. The largest effect size was 1.37 for the insight-oriented intervention, followed by 0.78 for the behavioural treatment and 0.71 for the cognitive-behavioural one.

Meta-analyses give little indication of the nature of the studies that are included in them, so some of the better-designed studies will be outlined. All these studies compare behavioural marital therapy with some other treatment. An early study by Neil Jacobson (1978) in the United States compared the effectiveness of eight weekly one- to 1½-hour sessions of two forms of marital behaviour therapy with a non-specific and a waiting-list control condition in 32 couples mainly recruited through advertisements for couples experiencing marital problems. Behavioural marital therapy consisted of communication and problem-solving training with contingency contracting. The two behavioural groups differed in terms of the type of contracting. One group used good faith or parallel contracts, in which partners agree to actions which are not dependent on whether the other person carries out their obligation; the other group used 'quid pro quo' contracts, in which one person only carries out their agreed action if the other person has already performed theirs. In the non-specific control condition a couple discussed their problem until they reached some agreement. The therapist only participated in these discussions by asking factual questions, by primarily restating the apparent feelings underlying what was said, by interpreting the couple's interaction and by disclosing relevant personal information. Jacobson (1978) reported that couples' expectations about the effectiveness of this treatment were similar to those of the couples receiving the behavioural treatment, although details of which items were used were not given. Couples were randomly assigned to the four conditions and to one of three therapists who each carried out the three treatments. Outcome was measured before and after treatment with the Marital Adjustment Test (Locke and Wallace 1959), the Marital Happiness Scale (Stuart and Stuart 1973) and the rate of positive and negative responses observed when solving a hypothetical as well as a real but minor marital problem (Weiss and Summers 1983). The Marital Adjustment Test was also given one, three and six months after treatment had ended. In general there was no difference in the effectiveness of the two behavioural treatments, and both of them were more effective than the two control conditions. In addition, the two behavioural treatments combined were more effective than the non-specific condition at follow-up.

Jacobson (1984) also compared the effectiveness of 12–16 one- to 1½-hour sessions of the two major components of behavioural marital therapy, those of behaviour exchange and the training of communication and problem-solving, with the two components combined and a waiting-list control condition in 36 married American couples. It was thought that while the behaviour exchange component may have a more immediate effect on outcome by improving the positiveness of the couples' interaction, communication and problem-solving training may have a more delayed impact through teaching couples how to solve their problems in the long term. The effects of therapy were assessed immediately before and after treatment by the Dyadic Adjustment Scale (Spanier 1976), a marital problems checklist (Weiss et al. 1973; Margolin et al. 1983) and a 14-day record of positive and negative behaviours noted by the spouse (Weiss and Perry 1983). The first two measures were also given six months later. Couples were randomly assigned to one of the four conditions. Surprisingly, the average number of sessions for the three treatments was not reported or taken into account. At post-test all three treatments showed greater marital satisfaction and fewer marital problems than the waiting-list control but there were no differences between the three treatments. The results concerning the ratio of positive responses shown by the spouse at home were more complicated, but generally the combined and the behaviour exchange treatment indicated more positive change than the other two conditions. At the six-month follow-up the combined and the communication and problem-solving treatments maintained their improvement more than the behaviour exchange treatment.

For this study, Jacobson and his colleagues reported the follow-up results for 43 couples at one year (Jacobson *et al.* 1985) and for 34 couples at two years (Jacobson *et al.* 1987). In both follow-up studies, there were no significant differences in marital satisfaction and the number of marital problems, although couples receiving the combined treatment were more likely to be happily married and less likely to be divorced or separated than those who received either component. For example, at the one-year follow-up three couples (21 per cent) in the behaviour exchange treatment and five couples (38 per cent) in the communication and problem-solving treatment divorced or separated, compared with none in the combined treatment.

In a German study Kurt Hahlweg and his colleagues (1982) compared the effects of 15 sessions of behavioural marital therapy with the component of communication training on its own and a waiting-list control in 85 married couples mainly recruited through radio announcements. Couples were randomly assigned to the three conditions and treated either as a couple on their own or in a group of couples. There were six therapists, each of whom carried out the two treatments. The effects of the treatments were assessed immediately before and after treatment with a relationship questionnaire, a list of problems, a general happiness rating and the frequency of positive and negative responses made when discussing a hypothetical and a real marital problem (Weiss and Summers 1983). The first three measures were also given six and 12 months after treatment. At post-test the two treatments were generally more effective than the waiting-list control. At both follow-ups there was a tendency for marital behavioural therapy to be more effective than communication training.

Several studies have investigated the effects of incorporating a cognitive intervention within behavioural marital therapy. In the United States Donald Baucom and Gregory Lester (1986) compared the effects of 12 weekly 1½-hour sessions of either behavioural marital therapy or combined cognitive and behavioural marital therapy with a waiting-list control in 24 maritally distressed couples. The behavioural treatment consisted of communication and problem-solving training followed by 'quid pro quo' contracting, while the cognitive treatment focused on the couples' attributions for marital problems and their expectations about each other and the marital relationship. Couples were randomly assigned to the three conditions. Two experienced therapists carried out both treatments. Outcome was assessed immediately before and after therapy with the Dyadic Adjustment Scale (Spanier 1976), a marital problems checklist (Weiss *et al.* 1973; Margolin *et al.* 1983), the Relationship Beliefs Inventory (Epstein and Eidelson 1981; see Baucom and Epstein 1990, pp. 442–4), the Irrational Beliefs Test (Jones 1968) and problem-solving, positive and negative verbal behaviour observed when solving two marital problems (Weiss and Summers 1983). The first four measures were also completed six months after therapy. In general there were no differences between the two treatments after therapy and at follow-up but both treatments were more effective than no treatment. Only couples in the combined treatment showed decreased irrational beliefs.

In a subsequent study Baucom and his colleagues (1990) compared the effects of 12 weekly sessions of four treatments with a waiting-list control in 60 maritally distressed couples. The four treatments were behavioural marital therapy on its own or combined with cognitive restructuring, emotional expressiveness training or both. Behavioural marital therapy consisted of problem-solving skills and 'quid pro quo' contracts, while emotional expressiveness training was based on Guerney's (1977) relationship enhancement programme and involved expressing emotions, responding empathically and switching between the two. It was anticipated that behavioural marital therapy on its own would be less effective than when combined with other components, and that the improvements shown should reflect the skills taught so that, for example, couples receiving the cognitive component should show greater cognitive change. Couples were randomly assigned to one of the five conditions and one of four therapists who carried out each of the treatments. General change immediately after treatment was assessed with the Dyadic Adjustment Scale while changes in behaviour, cognition and emotion were measured with various other tests such as the Marital Interaction Coding System (Weiss and Summers 1983) for behaviour, the Relationship Beliefs Inventory (Epstein and Eidelson 1981) for cognition and the Verbal Interaction Task (Guerney 1977) for emotion. The Dyadic Adjustment Scale and a self-report on marital problems were given at six months follow-up. Overall, the four treatments were more effective than no treatment and there were few differences between the treatments. The nature of improvement generally reflected the focus of the treatment so, for instance, cognitive restructuring resulted in lower irrational beliefs.

Kim Halford and his colleagues (1993) in Australia compared the effects of 12–15 weekly 1½-hour sessions of either behavioural marital therapy or enhanced behavioural marital therapy in 26 maritally distressed couples. Behavioural marital therapy consisted of behaviour exchange and communication and problem-solving training, while the enhanced treatment included cognitive restructuring, exploring feelings in stressful interactions and carrying out communication tasks in problematical situations at home. Note that this study does not simply evaluate the effects of adding a cognitive component as the enhanced treatment included other elements. Couples were randomly assigned to one of the two conditions and to one of five therapists, each of whom conducted both treatments. Outcome was assessed at the start and end of therapy and three months later with various measures including the Dyadic Adjustment Scale, the Relationship Beliefs Inventory and the number of negative responses in recorded interactions in the clinic and at home. In general, the two treatments did not differ in their effectiveness (apart from a greater decrease in negative responses for behavioural marital therapy) and both treatments produced improvement.

Finally, a number of studies have compared the effects of behavioural marital therapy with non-behavioural methods such as emotionally focused couple therapy and insight-oriented marital therapy. In Canada Susan Johnson and Leslie Greenberg (1985) evaluated the effects of eight weekly one-hour sessions of either behavioural or emotionally focused marital therapy with a waiting-list control in 45 maritally distressed couples recruited through a newspaper article. Couples were randomly assigned to one of the three conditions and to one of the six therapists carrying out one of the two treatments. The two treatments were monitored to ensure that they were appropriately implemented and distinguishable. Outcome was assessed before and after treatment and two months later with various self-report measures including the Dyadic Adjustment Scale and the Personal Assessment of Intimacy in Relationships Inventory (Schaefer and Olson 1981). Overall, the two treatments were more effective than the waiting-list control while the emotionally focused treatment was more effective on some of the measures (such as marital satisfaction and cohesion) than the behavioural treatment.

In another Canadian study Paul James (1991) compared the effects of 12 weekly one-hour sessions of emotionally focused couple therapy (on its own or combined with communication training) with a waiting-list control in 42 distressed couples recruited through newspaper articles. The communication training consisted of four sessions based on Guerney's Relationship Enhancement programme but which also included distinguishing primary from secondary emotions. Couples were randomly assigned to the three conditions. Fourteen postgraduate counselling students were randomly assigned to be trained in and to administer one or other treatment. The two treatments were monitored to ensure that they were appropriately administered and distinct. Various self-report measures such as the Dyadic Adjustment Scale, the Communication Scale (Fournier et al. 1983) and Target Complaints (Battle et al. 1966) were completed immediately before and after treatment and four months later. At post-test both treatments were better than the control condition in terms of relationship satisfaction and the three main relationship complaints. The combined treatment was superior to the control condition in communication at post-test and to the single treatment in relationship complaints at follow-up.

In the United States Douglas Snyder and Robert Wills (1989) compared the effects of about 19 sessions of behavioural marital therapy, insight-oriented marital therapy and a waiting-list control in 79 maritally distressed couples recruited through newspaper advertisements. The insight-oriented treatment emphasized the interpretation and resolution of intrapersonal and interpersonal emotional conflicts contributing to current marital difficulties. It also dealt with developmental issues, collusive interactions, incongruent expectations and maladaptive relationship rules. Couples were randomly assigned to the three conditions and to one of five therapists within the two treatments. Five eclectic therapists were trained to carry out both treatments and the two treatments were monitored to ensure that they were appropriately implemented and distinct. Outcome before and after treatment and six months later was assessed with both self-report measures such as the Global Distress Scale of the Marital Satisfaction Inventory (Snyder 1979) and observational measures of verbal agreement and positive non-verbal behaviour when discussing marital problems (Gottman *et al.* 1977). In general, both treatments showed a similar increase in improvement compared to the waiting-list control, which was maintained at follow-up.

Four years after treatment had ended Snyder and his colleagues (1991) found that 38 per cent of the behavioural marital therapy couples had divorced compared with only 3 per cent of the insight-oriented marital therapy couples. There were no differences between the two treatments in the percentages receiving additional marital or individual therapy subsequently. Commenting on these findings, Neil Jacobson (1991) noted that none of the 31 intervention techniques listed in the training manual for insight-oriented marital therapy were incompatible with behavioural marital therapy. He suggested that restricting the use of these techniques in the behavioural treatment may have led to this differential effect.

Studies evaluating the effectiveness of marital therapy have generally shown that while therapy is more effective than no treatment, there is little evidence that one form of treatment is consistently better than another. If one adopts the more stringent criterion that couples should only be considered improved if their subsequent score is one or more standard deviations above their pre-treatment score and falls above a cut-off point which indicates that they are within the range of non-distressed couples, then Neil Jacobson and his colleagues (1987) found that only 50 per cent of couples receiving behavioural marital therapy could be considered to be improved two years later. In other words, half the couples had not improved, indicating that there is considerable scope for enhancing the effectiveness of this, the most extensively evaluated, method. The results for insight-oriented marital therapy are more promising but so far are based on only one study.

SEPARATION COUNSELLING AND MEDIATION

Relationship or marital therapy is usually undertaken with couples who have not yet decided to separate or divorce. Separation or divorce interventions, on the other hand, typically involve couples who have decided to part. Various forms of such interventions may be distinguished. Mediation is concerned with trying to help separating couples to come to an agreed settlement over various disputes, such as custody of the children, without recourse to litigation. Reconciliation involves preventing couples from separating. Conciliation, counselling or therapy aims to help couples come to terms with their separation. Douglas Sprenkle and Cheryl Storm (1983) reviewed some of the earlier studies attempting to evaluate the outcome of these approaches and acknowledged the methodological weaknesses of many of them. Since then no new studies appear to have been published. Consequently, three of the better-designed studies covered in this earlier review will be outlined.

In the United States Jessica Pearson and Nancy Thoennes (1982) compared the effects of mediation with no mediation on 274 parents who were expected to contest child custody and visitation and who were randomly assigned to these two groups. The no mediation group were interviewed on three occasions: as soon as they had filed court documents indicating they disagreed with the custody and visit arrangements; shortly after the court had promulgated the final orders concerning these matters; and six to 12 months later. The mediation group were interviewed on four occasions: before and after mediation; soon after the court had promulgated final orders; and six to 12 months later.

The results were based on 54 individuals who did not receive mediation, 95 individuals who rejected the mediation offer and 125 individuals who mediated, of whom 61 reached agreement and 64 did not. No explanation was given as to why random assignment should have resulted in such different numbers in the mediation and no mediation groups other than that both parents were more likely to be interviewed in the mediation group than in the other two samples. No information was provided to show that the samples were equivalent on basic sociodemographic variables. Few details of the mediation intervention were given except that individuals were assigned to male–female teams consisting of lawyers and mental health professionals trained in mediation techniques.

The four groups were compared on various measures although whether the differences were statistically significant was not determined. In general, the mediation group had more positive outcomes than the no mediation group. For example, 82 per cent of the mediation group reached agreement compared to 53 per cent in the group rejecting mediation and 48 per cent in the no mediation group. About 50 per cent of the mediation group reported improved co-operation with their ex-partner compared with 18 per cent in the group rejecting mediation and 24 per cent in the no mediation group. However, it is not clear what effect the differing proportions of couples in these groups had on these results.

Margaret Hickman and Bruce Baldwin (1971) evaluated the effects of eight twice-weekly one-hour sessions of communication training provided by a counsellor or a text with a waiting-list control in 30 American couples who petitioned the Conciliation Court for help in resolving their marital difficulties. Ten couples were randomly assigned to each of the three groups and there was only one counsellor. Outcome was measured after treatment in terms of the change in participants' rating of four aspects of the relationship on each of 12 scales and whether they signed a court document agreeing to continue their marriage. On both these measures couples receiving communication training from the counsellor showed a significantly more positive outcome than those in the waiting-list control group. However, no information is given as to how seriously couples were considering divorce and there was no follow-up.

Jake Thiessen and his colleagues (1980) compared the effect of five three-hour weekly group sessions of communication training with no training on post-divorce adjustment as measured by the Fisher (1977) Divorce Adjustment Scale, in 28 American women who had been physically separated from their spouse for no more than nine months and for three months on average. Participants were assigned to the two conditions according to their availability and there was no follow-up assessment. Women in the treatment group reported significantly greater adjustment than those in the control group.

While the results of these few studies indicate that separation interventions may have beneficial effects, more and better-controlled studies need to be carried out to be more certain about the reliability of such effects.

SUMMARY

Various interventions have been developed to help individuals and couples try to resolve serious difficulties that have arisen in their relationship, to prevent these problems from arising and to cope with problems of separation. The effects of some of these interventions have been evaluated empirically, mainly by comparing them with no-treatment control conditions and to a lesser extent with treatments consisting of components constituting that treatment. Preventive interventions that have been found to be more effective than no treatment include the Relationship Enhancement, the Couple Communication and the Prevention and Relationship Enhancement Programs. Each of these programmes teaches couples to communicate more effectively. Interventions for seriously distressed couples that have been shown to be more effective than no treatment are behavioural, cognitive-behavioural, emotionally focused and insight-oriented couple therapy. A component common to these approaches is an attempt to help couples to decrease their more negative interactions. Separation interventions remain to be evaluated more rigorously.

References

Ainsworth, M. D. S., Blehar, M. C., Waters, E. and Wall, S. 1978: *Patterns of attachment: A psychological study of the strange situation.* Hillsdale, NJ: Erlbaum.

Anda, R., Williamson, D., Jones, D., Macera, C., Eaker, E., Glassman, A. and Marks, J. 1993: Depressed affect, hopelessness, and the risk of ischemic heart disease in a cohort of U.S. adults. *Epidemiology* 4, 285–94.

Anderson, S. A., Russell, C. S. and Schumm, W. R. 1983: Perceived marital quality and family life-cycle categories: A further analysis. *Journal of Marriage and the Family* 45, 127–39.

Anonymous 1903: Assortative mating in man. A cooperative study. *Biometrika* 2, 481–98.

Antill, J. K. 1983: Sex role complementarity versus similarity in married couples. *Journal of Personality and Social Psychology* 45, 145–55.

Arias, I., Samios, M. and O'Leary, K. D. 1987: Prevalence and correlates of physical aggression during courtship. *Journal of Interpersonal Violence* 2, 82–90.

Ashford, S. 1987: Family matters. In Jowell, R., Witherspoon, S. and Brook, L. (eds), *British social attitudes: The 1987 report.* Aldershot: Gower, 121–52.

Auerbach, R. and Kilmann, P. R. 1977: The effects of group systematic desensitization on secondary erectile failure. *Behavior Therapy* 8, 330–9.

Aylmer, R. C. 1986: Bowen family systems marital therapy. In Jacobson, N. S. and Gurman, A. S. (eds), *Clinical handbook of marital therapy.* New York: Guilford Press, 107–48.

Bach, G. R. and Wyden, P. 1969: *The intimate enemy: How to fight fair in love and marriage.* New York: Morrow.

Bakker, C. B. and Bakker-Radbau, M. K. 1973: *No trespassing.* San Francisco: Chandler and Sharp.

Barefoot, J. C. and Schroll, M. 1996: Symptoms of depression, acute myocardial infarction, and total mortality in a community sample. *Circulation* 93, 1976–80.

Barrera, M., Sandler, I. N. and Ramsay, T. B. 1981: Preliminary development of a scale of social support. *American Journal of Community Psychology* 9, 435–47.

Barrett-Lennard, G. T. 1962: Dimensions of therapist response as causal factors in therapeutic change. *Psychological Monographs: General and Applied* 76 (43, Whole No. 562).

Barrett-Lennard, G. T. 1964: The Relationship Inventory: Forms OS-M-64, OS-F-64 and MO-M-64 plus MO-F-64. Unpublished manuscript, University of New England, Australia.

Bartholomew, K. and Horowitz, L. M. 1991: Attachment styles among young adults: A test of a four-category model. *Journal of Personality and Social Psychology* **61**, 226–44.

Battle, C. G., Imber, S. D., Hoehen-Saric, R., Stone, A. R., Nash, E. R. and Frank, J. D. 1966: Target complaints as criteria of improvement. *American Journal of Psychotherapy* **20**, 184–92.

Baucom, D. H. and Epstein, N. 1990: *Cognitive behavioral marital therapy*. New York: Brunner/Mazel.

Baucom, D. H., Epstein, N. and Rankin, L. A. 1995: Cognitive aspects of cognitive-behavioral marital therapy. In Jacobson, N. S. and Gurman, A. S. (eds), *Clinical handbook of couple therapy*. New York: Guilford Press, 65–90.

Baucom, D. H. and Lester, G. W. 1986: The usefulness of cognitive restructuring as an adjunct to behavioral marital therapy. *Behavior Therapy* **17**, 385–403.

Baucom, D. H., Sayers, S. L. and Sher, T. G. 1990: Supplementing behavioral marital therapy with cognitive restructuring and emotional expressiveness training: An outcome investigation. *Journal of Consulting and Clinical Psychology* **58**, 636–45.

Beach, S. R. H. and O'Leary, K. D. 1993: Dysphoria and marital discord: Are dysphoric individuals at risk for marital adjustment? *Journal of Marital and Family Therapy* **19**, 355–68.

Beck, A. T. and Beck, R. W. 1972: Screening depressed patients in family practice: A rapid technic. *Postgraduate Medicine* **52**, 81–5.

Beck, A. T., Ward, C. H., Mendelson, M., Mock, J. and Erbaugh, J. 1961: An inventory for measuring depression. *Archives of General Psychiatry* **4**, 561–71.

Bem, S. L. 1974: The measurement of psychological androgyny. *Journal of Consulting and Clinical Psychology* **42**, 155–62.

Ben-Shlomo, Y., Davey Smith, G., Shipley, M. and Marmot, M.G. 1993: Magnitude and causes of mortality differences between married and unmarried men. *Journal of Epidemiology and Community Health* **47**, 200–5.

Bentler, P. M. 1968a: Heterosexual behavior assessment - I. Males. *Behaviour Research and Therapy* **6**, 21–5.

Bentler, P. M. 1968b: Heterosexual behavior assessment - II. Females. *Behaviour Research and Therapy* **6**, 27–30.

Bentler, P. M. and Newcomb, M. D. 1978: Longitudinal study of marital success and failure. *Journal of Consulting and Clinical Psychology* **46**, 1053–70.

Berg, J. H. and McQuinn, R. D. 1986: Attraction and exchange in continuing and non-continuing dating relationships. *Journal of Personality and Social Psychology* **50**, 942–52.

Berkman, L. F. and Syme, L. 1979: Social networks, host resistance, and mortality: A nine-year follow-up study of Alameda County residents. *American Journal of Epidemiology* **109**, 186–204.

Bernard, J. 1934: Factors in the distribution of marital success. *American Journal of Sociology* **40**, 49–60.

Berscheid, E., Dion, K., Walster, E. and Walster, G. W. 1971: Physical attractiveness and dating choice: A test of the matching hypothesis. *Journal of Experimental Social Psychology* **7**, 173–89.

Berscheid, E., Snyder, M. and Omoto, A. M. 1989: The Relationship Closeness Inventory: Assessing the closeness of interpersonal relationships. *Journal of Personality and Social Psychology* **57**, 792–807.

Bertillon, A. 1859: Mariage. In *Dictionnaire encyclopédique des sciences médicales* 2nd series.

Bertillon, M. J. 1879: Les célibataires, les veufs and les divorcés au point de vue du mariage. *Revue Scientifique* February, 776–83.

Bienvenu, M. J. 1970: Measurement of marital communication. *The Family Coordinator* **19**, 26–30.

Billings, A. 1979: Conflict resolution in distressed and nondistressed married couples. *Journal of Consulting and Clinical Psychology* **47**, 368–76.

Birchler, G. R., Weiss, R. L. and Vincent, J. P. 1975: Multimethod analysis of social reinforcement exchange between maritally distressed and nondistressed spouse and stranger dyads. *Journal of Personality and Social Psychology* **31**, 349–60.

Blau, P. M. 1964: *Exchange and power in social life*. New York: John Wiley.

Blazer, D. G. 1982: Social support and mortality in an elderly community population. *American Journal of Epidemiology* **115**, 684–94.

Blood, J. O., Jr. and Wolfe, D. M. 1960: *Husbands and wives: The dynamics of married living*. Westport, CT: Greenwood.

Booth, A. and Edwards, J. N. 1992: Starting over: Why remarriages are more unstable. *Journal of Family Issues* **13**, 179–94.

Booth, A. and Johnson, D. 1988: Premarital cohabitation and marital success. *Journal of Family Issues* **9**, 255–72.

Braiker, H. B. and Kelley, H. H. 1979: Conflict in the development of close relationships. In Burgess, R. L. and Huston, T. L. (eds), *Social exchange in developing relationships*. New York: Academic Press, 135–68.

Brock, G. W. and Joanning, H. 1983: A comparison of the Relationship Enhancement Program and the Minnesota Couple Communication Program. *Journal of Marital and Family Therapy* **9**, 413–21.

Broderick, J. E. and O'Leary, K. D. 1986: Contributions of affect, attitudes, and behavior to marital satisfaction. *Journal of Consulting and Clinical Psychology* **54**, 514–17.

Brook, L. and Witherspoon, S. 1987: *British Social Attitudes 1986 Survey Technical Report*. London: SCPR.

Bryman, A. and Cramer, D. 1997: *Quantitative data analysis with SPSS for Windows: A guide for social scientists*. London: Routledge.

Bumpass, L. L. and Sweet, J. A. 1972: Differentials in marital instability: 1970. *American Sociological Review* **37**, 754–66.

Bumpass, L. L. and Sweet, J. A. 1989: National estimates of cohabitation. *Demography* **26**, 615–25.

Bumpass, L. L., Sweet, J. A. and Cherlin, A. 1991: The role of cohabitation in declining rates of marriage. *Journal of Marriage and the Family* **53**, 913–27.

Burgess, E. W. and Cottrell, L., Jr. 1939: *Predicting success or failure in marriage*. New York: Prentice-Hall.

Burgess, E. W., Locke, H. J. and Thomes, M. M. 1971: *The family from institution to companionship*. New York: American Book.

Burgess, E. W. and Wallin, P. 1953: *Engagement and marriage*. Chicago: Lippincott.

Buss, D. M. 1984: Marital assortment for personality dispositions: Assessment with three different data sources. *Behavior Genetics* **14**, 111–23.

Buss, D. M *et al.* 1990: International preferences in selecting mates: A study of 37 cultures. *Journal of Cross-Cultural Psychology* **21**, 5–47.

Byrne, D. 1961: Interpersonal attraction and attitude similarity. *Journal of Abnormal and Social Psychology* **62**, 713–15.

Byrne, D. 1971: *The attraction paradigm*. New York: Academic Press.

Byrne, D. and Clore, G. L. 1967: Effectance arousal and attraction. *Journal of Personality and Social Psychology* **6** (4, Whole No. 638).

Byrne, D. and Nelson, D. 1965: Attraction as a linear function of proportion of positive reinforcements. *Journal of Personality and Social Psychology* **1**, 659–63.

Byrne, D. and Rhamey, R. 1965: Magnitude of positive and negative reinforcements as a determinant of attraction. *Journal of Personality and Social Psychology* **2**, 884–9.

Campbell, D. T. 1963: From description to experimentation: Interpreting trends as quasi-experiments. In Harris, C. W. (ed.), *Problems in measuring change*. Madison, WI: University of Wisconsin Press, 212–42.

Campbell, D. T. and Reichardt, C. S. 1991: Problems in assuming the comparability of pretest and posttest in autoregressive and growth models. In Snow, R. E. and Wiley, D. E. (eds), *Improving inquiry in social science: A volume in honor of Lee J. Cronbach*. London: Lawrence Erlbaum Associates, 201–19.

Campbell, D. T. and Stanley, J. C. 1966: *Experimental and quasi-experimental designs for research*. Chicago: Rand McNally.

Caserta, M. S. and Lund, D. A. 1993: Intrapersonal resources and the effectiveness of self-help groups for bereaved older adults. *The Gerontologist* **33**, 619–29.

Caspi, A., Herbener, E. S. and Ozer, D. J. 1992: Shared experiences and the similarity of personalities: A longitudinal study of married couples. *Journal of Personality and Social Psychology* **62**, 281–91.

Cate, R. M., Lloyd, S. A. and Henton, J. M. 1985: The effect of equity, equality, and reward level on the stability of students' premarital relationships. *Journal of Social Psychology* **125**, 715–21.

Cate, R. M., Lloyd, S. A., Henton, J. M. and Larson, J. H. 1982: Fairness and reward level as predictors of relationship satisfaction. *Social Psychology Quarterly* **45**, 177–81.

Cate, R. M., Lloyd, S. A. and Long, E. 1988: The role of rewards and fairness in developing premarital relationships. *Journal of Marriage and the Family* **50**, 443–52.

Centers, R., Raven, B. H. and Rodrigues, A. 1971: Conjugal power structure: A reexamination. *American Sociological Review* **36**, 264–78.

Christensen, A. 1988: Dysfunctional interaction patterns in couples. In Noller, P. and Fitzpatrick, M. A. (eds), *Perspectives on marital interaction*. Clevedon: Multilingual Matters, 31–52.

Christensen, A. and Heavey, C. L. 1990: Gender and social structure in the demand/withdraw pattern of marital conflict. *Journal of Personality and Social Psychology* **59**, 73–81.

Christensen, A., Jacobson, N. S. and Babcock, J. C. 1995: Integrative behavioral couple therapy. In Jacobson, N. S. and Gurman, A. S. (eds) *Clinical handbook of couple therapy*. New York: Guilford Press, 31–64.

Cimbalo, R. S., Faling, V., and Mousaw, P. 1976: The course of love: A cross-sectional design. *Psychological Reports* **38**, 1292–4.

Clark, A. L. and Wallin, P. 1965: Women's sexual responsiveness and the duration and quality of their marriages. *American Journal of Sociology* **71**, 187–96.

Clore, G. L. and Byrne, D. 1974: A reinforcement-affect model of attraction. In Huston, T. L. (ed.), *Foundations of interpersonal attraction*. New York: Academic Press, 143–70.

Cohen, J. 1969: *Statistical power analysis for the behavioral sciences*. New York: Academic Press.

Collins, N. L. and Read, S. J. 1990: Adult attachment, working models, and relationship quality in dating couples. *Journal of Personality and Social Psychology* 58, 644–63.

Cornoni-Huntley, J., Barbano, H, E., Brody, J. A., Cohen, B., Feldman, J. J., Kleinman, J. C. and Madans, J. 1983: National Health and Nutrition Examination I: Epidemiologic follow-up survey. *Public Health Reports* 98, 245–51.

Corrales, R. 1975: Power and satisfaction in early marriage. In Cromwell, R. E. and Olson, D. H. (eds), *Power in families*. New York: Wiley, 197–216.

Cramer, D. 1987: Lovestyles revisited. *Social Behavior and Personality* 15, 215–18.

Cramer, D. 1988: Self-esteem and facilitative close relationships: A cross-lagged panel correlation analysis. *British Journal of Social Psychology* 27, 115–26.

Cramer, D. 1990: Self-esteem and close relationships: A statistical refinement. *British Journal of Social Psychology* 29, 189–91.

Cramer, D. 1992a: *Personality and psychotherapy: Theory, practice and research*. Milton Keynes: Open University Press.

Cramer, D. 1992b: Nature of romantic love in female adolescents. *Journal of Psychology* 126, 679–82.

Cramer, D. 1993a: Living alone, marital status, gender and health. *Journal of Community and Applied Social Psychology* 3, 1–15.

Cramer, D. 1993b: Dimensions of romantic love in British female adolescents. *Journal of Social Psychology* 133, 411–13.

Cramer, D. 1998: *Fundamental statistics for social research: Step-by-step calculations and computer techniques using SPSS for Windows*. London: Routledge.

Cramer, D., Henderson, S. and Scott, R. 1996: Mental health and adequacy of social support: A four-wave panel study. *British Journal of Social Psychology* 35, 285–95.

Cramer, D., Henderson, S. and Scott, R. 1997: Mental health and desired social support: A four-wave panel study. *Journal of Social and Personal Relationships* 14, 761–75.

Crognier, E. 1977: Assortative mating for physical features in an African population from Chad. *Journal of Human Evolution* 6, 105–14.

Crowe, M. J. 1978: Conjoint marital therapy: A controlled outcome study. *Psychological Medicine* 8, 623–36.

Cupach, W. R. and Metts, S. 1986: Accounts of relational dissolution: A comparison of marital and non-marital relationships. *Communication Monographs* 53, 311–34.

Curry, T. J. and Kenny, D. A. 1974: The effects of perceived and actual similarity in values and personality in the process of interpersonal attraction. *Quality and Quantity* 8, 27–44.

Dare, C. 1986: Psychoanalytic marital therapy. In Jacobson, N. S. and Gurman, A. S. (eds), *Clinical handbook of marital therapy*. New York: Guilford Press, 13–28.

Davis, K. 1941: Intermarriage in caste societies. *American Anthropologist* 43, 376–95.

Davis, K. B. 1929: *Factors in the sex life of twenty-two hundred women*. New York: Harper and Brothers.

Davis, K. E. and Latty-Mann, H. 1987: Love styles and relationship quality: A contribution to validation. *Journal of Social and Personal Relationships* 4, 409–28.

DeLamater, J. and MacCorquodale, P. 1979: *Premarital sexuality: Attitudes, relationships, behavior*. Madison, WI: University of Wisconsin Press.

DeMaris, A. 1984: A comparison of remarriages with first marriages on satisfaction in marriage and its relationship to prior cohabitation. *Family Relations* **33**, 443–49.

Dentler, R. A. and Pineo, P. 1960: Sexual adjustment, marital adjustment and personal growth of husbands: A panel analysis. *Marriage and Family Living* **22**, 45–8.

Derogatis, L. R. 1983: *SCL-90-R: Administration, scoring and procedures manual - II for the (R)evised version.* Towson, MD: Clinical Psychometric Research.

Derogatis, L. R., Lipman, R. S., Covi, L. and Rickels, K. 1971: Neurotic symptom dimensions as perceived by psychiatrists and patients of various social classes. *Archives of General Psychiatry* **24**, 454–64.

Derogatis, L. R. and Melisaratos, N. 1979: The DSFI: A multidimensional measure of sexual functioning. *Journal of Sexual and Marital Therapy* **5**, 244–81.

Deutsch, M. and Solomon, L. 1959: Reactions to evaluations by others as influenced by self-evaluations. *Sociometry* **22**, 93–112.

Dion, K. K. and Dion, K. L. 1975: Self-esteem and romantic love. *Journal of Personality* **43**, 39–57.

Dion, K. L. and Dion, K. K. 1973: Correlates of romantic love. *Journal of Consulting and Clinical Psychology* **41**, 51–6.

Dittes, J. E. 1959: Attractiveness of group as a function of self-esteem and acceptance by group. *Journal of Abnormal and Social Pyschology* **59**, 77–82.

Drigotas, S. M. and Rusbult, C. E. 1992: Should I stay or should I go? A dependence model of breakups. *Journal of Personality and Social Psychology* **62**, 62–87.

Duck, S. 1995: Repelling the study of attraction. *The Psychologist* **8**, 60–3.

Dunn, R. L. and Schwebel, A. I. 1995: Meta-analytic review of marital therapy outcome research. *Journal of Family Psychology* **9**, 58–68.

Durkheim, E. 1952: *Suicide: A study in sociology* (J. A. Spaulding and J. Simpson, trans.). London: Routledge, Kegan & Paul. (Original work published 1897)

Dutton, D. G. 1972: Effect of feedback parameters on congruency versus positivity effects in reactions to personal evaluations. *Journal of Personality and Social Psychology* **24**, 366–72.

Ebrahim, S., Wannamethee, G., McCallum, A., Walker, M. and Shaper, A. G. 1995: Marital status, change in marital status, and mortality in middle-aged British men. *American Journal of Epidemiology* **142**, 834–42.

Eddy, J. M., Heyman, R. E. and Weiss, R. L. 1991: An empirical evaluation of the Dyadic Adjustment Scale: Exploring the differences between marital 'satisfaction' and 'adjustment'. *Behavioral Assessment* **13**, 199–220.

Edwards, A. L. 1953: *Manual for the Edwards Personal Preference Schedule.* New York: Psychological Corporation.

Edwards, J. N. and Booth, A. 1976: Sexual behavior in and out of marriage: An assessment of correlates. *Journal of Marriage and the Family* **38**, 73–81.

Elder, G. H., Jr. 1969: Appearance and education in marriage mobility. *American Sociological Review* **34**, 519–33.

Ellis, A. 1962: *Reason and emotion in psychotherapy.* Secaucus, NJ: Lyle Stuart.

Emanuels-Zuurveen, L. and Emmelkamp, P. M. G. 1996: Individual behavioural-cognitive therapy v. marital therapy for depression in maritally distressed couples. *British Journal of Psychiatry* **169**, 181–8.

England, J. L. and Kunz, P. R. 1975: The application of age-specific rates to divorce. *Journal of Marriage and the Family* **37**, 40–6.

Epstein, N. and Eidelson, R. J. 1981: Unrealistic beliefs of clinical couples: Their relationship to expectations, goals and satisfaction. *American Journal of Family Therapy* 9, 13–22.

Escudero, V., Rogers, L. E. and Gutierrez, E. 1997: Patterns of relational control and nonverbal affect in clinic and nonclinic couples. *Journal of Social and Personal Relationships* 14, 5–29.

Everaerd, W. and Dekker, J. 1981: A comparison of sex therapy and communication therapy: Couples complaining of orgasmic dysfunction. *Journal of Sex and Marital Therapy* 7, 278–89.

Everaerd, W. and Dekker, J. 1982: Treatment of secondary orgasmic dysfunction: A comparison of systematic desensitization and sex therapy. *Behaviour Research and Therapy* 20, 269–74.

Everaerd, W. and Dekker, J. 1985: Treatment of male sexual dysfunction: Sex therapy compared with systematic desensitization and rational emotive therapy. *Behaviour Research and Therapy* 23, 13–25.

Everson, S. A., Goldberg, D. E., Kaplan, G. A., Cohen, R. D., Pukkala, E., Tuomilehto, J. and Salonen, J. T. 1996: Hopelessness and risk of mortality and incidence of myocardial infarction and cancer. *Psychosomatic Medicine* 58, 113–21.

Eysenck, H. J. 1976: *Sex and personality*. London: Open Books.

Eysenck, H. J. and Eysenck, S. B. G. 1975: *Manual of the Eysenck Personality Questionnaire*. London: Hodder and Stoughton.

Eysenck, H. J. and Wakefield, JR., J. A. 1981: Psychological factors as predictors of marital satisfaction. *Advances in Behaviour Research and Therapy* 3, 151–92.

Farr, W. 1975: Marriage and mortality. In Humphreys, N. (ed.), *Vital statistics: A memorial volume of selections from the reports and writings of William Farr*. Metuchen, NJ: Scarecrow Press 438–41. (Original work published 1885.)

Faschingbauer, T. R. 1981: *Texas revised inventory of grief manual*. Houston, TX: Honeycomb.

Feingold, A. 1981: Testing equity as an explanation for romantic couples 'mismatched' on physical attractiveness. *Psychological Reports* 49, 247–50.

Feingold, A. 1988: Matching for attractiveness in romantic partners and same-sex friends: A meta-analysis and theoretical critique. *Psychological Bulletin* 104, 226–35.

Feingold, A. 1990: Gender differences in effects of physical attractiveness on romantic attraction: A comparison across five research paradigms. *Journal of Personality and Social Psychology* 59, 981–93.

Filsinger, E. E. 1983: A machine-aided marital observation technique: The Dyadic Interaction Scoring Code. *Journal of Marriage and the Family* 45, 623–32.

Filsinger, E. E. and Thoma, S. J. 1988: Behavioral antecedents of relationship stability and adjustment: A five-year longitudinal study. *Journal of Marriage and the Family* 50, 785–95.

Finch, J. 1989: Kinship and friendship. In Jowell, R., Witherspoon, S. and Brook, L. (eds), *British social attitudes: Special international report: The 6th report*. Aldershot: Gower, 87–103.

Fincham, F. D. and Bradbury, T. N. 1993: Marital satisfaction, depression, and attributions: A longitudinal analysis. *Journal of Personality and Social Psychology* 64: 442–52.

Fisher, B. F. 1977: Identifying and Meeting Needs of Formerly-Married People through a Divorce Adjustment Seminar. Unpublished doctoral dissertation, University of North Colorado (University Microfilms No. 77-11057).

Fitzpatrick, M. A. 1988: *Between husbands and wives: Communication in marriage.* Newbury Park, CA: Sage.

Fitzpatrick, M. A. and Best, P. G. 1979: Dyadic adjustment in traditional, independent, and separate relationships: A validation study. *Communication Monographs* **46**, 167–78.

Fitzpatrick, M. A. and Indvik, J. 1982: The instrumental and expressive domains of marital communication. *Human Communication Research* 8, 195–213.

Floyd, F. J., Markman, H. J., Kelly, S., Blumberg, S. L. and Stanley, S. M. 1995: Preventive intervention and relationship enhancement. In Jacobson, N. S. and Gurman, A. S. (eds) *Clinical handbook of couple therapy.* New York: Guilford Press, 212–26.

Fournier, D. G., Olson, D. H. and Druckman, J. M. 1983: Assessing marital and pre-marital relationships: The PREPARE/ENRICH Inventories. In Filsinger, E. E. (ed), *Marriage and family assessment.* Newbury Park, CA: Sage, 229–50.

Fowers, B. J. and Olson, D. H. 1986: Predicting marital success with PREPARE: A predictive validity study. *Journal of Marital and Family Therapy* 12, 403–13.

Frazier, P. A. and Esterly, E. 1990: Correlates of relationship beliefs: Gender, relationship experience and relationship satisfaction. *Journal of Social and Personal Relationships* 7, 331–52.

French, J. R. P., JR. and Raven, B. H. 1959: The bases of social power. In Cartwright, D. (ed.), *Studies in social power.* Ann Arbor, MI: University of Michigan Press, 150–67.

Geiss, S. K. and O'Leary, K. D. 1981: Therapist ratings of frequency and severity of marital problems: Implications for research. *Journal of Marriage and Family Therapy,* 7, 515–20.

Gelder, M. G., Bancroft, J. H. J., Gath, D. H., Johnston, D. W., Mathews, A. M. and Shaw, P. M. 1973: Specific and non-specific factors in behaviour therapy. *British Journal of Psychiatry* **123**, 445–62.

Gelder, M. G. and Marks, I. M. 1966: Severe agoraphobia: A controlled prospective trial of behaviour therapy. *British Journal of Psychiatry* **112**, 309–19.

Giblin, P. 1986: Research and assessment in marriage and family enrichment: A meta-analysis study. *Journal of Psychotherapy and the Family* 2, 79–96.

Giblin, P., Sprenkle, D. H. and Sheehan, R. 1985: Enrichment outcome research: A meta-analysis of premarital and family interventions. *Journal of Marital and Family Therapy* 11, 257–71.

Gigy, L. and Kelly, J. B. 1992: Reasons for divorce: Perspectives of divorcing men and women. *Journal of Divorce and Remarriage* **18**, 169–87.

Glenn, N. D. and Weaver, C. N. 1978. A multivariate, multisurvey study of marital happiness. *Journal of Marriage and the Family* **40**, 269–82.

Goldberg, D. P. 1972: *The detection of psychiatric illness by questionnaire.* London: Oxford University Press.

Goldstein, J. W. and Rosenfeld, H. M. 1969: Insecurity and preference for persons similar to oneself. *Journal of Personality* 37, 253–68.

Goode, W. J. 1956: *After divorce.* Glencoe, IL: Free Press.

Goode, W. J. 1993: *World changes in divorce patterns.* New Haven, CT: Yale University Press.

Goodrich, D. W., Ryder, R. G. and Raush, M. L. 1968: Patterns of newlywed marriage. *Journal of Marriage and the Family* 30, 383–91.

Gorer, G. 1971: *Sex and marriage in England today: A study of the views and experiences of the under-45s.* London: Nelson.

Gottman, J., Markman, H. and Notarius, C. 1977: The topography of marital conflict: A sequential analysis of verbal and nonverbal behavior. *Journal of Marriage and the Family* 39, 461–77.

Gottman, J., Notarius, C., Markman, H., Bank, S., Yoppi, B. and Rubin, M. E. 1976: Behavior exchange theory and marital decision making. *Journal of Personality and Social Psychology* 34, 14–23.

Gottman, J. M. 1979: *Marital interaction: Experimental investigations*. New York: Academic Press.

Gottman, J. M. 1993: The roles of conflict engagement, escalation, and avoidance in marital interaction: A longitudinal view of five types of couples. *Journal of Consulting and Clinical Psychology* 61, 6–15.

Gottman, J. M. and Krokoff, L. J. 1989: Marital interaction and satisfaction: A longitudinal view. *Journal of Consulting and Clinical Psychology* 57, 47–52.

Gottman, J. M. and Krokoff, L. J. 1990: Complex statistics are not always clearer than simple statistics: A reply to Woody and Costanzo. *Journal of Consulting and Clinical Psychology* 58, 502–5.

Gottman, J. M. and Levenson, R. W. 1992: Marital processes predictive of later dissolution: Behavior, physiology, and health. *Journal of Personality and Social Psychology* 63: 221–3.

Gottman, J. M. and Porterfield, A. L. 1981: Communicative competence in the nonverbal behavior of married couples. *Journal of Marriage and the Family* 43, 817–24.

Gove, W. R., Hughes, M. and Style, C. B. 1983: Does marriage have positive effects on the psychological well-being of the individual? *Journal of Health and Social Behavior* 24, 122–31.

Gray-Little, B. and Burks, N. 1983: Power and satisfaction in marriage: A review and critique. *Psychological Bulletin* 93, 513–38.

Greenberg, L. S. and Johnson, S. M. 1986: Emotionally focused couples therapy. In Jacobson, N. S. and Gurman, A. S. (eds), *Clinical handbook of marital therapy*. New York: Guilford Press, 253–76.

Greenberg, L. S. and Johnson, S. M. 1988: *Emotionally focused therapy for couples*. New York: Guilford Press.

Gross, L. 1944: A belief pattern scale for measuring attitudes toward romanticism. *American Sociological Review* 9, 463–72.

Grover, K. J., Russell, C. S., Schumm, W. R. and Paff-Bergen, L. A. 1985: Mate selection processes and marital satisfaction. *Family Relations* 34, 383–6.

Guerney, B. G., Jr. 1977: *Relationship enhancement: Skill-training programs for therapy, problem prevention, and enrichment*. San Francisco: Jossey-Bass.

Guerney, B., Jr., Brock, G. and Coufal, J. 1986: Integrating marital therapy and enrichment: The Relationship Enhancement approach. In Jacobson, N. S. and Gurman, A. S. (eds), *Clinical handbook of marital therapy*. New York: Guilford Press, 151–72.

Gurman, A. S. and Kniskern, D. P. 1977: Enriching research on marital enrichment programs. *Journal of Marriage and Family Counseling* 3, 3–11.

Gurman, A. S. and Kniskern, D. P. 1978: Research on marital and family therapy: Progress, perspective, and prospect. In Garfield, S. L. and Bergin, A. E. (eds), *Handbook of psychotherapy and behavior change: An empirical analysis*, 2nd edn. New York: Wiley, 817–901.

Hahlweg, K. and Markman, H. J. 1988: Effectiveness of behavioral marital therapy: Empirical status of behavioral techniques in preventing and alleviating marital distress. *Journal of Consulting and Clinical Psychology* 56, 440–7.

Hahlweg, K., Revenstorf, D. and Schindler, L. 1982: Treatment of marital distress: Comparing formats and modalities. *Advances in Behaviour Research and Therapy* 4, 57–74.

Halford, W. K., Hahlweg, K. and Dunne, M. 1990: The cross-cultural consistency of marital communication associated with marital distress. *Journal of Marriage and the Family* 52, 487–500.

Halford, W. K., Sanders, M. R. and Behrens, B. C. 1993: A comparison of the generalization of behavioral marital therapy and enhanced behavioral marital therapy. *Journal of Consulting and Clinical Psychology* 61, 51–60.

Hamilton, G. V. 1929: *A research in marriage.* New York: Albert and Charles Boni.

Hanson, B. S., Isacsson, S-O., Janzon, L. and Lindell, S-E. 1989: Social network and social support influence mortality in elderly men: The prospective population study of 'Men born in 1914', Malmo, Sweden. *American Journal of Epidemiology* 130, 100–11.

Harding, S., Phillips, D. and Fogarty, M. 1986: *Contrasting values in Western Europe: Unity, diversity and change.* London: Macmillan.

Harrison, G. A., Gibson, J. B. and Hiorns, R. W. 1976: Assortative marriage for psychometric, personality and anthropometric variation in a group of Oxfordshire villages. *Journal of Biosocial Sciences* 8, 145–53.

Hartman, L. M. and Daly, E. M. 1983: Relationship factors in the treatment of sexual dysfunction. *Behaviour Research and Therapy* 21, 153–60.

Haskey, J. 1982: The proportion of marriages ending in divorce. *Population Trends* 27, 4–8.

Haskey, J. 1989: Current prospects for the proportion of marriages ending in divorce. *Population Trends* 55, 34–7.

Hatfield, E. and Sprecher, S. 1986: Measuring passionate love in intimate relationships. *Journal of Adolescence* 9, 383–410.

Hazan, C. and Shaver, P. 1987: Romantic love conceptualized as an attachment process. *Journal of Personality and Social Psychology* 52, 511–24.

Heaton, T. B. and Albrecht, S. L. 1991: Stable unhappy marriages. *Journal of Marriage and the Family* 53, 747–58.

Heavey, C. L., Layne, C. and Christensen, A. 1993; Gender and conflict structure in marital interaction: A replication and extension. *Journal of Consulting and Clinical Psychology* 61, 16–27.

Helsing, K. J. and Szklo, M. 1981: Mortality after bereavement. *American Journal of Epidemiology* 114, 41–52.

Henderson, S., Byrne, D. G. and Duncan-Jones, P. 1981: *Neurosis and the social environment.* Sydney: Academic Press.

Hendrick, C. and Hendrick, S. 1986: A theory and method of love. *Journal of Personality and Social Psychology* 50, 392–402.

Hendrick, C. and Hendrick, S. 1989: Research on love: Does it measure up? *Journal of Personality and Social Psychology* 56, 784–94.

Hendrick, C., Hendrick, S., Foote, F. H. and Slapion-Foote, M. J. 1984: Do men and women love differently? *Journal of Social and Personal Relationships* 1, 177–95.

Hendrick, S. S. 1988: A generic measure of relationship satisfaction. *Journal of Marriage and the Family* 50, 93–8.

Hendrick, S. S., Hendrick, C. and Adler, N. L. 1988: Romantic relationships: Love, satisfaction, and staying together. *Journal of Personality and Social Psychology* 54, 980–8.

Herbst, P. G. 1952: The measurement of family relationships. *Human Relations* 5, 3–35.

Hickman, M. E. and Baldwin, B. A. 1971: Use of programmed instruction to improve communication in marriage. *Family Coordinator* 20, 121–5.

Hill, C. T., Rubin, Z. and Peplau, L. A. 1976: Breakups before marriage: The end of 103 affairs. *Journal of Social Issues* 32, 147–68.

Hill, R. 1945: Campus values in mate selection. *Journal of Home Economics* 37, 554–8.

Hinkle, D. E. and Sporakowski, M. J. 1975: Attitudes toward love: A reexamination. *Journal of Marriage and the Family* 37, 764–7.

Hobart, C. 1958: The incidence of romanticism during courtship. *Social Forces* 36, 362–7.

Hoem, B. and Hoem, J. M. 1988: The Swedish family: Aspects of contemporary developments. *Journal of Family Issues* 9, 397–424.

Homans, G. C. 1961: *Social behavior: Its elementary forms*. New York: Harcourt, Brace & World.

Hope Gonzales, M., Davis, J. M., Loney, G. L., Lukens, C. K. and Junghans, C. M. 1983: Interactional approach to interpersonal attraction. *Journal of Personality and Social Psychology* 44, 1192–7.

Hoyt, L. L. and Hudson, J. W. 1981: Personal characteristics important in mate preference among college students. *Social Behavior and Personality* 9, 93–6.

Hudson, J. W. and Henze, L. F. 1969: Campus values in mate selection: A replication. *Journal of Marriage and the Family* 31, 772–5.

Hudson, W. W. 1981: Development and use of indexes and scales. In Grinnell, R. M. (ed.), *Social work research and evaluation*. Itasca, IL: F. E. Peacock Publishers.

Hurlbert, D. F. and Whittaker, K. E. 1991: The role of masturbation in marital and sexual satisfaction: A comparative study of female masturbators and nonmasturbators. *Journal of Sex Education and Therapy* 17, 272–82.

Huston, T. L. and Vangelisti, A. L. 1991: Socioemotional behavior and satisfaction in marital relationships: A longitudinal study. *Journal of Personality and Social Psychology* 61, 721–33.

Izard, C. E. 1960: Personality similarity and friendship. *Journal of Abnormal and Social Psychology* 61, 47–51.

Jackson, D. N. 1967: *Personality Research Form Manual*. Goshen, NY: New York Research Psychologists Press.

Jacobs, L., Berscheid, E. and Walster, E. 1971: Self-esteem and attraction. *Journal of Personality and Social Psychology* 17, 84–91.

Jacobson, N. S. 1978: Specific and nonspecific factors in the effectiveness of a behavioral approach to the treatment of marital discord. *Journal of Consulting and Clinical Psychology* 46, 442–52.

Jacobson, N. S. 1984: A component analysis of behavioral marital therapy: The relative effectiveness of behavior exchange and communication/problem-solving training. *Journal of Consulting and Clinical Psychology* 52, 295–305.

Jacobson, N. S. 1991: Behavioral versus insight-oriented marital therapy: Labels can be misleading. *Journal of Consulting and Clinical Psychology* 59, 142–5.

Jacobson, N. S., Dobson, K., Fruzetti, A. E., Schmaling, K. B. and Salusky, S. 1991: Marital therapy as a treatment for depression. *Journal of Consulting and Clinical Psychology* 59, 547–57.

Jacobson, N. S., Follette, V. M., Follette, W. C., Holtzworth-Munroe, A., Katt, J. L.

and Schmaling, K. B. 1985: A component analysis of behavioral marital therapy: 1-year follow-up. *Behavior Research and Therapy* 23, 549–55.

Jacobson, N. S. and Holtzworth-Munroe, A. 1986: Marital therapy: A social learning-cognitive perspective. In Jacobson, N. S. and Gurman, A. S. (eds), *Clinical handbook of marital therapy*. New York: Guilford Press, 29–70.

Jacobson, N. S. and Margolin, G. 1979: *Marital therapy: Strategies based on social learning and behavior exchange principles*. New York: Brunner/Mazel.

Jacobson, N. S., Schmaling, K. B. and Holtzworth-Munroe, A. 1987: Component analysis of behavioral marital therapy: 2-year follow-up and prediction of relapse. *Journal of Marital and Family Therapy* 13, 187–95.

James, P. S. 1991: Effects of a communication training component added to an emotionally focused couples therapy. *Journal of Marital and Family Therapy* 17, 263–75.

Johnson, A. M., Wadsworth, J., Wellings, K. and Field, J. 1994: *Sexual attitudes and lifestyles*. London: Blackwell.

Johnson, D. J. and Rusbult, C. E. 1989: Resisting temptation: Devaluation of alternative partners as a means of maintaining commitment in close relationships. *Journal of Personality and Social Psychology* 57, 967–80.

Johnson, D. R., Amoloza, T. O. and Booth, A. 1992: Stability and developmental change in marital quality: A three-wave panel analysis. *Journal of Marriage and the Family* 54, 582–94.

Johnson, R. C., Defries, J. C., Wilson, J. R., McClearn, G. E., Vandenberg, S. G., Ashton, G. C., Mi, M. P. and Rashad, M. N. 1976: Assortative marriage for specific cognitive abilities in two ethnic groups. *Human Biology* 48, 343–52.

Johnson, S. M. and Greenberg, L. S. 1985: Differential effects of experiential and problem-solving interventions in resolving marital conflict. *Journal of Consulting and Clinical Psychology* 53, 175–84.

Johnson, S. M. and Greenberg, L. S. 1995: The emotionally focused approach to problems in adult attachment. In Jacobson, N. S. and Gurman, A. S. (eds) *Clinical handbook of couple therapy*. New York: Guilford Press, 121–41.

Joiner, T. E., Jr. and Metalsky, G. I. 1995: A prospective test of an integrative interpersonal theory of depression: A naturalistic study of college roommates. *Journal of Personality and Social Psychology* 69, 778–88.

Jones, R. G. 1968: A factored measure of Ellis' Irrational Belief System, with Personality and Maladjustment Correlates. Unpublished doctoral dissertation, University of Texas (University Microfilms No. 69–6443).

Jones, S. C. 1973: Self- and interpersonal evaluations: Esteem theories versus consistency theories. *Psychological Bulletin* 79, 185–99.

Jorgensen, S. R. and Klein, D. M. 1979: Sociocultural heterogamy, dissensus, and conflict in marriage. *Pacific Sociological Review* 22, 51–75.

Joung, I. M. A., Van De Mheen, H., Stronks, K., Van Poppel, F. W. A. and Mackenbach, J. P. 1994: Differences in self-reported morbidity by marital status and by living arrangement. *International Journal of Epidemiology* 23, 91–7.

Jowell, R., Witherspoon, S. and Brook, L. 1987: *British social attitudes: The 1987 report*. Aldershot: Gower.

Jowell, R., Witherspoon, S. and Brook, L. 1989: *British social attitudes: Special international report: The 6th report*. Aldershot: Gower.

Kahn, M. 1970: Nonverbal communication and marital satisfaction. *Family Process* 9, 449–56.

Kanin, E. J. and Davidson, K. R. 1972: Some evidence bearing on the aim-inhibition hypothesis of love. *Sociological Quarterly* 13, 210–17.

Kanin, E. J., Davidson, K. R. and Scheck, S. R. 1970: A research note on male-female differentials in the experience of heterosexual love. *Journal of Sex Research* 6, 64–72.

Kaplan, G. A., Roberts, R. E., Camacho, T. C. and Coyne, J. C. 1987: Psychosocial predictors of depression: Prospective evidence from the Human Population Laboratory studies. *American Journal of Epidemiology* 125, 206–20.

Katz, I., Glucksberg, S. and Krauss, R. 1960: Need satisfaction and Edwards PPS scores in married couples. *Journal of Consulting Psychology* 24, 205–8.

Kelley, H. H. and Thibaut, J. W. 1978: Interpersonal relations: A *theory of interdependence*. New York: Wiley.

Kelly, E. L. and Conley, J. J. 1987: Personality and compatibility: A prospective analysis of marital stability and marital satisfaction. *Journal of Personality and Social Psychology* 52, 27–40.

Kenny, D. A. 1975: Cross-lagged panel correlation: A test for spuriousness. *Psychological Bulletin* 82, 887–903.

Kitson, G. C. and Sussman, M. B. 1982: Marital complaints, demographic characteristics, and symptoms of mental distress in divorce. *Journal of Marriage and the Family* 44, 87–101.

Knox, D. 1970: *Marriage happiness: A behavioural approach to counseling*. Champaign, IL: Research Press.

Knox, D. H., JR., and Sporakowski, M. J. 1968: Attitudes of college students toward love. *Journal of Marriage and the Family* 30, 638–42.

Kobrin, F. E. and Hendershot, G. E. 1977: Do family ties reduce mortality? Evidence from the United States, 1966–1968. *Journal of Marriage and the Family* 39, 373–80.

Krause, N. 1986: Social support, stress, and well-being among older adults. *Journal of Gerontology* 41, 512–19.

Krause, N., Liang, J. and Yatomi, N. 1989: Satisfaction with social support and depressive symptoms: A panel analysis. *Psychology and Aging* 4, 88–97.

Ktsanes, T. 1955: Mate selection on the basis of personality type: A study utilizing an empirical typology of personality. *American Sociological Review* 20, 547–51.

Kurdek, L. A. 1991a: The relations between reported well-being and divorce history, availability of a proximate adult, and gender. *Journal of Marriage and the Family* 53, 71–8.

Kurdek, L. A. 1991b: Sexuality in homosexual and heterosexual couples. In McKinney, K. and Sprecher, S. (eds), *Sexuality in close relationships*. Hillsdale, NJ: Lawrence Erlbaum Associates, 177–91.

Kurdek, L. A. 1992: Relationship stability and relationship satisfaction in cohabiting gay and lesbian couples: A prospective longitudinal test of the contextual and interdependence models. *Journal of Social and Personal Relationships* 9, 125–42.

Kurdek, L. A. 1993: Predicting marital dissolution: A 5-year prospective longitudinal study of newlywed couples. *Journal of Personality and Social Psychology* 64, 221–42.

Kurdek, L. A. 1994: Conflict resolution styles in gay, lesbian, heterosexual nonparent, and heterosexual parent couples. *Journal of Marriage and the Family* 56, 705–22.

Kurdek, L. A. 1995: Predicting change in marital satisfaction from husbands' and wives' conflict resolution styles. *Journal of Marriage and the Family* 57, 153–64.

Kurdek, L. A. and Schmitt, J. P. 1986: Relationship quality of partners in heterosexual married, heterosexual cohabiting, and gay and lesbian relationships. *Journal of Personality and Social Psychology* 51, 711–20.

Lackner, J. B., Joseph, J. G., Ostrow, D. G., Kessler, R. C., Eshleman, S., Wortman, C. B., O'Brien, K., Phair, J. P. and Chmiel, J. 1993: A longitudinal study of psychological distress in a cohort of gay men: Effects of social support and coping strategies. *Journal of Nervous and Mental Disease* 181, 4–12.

Lantz, H. R., Britton, M., Schmitt, R. L. and Snyder, E. C. 1968: Pre-industrial patterns in colonial family in America: A content analysis of colonial magazines. *American Sociological Review* 33, 413–27.

Lantz, H. R., Schmitt, R. L. and Herman, R. 1973: The pre-industrial family in America: A further examination of early magazines. *American Journal of Sociology* 79, 566–88.

Larsen, A. S. and Olson, D. H. 1989: Predicting marital satisfaction using PREPARE: A replication study. *Journal of Marital and Family Therapy* 15, 311–22.

Lasswell, T. E. and Lasswell, M. E. 1976: I love you but I'm not in love with you. *Journal of Marriage and Family Counseling*, 38, 211–24.

Laumann, E. O., Gagnon, J. H., Michael, R. T. and Michaels, S. 1994: *The social organization of sexuality: Sexual practices in the United States*. Chicago: University of Chicago Press.

Lazarsfeld, P. F. and Merton, R. K. 1954: Friendship as a social process: A substantive and methodological analysis. In Berger, M., Abels, T. and Page, C. H. (eds), *Freedom and control in modern society*. New York: Van Nostrand, 18–66.

Lee, J. A. 1973: *Colors of love: An exploration of the ways of loving*. Toronto: New Press.

Lee, J. A. 1975: Styles of loving. *Psychology Today* (UK edn) 1, 20–7.

Lee, J. A. 1976: *Lovestyles*. London: Dent.

Leonard, R. L., Jr. 1975: Self-concept and attraction for similar and dissimilar others. *Journal of Personality and Social Psychology* 31, 926–9.

Letourneau, C. 1891: *The evolution of marriage and of the family*. London: Walter Scott.

Levenson, R. W. and Gottman, J. M. 1983: Marital interaction: Physiological linkage and affective exchange. *Journal of Personality and Social Psychology* 45, 587–97.

Levinger, G. 1964: Note on need complementarity in marriage. *Psychological Bulletin* 61, 153–7.

Levy, M. B. and Davis, K. E. 1988: Lovestyles and attachment styles compared: Their relations to each other and to various relationship characteristics. *Journal of Social and Personal Relationships* 5, 439–71.

Lewis, R. A., and Burr, W. R. 1975: Premarital coitus and commitment among college students. *Archives of Sexual Behavior* 4, 73–9.

Lillard, L. A. and Waite, L. J. 1995: 'Til death do us part': Marital disruption and mortality. *American Journal of Sociology* 100, 1131–56.

Lipetz, M. E., Cohen, I. H., Dworkin, J. and Rogers, L. R. 1970: Need complementarity, marital stability, and marital satisfaction. In Gergen, K. J. and Marlowe, D. (eds), *Personality and social behavior*. Reading, MA: Addison-Wesley, 201–12.

Locke, H. J. and Wallace, K. M. 1959: Short marital-adjustment and prediction tests: Their reliability and validity. *Marriage and Family Living* 21, 251–5.

Lombardo, J. P., Weiss, R. F. and Buchanan, W. 1972: Reinforcing and attracting functions of yielding. *Journal of Personality and Social Psychology* 24, 359–68.

LoPiccolo, J. and Steger, J. C. 1974: The Sexual Interaction Inventory: A new instrument for assessment of sexual dysfunction. *Archives of Sexual Behavior* 3, 163–71.

Lowenthal, M. J. and Haven, C. 1968: Interaction and adaptation: Intimacy as a critical variable. *American Sociological Review* 33, 20–30.

Lund, M. 1985: The development of investment and commitment scales for predicting continuity of personal relationships. *Journal of Social and Personal Relationships* 2, 3–23.

McCrae, R. R. and Costa, P. T., Jr. 1988: Psychological resilience among widowed men and women: A 10-year follow-up of a national sample. *Journal of Social Issues* 44, 129–42.

McGinnis, R. 1958: Campus values in mate selection. *Social Forces* 36, 368–73.

McGonagle, K. A., Kessler, R. C. and Gotlib, I. H. 1993: The effects of marital disagreement style, frequency, and outcome on marital disruption. *Journal of Social and Personal Relationships* 10, 385–404.

McKillip, J. and Riedel, S. L. 1983: External validity of matching on physical attractiveness for same and opposite sex couples. *Journal of Applied Social Psychology* 13, 328–37.

Margolin, G., Talovic, S. and Weinstein, C. D. 1983: Areas of Change Questionnaire: A practical approach to marital assessment. *Journal of Consulting and Clinical Psychology* 51, 920–31.

Margolin, G. and Wampold, B. E. 1981: Sequential analysis of conflict and accord in distressed and nondistressed marital partners. *Journal of Consulting and Clinical Psychology* 49, 554–67.

Markman, H. J. 1979: Application of a behavioral model of marriage in predicting relationship satisfaction of couples planning marriage. *Journal of Consulting and Clinical Psychology* 47, 743–9.

Markman, H. J. 1981: Prediction of marital distress: A 5-year follow-up. *Journal of Consulting and Clinical Psychology* 49, 760–2.

Markman, H. J. 1984: The longitudinal study of couples' interactions: Implications for understanding and predicting the development of marital distress. In Hahlweg, K. and Jacobson, N. S. (eds) *Marital interaction: Analysis and modification.* New York: Guilford Press, 253–81.

Markman, H. J. and Floyd, S. 1980: Possibilities for the prevention of marital discord: A behavioral perspective. *American Journal of Family Therapy* 8, 29–48.

Markman, H. J., Floyd, F. J., Stanley, S. M. and Storaasli, R. D. 1988: Prevention of marital distress: A longitudinal investigation. *Journal of Consulting and Clinical Psychology* 56, 210–17.

Markman, H. J., Renick, M. J., Floyd, F. J., Stanley, S. M. and Clements, M. 1993: Preventing marital distress through communication and conflict management training: A 4- and 5-year follow-up. *Journal of Consulting and Clinical Psychology* 61, 70–7.

Markman, H. J., Stanley, S. and Blumberg, S. L. 1994: *Fighting for your marriage: Positive steps for preventing divorce and preserving a lasting love.* San Francisco: Jossey-Bass.

Marks, I. M., Gelder, M. G. and Edwards, G. 1968: Hypnosis and desensitization for phobias: A controlled prospective trial. *British Journal of Psychiatry* 114, 1263–74.

Marmar, C. R., Horowitz, M. J., Weiss, D. S., Wilner, N. R. and Kaltreider, N. B. 1988: A controlled trial of brief psychotherapy and mutual-help group treatment of conjugal bereavement. *American Journal of Psychiatry* 145, 203–9.

Martin, C. T. and Bumpass, L. L. 1989: Recent trends in marital disruption. *Demography* **26**, 37–51.

Mascie-Taylor, C. G. N. and Vandenberg, S. G. 1988: Assortative mating for IQ and personality due to propinquity and personal preference. *Behavior Genetics* **18**, 339–45.

Masters, W. H. and Johnson, V. E. 1970: *Human sexual inadequacy*. Boston: Little, Brown.

Mathews, V. D. and Mihanovich, C. S. 1963: New orientations on marital adjustment. *Marriage and Family Living* **25**, 300–4.

Meyer, J. P. and Pepper, S. 1977: Need compatibility and marital adjustment in young married couples. *Journal of Personality and Social Psychology* **35**, 331–42.

Michaels, J. W., Acock, A. C. and Edwards, J. N. 1986: Social exchange and equity determinants of relationship commitment. *Journal of Social and Personal Relationships* **3**, 161–75.

Michaels, J. W., Edwards, J. N. and Acock, A. C. 1984: Satisfaction in intimate relationships as a function of inequality, inequity, and outcomes. *Social Psychology Quarterly* **47**, 347–57.

Millar, F. E. and Rogers, L. E. 1988: Power dynamics in marital relationships. In Noller, P. and Fitzpatrick, M. A. (eds), *Perspectives on marital interaction*. Clevedon: Multilingual Matters, 78–97.

Miller, S., Nunnally, E. W. and Wackman, D. B. 1975: Alive and aware: *Improving communication in relationships*. Minneapolis, MN: Interpersonal Communications Program, Inc.

Miller, S., Nunnally, E. W. and Wackman, D. B. 1976: Minnesota Couples Communication Program (MCCP): Premarital and marital groups. In Olson, D. (ed.) *Treating relationships*. Lake Mills, IA: Graphic Publishing Co., 21–39.

Munro, B. and Adams, G. R. 1978: Love American style: A test of role structure theory on changes in attitudes toward love. *Human Relations* **31**, 215–28.

Murray, H. A. 1938: *Explorations in personality*. New York: Oxford University Press.

Murray, H. A. 1943: *Thematic Apperception Test*. Cambridge, MA: Harvard University Press.

Murstein, B. I. 1967: Empirical tests of role, complementary needs, and homogamy theories of marital choice. *Journal of Marriage and the Family* **29**, 689–96.

Murstein, B. I. 1970: Stimulus-value-role: A theory of marital choice. *Journal of Marriage and the Family* **32**, 465–81.

Murstein, B. I. 1972: Physical attractiveness and marital choice. *Journal of Personality and Social Psychology* **22**, 8–12.

Murstein, B. I. 1976: The theory of complementary needs. In Murstein, B. I. *Who will marry whom? Theories and research in marital choice*. New York: Springer, 41–73.

Murstein, B. I. 1977: The stimulus-value-role (SVR) theory of dyadic relationships. In Duck, S. (ed.) *Theory and practice in interpersonal attraction*. London: Academic Press, 105–27.

Murstein, B. I. and Beck, G. D. 1972: Person perception, marriage adjustment, and social desirability. *Journal of Consulting and Clinical Psychology* **39**, 396–403.

Murstein, B. I., Cerreto, M. and MacDonald, M. G. 1977: A theory and investigation of the effect of exchange-orientation on marriage and friendship. *Journal of Marriage and the Family* **39**, 543–8.

Murstein, B. I. and Christy, P. 1976: Physical attractiveness and marriage adjustment in middle-aged couples. *Journal of Personality and Social Psychology* **34**, 537–42.

Myers, R. J. 1963: An instance of the pitfalls prevalent in graveyard research. *Biometrics* **19**, 638–50.

Newcomb, T. M. 1961: *The acquaintance process*. New York: Holt, Rinehart and Winston.

Noller, P. 1980: Misunderstandings in marital communication: A study of couples' nonverbal communication. *Journal of Personality and Social Psychology* **39**, 1135–48.

Noller, P. 1981: Gender and marital adjustment level differences in decoding messages from spouses and strangers. *Journal of Personality and Social Psychology* **41**, 272–8.

Noller, P., Feeney, J. A., Bonnell, D. and Callan, V. J. 1994: A longitudinal study of conflict in early marriage. *Journal of Social and Personal Relationships* **11**, 233–52.

Noller, P. and White, A. 1990: The validity of the Communication Patterns Questionnaire. *Psychological Assessment: Journal of Consulting and Clinical Psychology* **2**, 478–82.

Norman, W. T. 1963: Toward an adequate taxonomy of personality attributes: Replicated factor structure in peer nomination personality ratings. *Journal of Abnormal and Social Psychology* **66**, 574–83.

Norton, R. 1983: Measuring marital quality: A critical look at the dependent variable. *Journal of Marriage and the Family* **45**, 141–51.

Office of Population Censuses and Surveys 1995: *Marriage and divorce statistics: Review of the Registrar General on marriages and divorces in England and Wales, 1993*. London: HMSO.

O'Leary, K. D., Barling, J., Arias, I., Rosenbaum, A., Malone, J. and Tyree, A. 1989: Prevalence and stability of physical aggression between spouses: A longitudinal analysis. *Journal of Consulting and Clinical Psychology* **57**, 263–8.

O'Leary, K. D. and Beach, S. R. H. 1990: Marital therapy: A viable treatment for depression and marital discord. *American Journal of Psychiatry* **147**, 183–6.

O'Leary, K. D., Fincham, F. and Turkewitz, H. 1983: Assessment of positive feelings toward spouse. *Journal of Consulting and Clinical Psychology* **51**, 949–51.

O'Leary, K. D., Malone, J. and Tyree, A. 1994: Physical aggression in early marriage: Prerelationship and relationship effects. *Journal of Consulting and Clinical Psychology* **62**, 594–602.

O'Leary, K. D. and Turkewitz, H. 1981: A comparative outcome study of behavioral marital therapy and communication therapy. *Journal of Marital and Family Therapy* **7**, 159–69.

Olson, D. H. and Cromwell, R. E. 1975: Methodological issues in family power. In Cromwell, R. E. and Olson, D. H. (eds), *Power in families*. New York: Wiley, 131–50.

Olson, D. H. and Ryder, R. G. 1970: Inventory of Marital Conflicts (IMC): An experimental interaction procedure. *Journal of Marriage and the Family* **32**, 443–8.

Orden, S. R. and Bradburn, N. M. 1968: Dimensions of marriage happiness. *American Journal of Sociology* **73**, 715–31.

Osmond, M. W. and Martin, P. Y. 1978: A contingency model of marital organization in low income families. *Journal of Marriage and the Family* **40**, 315–29.

Oxman, T. E., Berkman, L. F., Kasl, S., Freeman, D. H., Jr. and Barrett, J. 1992: Social support and depressive symptoms in the elderly. *American Journal of Epidemiology* **135**, 356–68.

Palmer, J. 1969: Vindication, Evaluation, and the Effect of the Stranger's Competence on the Attitude Similarity-Attraction Function. Unpublished doctoral dissertation, University of Texas.

Patterson, G. R. and Hops, H. 1972: Coercion, a game for two: Intervention techniques for marital conflict. In Ulrich, R. E. and Mountjoy, P. T. (eds), *The experimental analysis of social behavior*. New York: Appleton-Century-Crofts, 424–40.

Pearson, J. and Thoennes, N. 1982: The benefits outweigh the costs. *Family Advocate* 4, 26, 28–32.

Pearson, K. and Lee, A. 1903: On the laws of inheritance in man: I Inheritance of physical characters. *Biometrika* 2, 46–398.

Phillips, K., Fulker, D. W., Carey, G. and Nagoshi, C. T. 1988: Direct marital assortment for cognitive and personality variables. *Behavior Genetics* 18, 347–56.

Pierce, R. A. 1970: Need similarity and complementarity as determinants of friendship choice. *Journal of Psychology* 76, 231–8.

Pike, G. R. and Sillars, A. L. 1985: Reciprocity of marital communication. *Journal of Social and Personal Relationships* 2, 303–24.

Pineo, P. C. 1961: Disenchantment in the later years of marriage. *Marriage and Family Living* 23, 3–11.

Pinney, E. M., Gerrard, M. and Denney, N. W. 1987: The Pinney Sexual Satisfaction Inventory. *Journal of Sex Research* 23, 233–51.

Preston, S. H. and McDonald, J. 1979: The incidence of divorce within cohorts of American marriages contracted since the Civil War. *Demography* 16, 1–25.

Price, R. A. and Vandenberg, S. G. 1979: Matching for physical attractiveness in married couples. *Personality and Social Psychology Bulletin* 5, 398–400.

Price, R. A. and Vandenberg, S. G. 1980: Spouse similarity in American and Swedish couples. *Behavior Genetics* 10, 59–71.

Radloff, L. S. 1977: The CES-D Scale: A self-report depression scale for research in the general population. *Applied Psychological Measurement* 1, 385–401.

Rands, M., Levinger, G. and Mellinger, G. D. 1981: Patterns of conflict resolution and marital satisfaction. *Journal of Family Issues* 2, 297–321.

Raush, H. L., Barry, W. A., Hertel, R. K. and Swain, M. A. 1974: *Communication, conflict and marriage: Explorations in the theory and study of intimate relationships*. San Francisco: Jossey-Bass.

Raven, B. H., Centers, R. and Rodrigues, A. 1975: The bases of conjugal power. In Cromwell, R. E. and Olson, D. H. (eds), *Power in families*. New York: Wiley, 217–32.

Rettig, K. D. and Bubolz, M. M. 1983: Interpersonal resource exchanges as indicators of quality of marriage. *Journal of Marriage and the Family* 45, 497–509.

Revenstorf, D., Vogel, B., Wegener, C., Hahlweg, K. and Schindler, L. 1980: Escalation phenomena in interaction sequences: An empirical comparison of distressed and non-distressed couples. *Behavior Analysis and Modification* 2, 97–115.

Rhyne, D. 1981: Bases of marital satisfaction among men and women. *Journal of Marriage and the Family* 43, 941–55.

Richardson, H. M. 1939: Studies of mental resemblance between husbands and wives and between friends. *Psychological Bulletin* 36, 104–20.

Roach, A. J., Frazier, L. P. and Bowden, S. R. 1981: The Marital Satisfaction Scale. *Journal of Marriage and the Family* 40, 537–46.

Roberts, L. J. and Krokoff, L. J. 1990: A time-series analysis of withdrawal, hostility, and displeasure in satisfied and dissatisfied marriages. *Journal of Marriage and the Family* 52, 95–105.

Rogosa, D. 1980: A critique of cross-lagged correlation. *Psychological Bulletin* **88**, 245–58.

Rollins, B. C. and Cannon, K. L. 1974: Marital satisfaction over the family life cycle: A reevaluation. *Journal of Marriage and the Family* **36**, 271–82.

Rosenberg, M. 1965: *Society and the adolescent self-image*. Princeton, NJ: Princeton University Press.

Rosenthal, R. and Rubin, D. B. 1982: A simple, general purpose display of magnitude of experimental effect. *Journal of Educational Psychology* **74**, 166–9.

Rosow, I. 1957: Issues in the concept of need-complementarity. *Sociometry* **20**, 216–33.

Rubin, Z. 1970: Measurement of romantic love. *Journal of Personality and Social Psychology* **16**, 265–73.

Rusbult, C. E. 1980: Commitment and satisfaction in romantic associations: A test of the investment model. *Journal of Experimental Social Psychology* **16**, 172–86.

Rusbult, C. E. 1983: A longitudinal test of the investment model: The development (and deterioration) of satisfaction and commitment in heterosexual involvements. *Journal of Personality and Social Psychology* **45**, 101–17.

Rusbult, C. E., Johnson, D. J. and Morrow, G. D. 1986: Predicting satisfaction and commitment in adult romantic involvements: An assessment of the generalizability of the investment model. *Social Psychology Quarterly* **49**, 81–9.

Sampson, E. E. and Insko, C. A. 1964: Cognitive consistency and performance in the autokinetic situation. *Journal of Abnormal and Social Psychology* **68**, 184–92.

Sarason, I. G., Levine, H. M., Basham, R. B. and Sarason, B. R. 1983: Assessing social support: The Social Support Questionnaire. *Journal of Personality and Social Psychology* **44**, 127–39.

Schaefer, M. T. and Olson, D. H. 1981: Assessing intimacy: The PAIR inventory. *Journal of Marital and Family Therapy* **1**, 47–60.

Schenk, J., Pfrang, H. and Rausche, A. 1983: Personality traits versus the quality of the marital relationship as the determinant of marital sexuality. *Archives of Sexual Behavior* **12**, 31–42.

Schiavi, R. C., Derogatis, L. R., Kuriansky, J., O'Connor, D. and Sharpe, L. 1979: The assessment of sexual function and marital interaction. *Journal of Sex and Marital Therapy* **5**, 169–224.

Schiller, B. 1932: A quantitative analysis of marriage selection in a small group. *Journal of Social Psychology* **3**, 297–319.

Schoen, R. 1975: Constructing increment-decrement life tables. *Demography* **12**, 313–24.

Schoen, R. 1992: First unions and the stability of first marriages. *Journal of Marriage and the Family* **54**, 281–4.

Schoen, R. and Baj, J. 1984: Twentieth-century cohort marriage and divorce in England and Wales. *Population Studies* **38**, 439–49.

Schoen, R. and Nelson, V. E. 1974: Marriage, divorce, and mortality: A life table analysis. *Demography* **11**, 267–90.

Schoen, R., Urton, W., Woodrow, K. and Baj, J. 1985: Marriage and divorce in twentieth century American cohorts. *Demography* **22**, 101–14.

Schoen, R. and Weinick, R. M. 1993: The slowing metabolism of marriage: Figures from 1988 U.S. marital status life tables. *Demography* **30**, 737–46.

Schooler, N., Hogarty, G. E. and Weissman, M. M. 1979: Social Adjustment Scale II (SAS-II). In Hargreaves, W. A., Atkinson, C. C. and Sorenson, J. E. (eds), *Resource material for community mental health program evaluators.* Washington, DC: U.S. Government Printing Office, 290–303.

Schumm, W. R., Anderson, S. A. and Griffin, C. L. 1983: The Marital Communication Inventory. In Filsinger, E. E. (ed.) *Marriage and family assessment: A sourcebook for family therapy.* Beverly Hills, CA: Sage, 191–208.

Schumm, W. R., Paff-Bergen, L. A., Hatch, R. C., Obiorah, F. C., Copeland, J. E., Meens, L. D. and Bugaighis, M. A. 1986: Concurrent and discriminant validity of the Kansas Marital Satisfaction Scale. *Journal of Marriage and the Family* 48, 381–8.

Schutz, W. C. 1967: *MATE, a FIRO scale: Husband's form, wife's form.* Palo Alto, CA: University of California Press.

Sears, R. R. 1977: Sources of life satisfactions of the Terman gifted men. *American Psychologist* 32, 119–28.

Seyfried, B. A. and Hendrick, C. 1973: When do opposites attract? When they are opposite in sex and sex-role attitudes. *Journal of Personality and Social Psychology* 25, 15–20.

Shaver, P. R. and Hazan, C. 1988: A biased overview of the study of love. *Journal of Social and Personal Relationships* 5, 473–501.

Shaw, B. F. 1977: Comparison of cognitive therapy and behavior therapy in the treatment of depression. *Journal of Consulting and Clinical Psychology* 45, 543–51.

Sheps, M. C. 1961: Marriage and mortality. *American Journal of Public Health* 51, 547–55.

Simpson, J. A. 1990: Influence of attachment styles on romantic relationships. *Journal of Personality and Social Psychology* 59, 971–80.

Skolnick, P. 1971: Reactions to personal evaluations: A failure to replicate. *Journal of Personality and Social Psychology* 18, 62–7.

Slater, E. and Woodside, M. 1951: *Patterns of marriage: A study of marriage relationships in the urban working class.* London: Cassell.

Sloane, R. B., Staples, F. R., Cristol, A. H., Yorkston, N. J. and Whipple, K. 1975: *Psychotherapy versus behavior therapy.* Cambridge, MA: Harvard University Press.

Smith, D. A., Vivian, D. and O'Leary, K. D. 1990: Longitudinal prediction of marital discord from premarital expressions of affect. *Journal of Consulting and Clinical Psychology* 58, 790–8.

Snyder, D. K. 1979: Multidimensional assessment of marital satisfaction. *Journal of Marriage and the Family* 41, 813–23.

Snyder, D. K. and Wills, R. M. 1989: Behavioral versus insight-oriented marital therapy: Effects on individual and interspousal functioning. *Journal of Consulting and Clinical Psychology* 57, 39–46.

Snyder, D. K., Wills, R. M. and Grady-Fletcher, A. 1991: Long-term effectiveness of behavioral versus insight-oriented marital therapy: A 4-year follow-up study. *Journal of Consulting and Clinical Psychology* 59, 138–141.

Solomon, Z. 1986: Self acceptance and the selection of a marital partner – an assessment of the SVR model of Murstein. *Social Behavior and Personality* 14, 1–6.

Sorensen, R. C. 1973: *Adolescent sexuality in contemporary America: Personal values and sexual behavior ages thirteen to nineteen.* New York: World.

Spanier, G. B. 1976: Measuring dyadic adjustment: New scales for assessing the quality of marriage and similar dyads. *Journal of Marriage and the Family* 38, 15–28.

Spanier, G. B., Lewis, R. A. and Cole, C. L. 1975: Marital adjustment over the family life cycle: The issue of curvilinearity. *Journal of Marriage and the Family* 37, 263–75.

Spanier, G. B., Sauer, W. and Larzelere, R. 1979: An empirical evaluation of the family life cycle. *Journal of Marriage and the Family* 41, 27–38.

Spielberger, C. D. 1983: *Manual for the State-Trait Anxiety Inventory*. Palo Alto, CA: Consulting Psychologists Press.

Sprecher, S. 1988: Investment model, equity, and social support determinants of relationship commitment. *Social Psychology Quarterly* 51, 318–28.

Sprecher, S. and Metts, S. 1989: Development of the 'Romantic Beliefs Scale' and examination of the effects of gender and gender-role orientation. *Journal of Social and Personal Relationships* 6, 387–411.

Sprenkle, D. H. and Storm, C. L. 1983: Divorce therapy outcome research: A substantive and methodological review. *Journal of Marital and Family Therapy* 9, 239–58.

Sternberg, R. J. 1986: A triangular theory of love. *Psychological Review* 93, 119–35.

Stevens, G., Owen, D. and Schaefer, E. C. 1990: Education and attractiveness in marriage choices. *Social Psychology Quarterly* 53, 62–70.

Straus, M. A. 1979: Measuring intrafamily conflict and violence: The Conflict Tactics (CT) Scales. *Journal of Marriage and the Family* 41, 75–88.

Straus, M. A. 1990a: Measuring intrafamily conflict and violence: The Conflict Tactics (CT) Scales. In Straus, M. A. and Gelles, R. J. (eds), *Physical violence in American families: Risk factors and adaptations to violence in 8,145 families*. New Brunswick, NJ: Transaction Publishers, 29–47.

Straus, M. A. 1990b: New scoring methods for violence and new norms for the Conflict Tactics Scale. In Straus, M. A. and Gelles, R. J. (eds), *Physical violence in American families: Risk factors and adaptations to violence in 8,145 families*. New Brunswick, NJ: Transaction Publishers, 535–59.

Stravynski, A., Gaudette, G., Lesage, A., Arbel, N., Petit, P., Clerc, D., Fabian, J., Lamontagne, Y., Langlois, R., Lipp, O. and Sidoun, P. 1997: The treatment of sexually dysfunctional men without partners: A controlled study of three behavioural group approaches. *British Journal of Psychiatry* 170, 338–44.

Strupp, H. H. and Hadley, S. W. 1979: Specific vs nonspecific factors in psychotherapy: A controlled study of outcome. *Archives of General Psychiatry* 36, 1125–36.

Stuart, R. B. and Stuart, F. 1973: *Marital Pre-Counseling Inventory*. Champaign, IL: Research Press.

Sullaway, M. and Christensen, A. 1983: Assessment of dysfunctional interaction patterns in couples. *Journal of Marriage and the Family* 45, 653–60.

Swan, W. B., Jr., Wenzlaff, R. M. and Tafarodi, R. W. 1992: Depression and the search for negative evaluations: More evidence of the role of self-verification strivings. *Journal of Abnormal Psychology* 101, 314–17.

Swensen, C. H. 1972: The behavior of love. In Otto, H. A. (ed.), *Love today: A new exploration*. New York: Association Press, 86–101.

Szinovacz, M. E. 1983: Using couple data as a methodological tool: The case of marital violence. *Journal of Marriage and the Family* 45, 633–44.

Taylor, P. A. and Glenn, N. D. 1976: The utility of education and attractiveness for females' status attainment through marriage. *American Sociological Review* 41, 484–98.

Terman, L. M. 1938: *Psychological factors in marital happiness*. New York: McGraw-Hill.

Terman, L. M. and Buttenweiser, P. 1935: Personality factors in marital compatibility: I and II. *Journal of Social Psychology* 6, 143–71, 267–89.

Tharp, R. G. 1964: Reply to Levinger's note. *Psychological Bulletin* 61, 158–60.

Thibaut, J. W. and Kelley, H. H. 1959: *The social psychology of groups*. New York: John Wiley.

Thiessen, J. D., Avery, A. W. and Joanning, H. 1980: Facilitating postdivorce adjustment among women: A communication skills training approach. *Journal of Divorce* 4, 35–44.

Thoits, P. 1987: Gender and marital status differences in control and distress: Common stress versus unique stress explanations. *Journal of Health and Social Behavior* 28, 7–22.

Thomson, E. and Colella, U. 1992: Cohabitation and marital stability: Quality or commitment? *Journal of Marriage and the Family* 54, 259–67.

Thornton, A 1989: Changing attitudes toward family issues in the United States. *Journal of Marriage and the Family* 51, 873–93.

Trost, J. 1967: Some data on mate-selection: Complementarity. *Journal of Marriage and the Family* 29, 730–8.

Tudiver, F., Hilditch, J., Permaul, J. A. and McKendree, D. J. 1992: Does mutual help facilitate newly bereaved widowers? Report of a randomized controlled trial. *Evaluation and the Health Professions* 15, 147–62.

Tzeng, M-S 1992: The effects of socioeconomic heterogamy and changes in marital dissolution for first marriages. *Journal of Marriage and the Family* 54, 609–19.

U.S. Bureau of the Census 1995: *Statistical Abstract of the United States 1995: The National Data Book*. Washington, DC: U.S. Government Printing Office.

Udry, J. R. 1977: The importance of being beautiful: A reexamination and racial comparison. *American Journal of Sociology* 83, 154–60.

Udry, J. R. 1981: Marital alternatives and marital disruption. *Journal of Marriage and the Family* 43, 889–97.

Ulrich-Jakubowski, D., Russell, D. W. and O'Hara, M. W. 1988: Marital adjustment difficulties: Cause or consequence of depressive symptomatology? *Journal of Social and Clinical Psychology* 7, 312–18.

United Nations 1995: *Demographic Yearbook 1993*. New York: United Nations Publishing Services.

Vachon, M. L. S., Lyall, W. A. L., Rogers, J., Freedman-Letofsky, K. and Freeman, S. J. J. 1980: A controlled study of self-help intervention for widows. *American Journal of Psychiatry* 137, 1380–4.

Vachon, M. L. S., Rogers, J., Lyall, W. A., Lancee, W. J., Sheldon, A. R. and Freeman, S. J. J. 1982: Predictors and correlates of adaptation to conjugal bereavement. *American Journal of Psychiatry* 139, 998–1002.

Vaillant, C. O. and Vaillant, G. E. 1993: Is the U-curve of marital satisfaction an illusion? A 40-year study of marriage. *Journal of Marriage and the Family* 55, 230–9.

Vera, H., Berardo, D. H. and Berardo, F. M. 1985: Age heterogamy in marriage. *Journal of Marriage and the Family* 47, 553–66.

Veroff, J., Kulka, R. A. and Douvan, E. 1981: *Mental health in America: Patterns of help-seeking from 1957 to 1976*. New York: Basic Books.

Vincent, J. P., Friedman, L. C., Nugent, J. and Messerly, L. 1979: Demand characteristics in observations of marital interaction. *Journal of Consulting and Clinical Psychology* 47, 557–66.

Wagner, R. V. 1975: Complementary needs, role expectations, interpersonal attraction and the stability of working relationships. *Journal of Personality and Social Psychology* 32, 116–24.

Walster, E., Aronson, V., Abrahams, D. and Rottman, L. 1966: Importance of physical attractiveness in dating behavior. *Journal of Personality and Social Psychology* 4, 508–16.

Walster, E., Berscheid, E. and Walster, G. W. 1973: New directions in equity research. *Journal of Personality and Social Psychology* 25, 151–76.

Walster, E., Walster, G. W. and Berscheid, E. 1978a: *Equity: Theory and research.* Boston: Allyn and Bacon.

Walster, E., Walster, G. W. and Traupmann, J. 1978b: Equity and premarital sex. *Journal of Personality and Social Psychology* 36, 82–92.

Wampler, K. S. 1982: The effectiveness of the Minnesota Couple Communication Program: A review of research. *Journal of Marital and Family Therapy* 8, 345–55.

Wampler, K. S. and Sprenkle, D. H. 1980: The Minnesota Couple Communication Program: A follow-up study. *Journal of Marriage and the Family* 42, 577–84.

Watkins, M. P. and Meredith, W. 1981: Spouse similarity in newlyweds with respect to specific cognitive abilities, socioeconomic status, and education. *Behavior Genetics* 11, 1–21.

Watson, D. and Friend, A. 1969: Measurement of social evaluative anxiety. *Journal of Consulting and Clinical Psychology* 33, 458–65.

Watzlawick, P., Beavin, J. H. and Jackson, D. D. 1967: *Pragmatics of human communication: A study of interaction patterns, pathologies and paradoxes.* New York: Norton.

Weiss, L. and Lowenthal, M. F. 1975: Life-course perspectives on friendship. In Lowenthal, M. F., Thurnher, M. and Chiriboga, D. (eds) *Four stages of life: A comparative study of women and men facing transitions.* San Francisco: Jossey-Bass, 48–61.

Weiss, R. L., Hops, H. and Patterson, G. R. 1973: A framework for conceptualizing marital conflict, a technology for altering it, some data for evaluating it. In Hamerlynck, L. A., Handly, L. C. and Mash, E. J. (eds) *Behavior change: Methodology, concepts, and practice.* Champaign, IL: Research, 309–42.

Weiss, R. L. and Perry, B. A. 1983: The Spouse Observation Checklist: Development and clinical applications. In Filsinger, E. E. (ed.), *Marriage and family assessment: A sourcebook for family therapy.* Beverly Hills, CA: Sage, 65–84.

Weiss, R. L. and Summers, K. J. 1983: Marital Interaction Coding System-III. In Filsinger, E. E. (ed.), *Marriage and family assessment: A sourcebook for family therapy.* Beverly Hills, CA: Sage, 85–115.

Weissman, M. M. and Bothwell, S. 1976: Assessment of social adjustment by patient self-report. *Archives of General Psychiatry* 33, 1111–15.

Weissman, M. M., Kasl, S. V. and Klerman, G. L. 1976: Follow-up of depressed women after maintenance treatment. *American Journal of Psychiatry* 133, 757–60.

Weissman, M. M., Klerman, G. L., Paykel, E. S., Prusoff, B. and Hanson, B. 1974: Treatment effects on the social adjustment of depressed patients. *Archives of General Psychiatry* 30, 771–8.

Whyte, M. K. 1990: *Dating, mating, and marriage.* New York: Aldine de Gruyter.

Wiener, D. N. 1948: Subtle and obvious keys for the MMPI. *Journal of Consulting and Clinical Psychology* 12, 164–70.

Winch, R. F. 1955a: The theory of complementary needs in mate-selection: A test of one kind of complementariness. *American Sociological Review* 20, 52–6.

Winch, R. F. 1955b: The theory of complementary needs in mate-selection: Final results on the test of the general hypothesis. *American Sociological Review* 20, 552–5.

Winch, R. F. 1958: *Mate-selection: A study of complementary needs.* New York: Harper.

Winch, R. F. 1967: Another look at the theory of complementary needs in mate-selection. *Journal of Marriage and the Family* 29, 756–62.

Winch, R. F., Ktsanes, T. and Ktsanes, V. 1954: The theory of complementary needs in mate selection: An analytic and descriptive study. *American Sociological Review* 19, 241–9.

Winch, R. F., Ktsanes, T. and Ktsanes, V. 1955: Empirical elaboration of the theory of complementary needs in mate-selection. *Journal of Abnormal and Social Psychology* 51, 508–13.

Winslow, C. N. 1937: A study of the extent of agreement between friends' opinions and their ability to estimate the opinions of each other. *Journal of Social Psychology* 8, 433–42.

Wolpe, J. 1958: *Psychotherapy by reciprocal inhibition.* Stanford, CA: Stanford University Press.

Woody, E. Z. and Costanzo, P. R. 1990: Does marital agony precede marital ecstasy? A comment on Gottman and Krokoff's 'Marital interaction and satisfaction: A longitudinal view'. *Journal of Consulting and Clinical Psychology* 58, 499–501.

Wright, P. H. 1969: A model and a technique for studies of friendship. *Journal of Experimental Social Psychology* 5, 295–309.

Yesavage, J. A., Brink, T. L., Rose, R. L., Lum, O., Huang, V., Adey, M. and Leirer, V. O. 1983: Development and validation of a geriatric screening scale: A preliminary report. *Journal of Psychiatric Research* 17, 37–49.

Zalokar, J. B. 1960: Marital status and major causes of death in women. *Journal of Chronic Diseases* 11, 50–60.

Zilboorg, G. 1936: Suicide among civilized and primitive races. *American Journal of Psychiatry* 92, 1347–69.

Zimmer, D. 1987: Does marital therapy enhance the effectiveness of treatment for sexual dysfunction? *Journal of Sex and Marital Therapy* 13, 193–209.

Author index

Subject index